ALSO BY ALECIA SWASY

Soap Opera: The Inside Story of Procter & Gamble

CHANGING
FOCUS

CHANGING
FOCUS

Kodak and the Battle
to Save a Great
American Company

ALECIA SWASY

TIMES BUSINESS

RANDOM HOUSE

Library of Congress Cataloging-in-Publication Data

Swasy, Alecia.
Changing focus : Kodak and the battle to save a great
American company / Alecia Swasy.
        p.   cm.
Includes index.
ISBN 0-8129-2463-0
1. Eastman Kodak Company. 2. Photographic industry—
United States. 3. Camera industry—United States.
4. Photographic film industry—United States.
5. Photographic chemicals industry—United States.
I. Title.
HD9708.U64E277   1997
338.7'681418'0973—dc21   96-50345

Random House website address:
http://www.randomhouse.com/
Printed in the United States of America on acid-free paper
98765432
First Edition

Book design by Mina Greenstein

For two great sisters,
ALEXIS HILL and AMY KASE.
And in memory of
PAT STRICHARCHUK

CONTENTS

CHANGING
FOCUS

INTRODUCTION

From Christmas morning around the tree to June afternoon weddings, America has captured its memories on Kodak film. The familiar yellow box has chronicled baby's first steps in the living room and Neil Armstrong's first steps on the moon. The film immortalized our historic moments of triumph and tragedy, from a returning World War II soldier stealing a kiss from a woman in Times Square to a stoic John F. Kennedy, Jr., saluting his father's casket. The scenes are forever stamped in our minds because of Kodak film.

Photography in the twentieth century also became an informal economic indicator of the prosperity of American households. Kodak founder George Eastman, who created the first batches of film in his mother's kitchen sink, taught young families to capture their pieces of the American dream in snapshots. Like a new car in the driveway, photo albums brimming with pictures of summertime smiles at the beach and caps and gowns of springtime graduation days became symbols of good times for the middle class. Indeed, any memorable scene was dubbed "a Kodak moment."

For generations of families in Rochester, New York, the Eastman Kodak Company represented their piece of the American dream. They could walk to work at the headquarters on State Street or the factory gates of Kodak Park, where machines churned out enough film in a year to stretch to the moon and back. Kodak seemed to offer a lifetime promise of security. Economic paternalism felt especially good to those who remembered the Depression, so they gave Kodak thirty or forty years in return for the company's care. It brought good paychecks and lavish benefits. At one time, Kodak perks included free bowling alleys, banking, and a bakery. Employees proudly wore their Koda-sneakers, white canvas shoes with the familiar yellow-and-red logo on the tongue. The yearly bonus, paid in mid-March, was so hefty that locals celebrated St. Kodak's Day rather than St. Patrick's Day. Rochester's generous patriarch was "the Yellow Father."

It was a gentle world for Kodak employees because Kodak was the unrivaled king of world photography. Its virtual monopoly on photographic film meant managers simply had to make sure the production machines were running twenty-four hours a day. In the early 1980s, one young employee was told: "You may think of this as a corporation, but it's really more of a country club." Managers golfed in the afternoons. Even the CEO dozed off during business reviews.

This is the story of how Eastman Kodak finally had to wake up. It is a snapshot of Rochester, its corporate father, and the people who depended on the company for jobs—and how they had to figure out how to cope when their paternalistic company was forced to change, firing thousands and stunning thousands more with new demands for a more competitive business era. It is a portrait of a classic northeastern industrial town and its people going through wrenching changes, struggling to recover and move forward after years of upheaval.

A similar picture is developing in many cities across America, as hundreds of other employers go through such restructurings. They are trying both to keep pace with the rapidly changing global economy and to reap fatter profits for shareholders. The same scene can be found in Dayton, Ohio, as the old NCR company is dismantled after a botched buyout by AT&T. Or in southern California, where the defense workers who built America's mighty military aircraft now find they are unnecessary in a post–Cold War world. It's a scene that can be found in Appalachia's once-booming coalfields, where the mine bosses who once ruled—then fired—thousands of miners now find their college degrees no longer insulate them from layoffs. Or in the office buildings of Washington, D.C., where government workers, once protected by inertia and bureaucracy, now find they are not wanted in the new era of small government. They all look for a way back into the mainstream. In Cincinnati, unemployed managers gather in a Methodist church to sharpen their computer skills. In Newark, Delaware, meetings of the local job search support group begin and end with a prayer for help. In suburban Philadelphia, former managers loiter in libraries, poring over the want ads, hoping someone needs them. On each business day in 1995, about 1,686 American workers learned they would lose their jobs. And the layoffs continue as big and small companies purge their workforces to stay competitive in a global marketplace and increase profits to shareholders.

Kodak is emblematic of American business in the twentieth century. Like General Motors, IBM, and many other capitalist icons, Kodak took its success for granted. Its managers believed that Americans would never buy any film except for the little yellow box, ignoring their Japanese rival Fuji Film's inroads until it had eaten up a large chunk of Kodak's domestic market. Kodak's board of directors and its senior management paid little attention to the changing marketplace or to the performance of their own people. When Kodak did try to diversify to counter problems in its core photography businesses, it had difficulty coping outside insular Rochester and made many costly wrong turns.

Like many companies, Kodak then had to undo some of those excesses. This meant cutting costs as fast as possible. Thousands of workers lost their jobs. Employees who had logged decades at the Yellow Father became the casualties recorded as mere statistics in daily newspaper headlines about downsizing, rightsizing, and the reengineering of corporate America. The layoffs gave a quick boost to Kodak's sagging stock price and quieted Wall Street's demands for improved quarterly numbers, but the decision proved to be a hasty and inadequate attempt to mask decades of bad management.

The downsizing is a traumatic wake-up call for millions of once-comfortable middle-class, white-collar workers. Those who were laid off lost the anchor that held the rest of their lives in place. They face a traumatic journey to find life outside the company's care. Finding a new job isn't easy, as the U.S. economy creates more lower-paying service jobs than the higher-paying manufacturing positions that used to be plentiful. Beyond that, the experience of a layoff changes lives in ways far beyond the most immediate impact of a lost paycheck. The fired must recast their dreams, starting with the basic question of how to survive without the identity of an office and a title at Kodak, to the more profound question of whether they will ever feel secure again.

The stories of seven Kodak workers who were laid off in 1993 provide a picture of what's in store for many Americans who once believed that a job in corporate America meant security for life. There is a new world out there for most U.S. workers, as companies rely more on temporary workers and less on loyalty and tenure. Careers for many are a series of stops in lower-paying jobs, not decades of promotions and salary increases at one company. Their journeys often leave them searching for something else to hang on to.

It is a wrenching time, even for those who escaped the layoffs and continue to work inside Kodak, now striving to reinvent itself to focus with renewed clarity on its traditional business of photography. Their progress and frustrations offer a glimpse of life in a post-downsizing company, showing other firms and employees now in the throes of reorganization what's ahead. Their successes and failures offer guidance and a measure of hope that upheaval can be followed by recovery. And they show how both corporate America and all of those inside must reshape themselves to fit into a new American dream.

PART ONE

The Gang That Couldn't Shoot Straight

I

Country Club

For Kay Whitmore, the beginning of the end came when he boarded the Kodak corporate jet for Fort Lauderdale in May 1993. As chief executive officer of Eastman Kodak, Whitmore had to chair the company's annual meeting, a spring ritual that was usually a social affair for shareholders and retirees. But this meeting would be different for Whitmore, a tall gray-haired man who looked more like a preacher than a chief executive. Kodak's cost-cutting chief financial officer had just resigned after a dispute with Whitmore. Kodak investors were so angry about the resignation that some suggested Whitmore should just leave, too. The CEO had been on a whirlwind tour of the country, meeting with investor groups, trying to convince them that he had a plan to turn around Kodak, which had recently reported a quarterly loss of more than $1.8 billion.

Fatigued as he was, he now had to convince the rest of the company's shareholders that he was up to the job. They were skeptical. And fed up. Kodak's stock performance lagged the Standard & Poor's 500 index by 50 percent, a dramatic change from the early 1980s and 1970s when Kodak routinely made big profits and outperformed other large companies. The several hundred investors gathered inside the Broward County Convention Center wanted to know if Whitmore had the stomach to slash thousands more from Kodak's workforce and cut sacred research-and-development spending to stop the hemorrhaging. The meeting was their chance to demand answers. Knowing there would be angry shareholders in the audience, but hoping to defuse some of the tension, Whitmore had rehearsed a carefully worded speech. Associates say he was was edgy during the week leading up to the meeting. Normally a patient and amiable Mormon, he was curt when rehearsing the speech. He clearly wasn't looking forward to the meeting. Whitmore looked tired when he took the podium and began to speak.

"We are driving for change in Kodak today," he told the group. Step by step, he gave a quick outline of his ten-point plan to improve cash flow, reduce spending, and review all of Kodak's businesses. His tactic of opening the meeting with promises to change seemed to mollify some in the audience. But many share-holders—John Ragusa, for one—weren't satisfied. He rose to interrupt Whitmore's planned agenda with a speech of his own.

"We are not looking at poor performance for a single month or quarter or year," Ragusa said. "We're addressing a decade of measurable, sustained underperformance." He reminded his fellow stakeholders that the people responsible "for this mess" were seated at the front of the auditorium: "the board of directors and the key executives they've appointed to run Eastman Kodak. All of these people have done a completely unsatisfactory job in discharging their duties." He likened them to common looters for their draining of the corporate treasury.

Ragusa went on and on about Kodak's problems. The audience listened as Whitmore grew increasingly agitated over Ragusa's long-winded speech. Finally, the CEO interrupted:

"Mr. Ragusa, I would remind you of the time—"

Ragusa snapped back: "Well, I'll remind you that you're an employee here."

And a well-paid one at that. Ragusa scolded Whitmore for taking home year after year of raises and a compensation package worth more than a million dollars annually.

Whitmore was getting fed up. He showed his temper a bit by threatening to have Ragusa removed from the auditorium because he was taking up too much time. Undaunted, Ragusa continued with his lecture. He reviewed how other poor-performing, overpaid CEOs in corporate America had met un-timely career ends when shareholders like him had had enough.

"Jim Robinson finally got run off from American Express," Ragusa said, reading off a list of boardroom obituaries. "John Akers finally got run off from IBM. And after only twenty-four months, Bob Stempel got run off from General Motors. Kay Whitmore and his crew are not irreplaceable."

The shareholder's remarks were practically heresy in the formerly benevolent and clublike world of Eastman Kodak, where lifetime employment was a given—especially for those like Whitmore, a well-liked engineer who had climbed up through the manufacturing ranks to become chief executive. But 1993 was a turning point. Kodak's investors finally said they'd had it with the mismanagement and overspending that had racked up more than $10 billion in debt on the firm's once pristine balance sheet. And while thousands of workers had been laid off in numerous restructurings, senior management was just starting to feel the heat.

The tumultuous 1993 events were a far cry from the early days of the company. George Eastman had scrimped and saved for every penny to learn photography as a hobby, then to build Kodak into the country's leading supplier of film for amateur and professional photographers.

When the young Eastman was six, his family moved to Rochester, where his father started a school that advertised itself as a place to learn about "making money and becoming useful in the world." The family hit hard times when Mr. Eastman died; George's mother, Maria Kilbourn Eastman, had to take in boarders to help pay the bills. George took his first job in 1868, when he was thirteen, earning $3 a week doing office jobs for an insurance agency. He later said that seeing his mother struggle created his fear of poverty. He kept meticulous records of his finances. They show a monthly budget for rent and food payments to his mother, and few indulgences, except for some ice cream on July 12, 1868. He would sometimes root through the trash at Bausch & Lomb, a Rochester eyeglasses company, looking for anything useful that he could sell for cash.

Eastman eventually became a junior bookkeeper at the Rochester Savings Bank, earning $1,400 a year. His new income allowed him an indulgence in 1877: he bought $94.36 worth of equipment and lenses from a local photographer, George H. Monroe, who became his teacher. Eastman loved photography and researched earlier inventors' work to learn how to make pictures. In his day it was a messy and cumbersome hobby, requiring the photographer to coat glass plates with light-sensitive chemicals and then perform tedious developing work. Eastman experimented at night in his mother's kitchen, trying to make his own photographic dry plates instead of the wet ones. He filed for his first U.S. patent in 1879, for a gadget that prepared dry gelatin plates.

He was in good company in the era of Alexander Graham Bell and his telephone, Thomas Edison and the electric light and talking machine, and other inventor-entrepreneurs. But Eastman needed money to build a business around his device. He turned to one of his mother's boarders, Colonel Henry Strong, a whip manufacturer, who became his first partner with an investment of $5,000, the same as Eastman's. The offices of the Eastman Dry Plate Company were in a rented loft of a State Street factory.

Early production grew, but Eastman ran into trouble after a long winter that kept photographers from going outdoors to use their cameras. When spring came, they found that the plates were no longer light sensitive, so their pictures were ruined. Eastman recalled the plates and replaced each one free of charge. The problem was in the gelatin used to coat the plates. Gelatin was made from cow bones and hides. The cows had apparently eaten something that affected the gelatin. The recall nearly drove Eastman out of business, but later he often said that it saved his reputation.

Eastman had set four business principles when he started his company: produce large quantities by machine; keep prices low; use foreign and domestic distribution; and advertise the product. After the plate debacle, he added another: control the supply of raw materials. For years, the company kept its own cattle yards to ensure a supply of untainted hides and bones. And Eastman started a chemical company in Kingsport, Tennessee, to produce a steady supply of ingredients for film. He was also adamant about not running up debts. Because "one is more independent if one can finance out of earnings." He believed that debt "is connected with eventual poverty."

By 1884, Eastman was perfecting a simple replacement for glass photographic plates: a roll of film. "I believe in the future of the film business," he wrote in a November 1884 letter.

By 1888, he was selling a camera for $25. It held a roll of film, enough for one hundred prints, which consumers could have developed by sending the entire camera back to Rochester. There it was reloaded with film and returned, along with the developed pictures. The camera was Eastman's model for what became a familiar Kodak ad slogan: "You press the button, we do the rest." It was a major improvement that made photography more accessible to ordinary families. Eastman wanted more advances and soon hired a chemist to develop new products, even if they took "a day, a week, month or a year."

He gave his products the brand name Kodak, which he made up. He started with the letter K, his favorite because it was the first letter of his mother's family name, Kilbourn. And it is "forceful, direct and arresting. I decided to use it twice for emphasis, to begin the name and to end it. Then I filled in the other letters to make the word short and catchy as to sound." Kodak became part of the English language. Photographers became known as Kodakers and "to Kodak" was a verb. Kodak's Brownie cameras were everywhere. Eastman had accomplished his mission to make the camera "as easy a recorder as the pencil."

Early praise came from surprising places. The warden of the Illinois State Penitentiary in Joliet wrote in February 1886 to thank Eastman for making it easier to make mug shots of the 1,600 convicts. "If a convict should escape from us today, I would have 200 of his photographs in the mails tomorrow morning, carrying his features to every prominent police official and detective in the country."

Eastman's letters show how persistent he was about spreading amateur photography around the globe. He distributed products overseas beginning in 1885, and built a plant in England in 1891. In the United States, he sent his salesmen to small towns to demonstrate products. He wasn't a patient man. To salesman David Cooper he wrote: "You and Jones were sent to New York to canvass the town, and you won't make much headway if one sits on his backside all day." Eastman demanded to see a list of customers that the team visited. He wrote to one salesman in Kansas City to question his expense account of $3 a day.

The company grew because photography was spreading to the mass market. Eastman helped promote it by advertising his cameras. By the turn of the century, he was the biggest advertiser in the country. He got product endorsements from famous people like Arctic explorer Robert Edwin Peary, who took a Kodak camera with him to the North Pole. Selling photography became easier as people took weekends off from work. And Kodak's advertising focused on the expanding middle class. "Keep a Kodak story of the children," read a 1920 advertisement.

Eastman also saw opportunity in partnerships with other inventors. In the late 1920s, Edison was working on a motion-picture camera; Eastman invented a continuous roll of film to use with it. Hollywood also got a boost when Eastman helped Walt Disney, then a young filmmaker in need of money, finance one of his films.

As the country grew, so did Kodak. The company's success made Eastman a millionaire. Money wasn't all-important to the entrepreneur and his once-impoverished family. When he told his mother the news that he'd made his first million, she replied: "That's nice, George." Indeed, he shared his surplus with his employees. He set up an accident and pension fund and a wage dividend, an annual bonus paid to all workers. Part of his motivation was a strong sense of paternalism. But he also feared that unions would try to organize his workers, so he was generous to his employees, hoping they would never feel the need to join.

He spoke often about the importance of treating employees as owners of the enterprise. And his work laid the foundation for Kodak's paternalism and the sense of entitlement among its employees, which seemed to work fine in a world where there was little worry about competition from other products. And the owner held a controlling interest in the enterprise, so he didn't have to worry about grumblings from other shareholders. Eastman believed that others who helped him build his business should share in its successes and become owners as well, so his became a company that took care of its people. "Our employees are content and loyal and we desire above all things to keep them so. We are running a very complicated and difficult business. I know of none more dependent on the good feeling and faithfulness of its employees." Eastman donated 10,000 shares of his Kodak stock to start an employee stock plan.

As Kodak grew, Eastman devoted more time to his other interests. He went bicycling in Russia and photographed wild animals while on safari in Africa. He once photographed a charging rhino, telling the hunter in his party to hold his fire until the last possible moment. When asked why he would risk his life by standing in front of an angry beast, Eastman replied: "You have to trust in your organization."

He displayed his photographs for guests at his massive Georgian-style mansion on Rochester's East Avenue, which he shared with his mother until her death in 1907. The house had a screening room for home movies, nine fireplaces, thirteen bathrooms, and an elevator so Mrs. Eastman wouldn't have to use the stairs. Imported marble from Switzerland covered the conservatory floor. A household chart from the 1920s shows that he employed more than thirty people to run the mansion, ranging from a third-floor maid to dairymen to tend the herd of Jersey and Brown Swiss cows that filled the backyard.

Eastman was part of an era in which businessmen helped the government improve ties with foreign lands. Acting the diplomat, he invited prominent Japanese to his house; Viscount Shibusawa, a philanthropist, visited in 1921. At that point, Japan wasn't an economic threat, so there was an emphasis on diplomacy and being good neighbors, rather than a rancorous debate about opening closed markets. The party dined on guinea hen breasts and creamed lobster with Paul Rouget 1904 as a violinist played Vivaldi. He would invite a hundred people for concerts featuring singers from the New York Metropolitan Opera. There were lively debates about topics ranging from plumbing to suicide. Eastman even subscribed to *Vogue* to learn more about women's fashions.

He often invited women to dinner, but the lifelong bachelor never seemed interested in a more serious relationship. Historian Curt Gerling put it bluntly, writing that he doubted Eastman "ever went to bed with a babe in his life." Henry Clune, who worked fifty years as a reporter at Gannett's Rochester newspapers, recalled one of Eastman's grand dinner parties, at which all the guests dressed in formal attire. One of Eastman's favorite opera singers wore a strapless gown that night. The curious inventor eyed the dress from across the room and moved closer to ask a question: "What is it that holds up that gown?" The singer replied: "Only your age, Mr. Eastman."

He was interested in some things to the point of obsession. He kept detailed logs of every rose he grew, noting which buds bloomed and which ones failed. He even recorded the amount of sausage produced from each pig he raised.

In his library, he wore small oval wire-rimmed glasses and studied the *Oxford Book of English Prose* and the works of Rudyard Kipling. The great promotor of photography was surprisingly shy about having his own picture taken. When he ordered bookplates for his library, he insisted that his picture not appear. Instead, the plate featured a man reading in a chair in front of a fireplace, his face hidden from view.

By 1924, Eastman had retired from day-to-day management of the company and given away millions to various charities and universities. He had developed arteriosclerosis and arthritis of the spine. In March 1932, he shot himself. He left a note that said: "My work is done. Why wait?" The coroner deemed the death suicide while temporarily insane. Eastman was cremated and his remains were buried near his film plant at Kodak Park.

In the years following Eastman's death, his company continued to build on his dream of making photography simple for everyone. The returnable camera was replaced with simpler cameras that consumers reloaded themselves. They returned only the roll of film to Kodak for processing. By 1935, Kodak was producing Kodachrome film, a color film first used for motion pictures and then for slides and home movie cameras. By the 1940s, Kodacolor film for prints was made available for consumers. Families of the 1950s could record their baby boom with Kodak's Brownie eight-millimeter movie camera. Other products made Kodak a familiar name in the workplace, too. Kodak's Carousel slide projectors became a fixture in every office of the 1960s. The U.S. government found Kodak's advances in lenses and specialized photography useful. A spy satellite called *Corona,* which monitored the Soviet Union and China in the 1960s, was equipped with a Kodak camera that took pictures whose resolution was high enough to show a line of people at Lenin's tomb.

Above all else, though, it was film that fueled Kodak's growth in the booming post–World War II U.S. economy. Foreign competitors, like Agfa in Europe and Fuji and Konica in Japan, weren't selling their products in the United States. Kodak was king in photography. In 1962, the firm's U.S. sales exceeded $1 billion and it employed 75,000 people worldwide. The same year, John Glenn took his place in history as the first American to orbit the earth. Kodak film brought his adventures back to everyone back home. By the following year, Kodak introduced its first Instamatic, an easy-to-load camera that used cartridges of film. More than 50 million Instamatic cameras were produced by 1970.

Sales of Kodak film were boosted by the company's move into television and sponsorship of all-American programs like *The Adventures of Ozzie and Harriet* and the *Ed Sullivan Show.* Kodak ads reminded consumers that all they needed was film, a camera, and "a little thoughtfulness" to make beautiful memories.

The company's success fueled an arrogance that, in hindsight, is truly remarkable. Few inside were willing to believe that any on the outside could contribute to the industry. Edwin Land, an inventor who developed a method of instant photography that didn't require any chemicals or processing for the film, tried to sell his idea to Kodak in the 1940s, but senior management rebuffed him. Land's invention became the Polaroid camera.

At times, this arrogance eroded the company's commitment to quality. Dick Streeter, who worked in a variety of Kodak assembly-line and staff jobs over two decades, recalls inspecting cameras in the late 1960s. His job was to tap on the lenses of a stack of cameras to make sure they stayed in place. If the lens dropped out of two or three cameras, he was told to reject the entire tray of a hundred cameras. "One day, I got five or six that fell out," he said. "I was rejecting things like crazy." Finally, his supervisor came over and questioned him; as a result, the engineers changed the requirements, so that a tray would be rejected if seven lenses fell out. Streeter continued to reject trays, because he was finding seven broken cameras. Next the requirement was raised to ten. He continued to reject trays of cameras.

His exasperated boss finally said: "You don't understand. Christmas is coming."

Streeter argued: "What if someone sticks their film in and they're taking pictures at a wedding or something else they'll never duplicate and the lens pops out?"

His boss replied: "If that happens, she'll take it to the camera store and the camera store will give her another one."

In another job, Streeter discovered that Kodak's "autofocus" slide projectors wouldn't focus unless you clipped the wires and focused them manually. Even senior managers in manufacturing admit that the company's philosophy in those days was to pay little attention to equipment and concentrate on the giant film-making process. Then as now film generated the bulk of the company's profits. It makes enough film every year to circle the equator thirty times. The manufacturing plant operates twenty-four hours a day.

"No matter what they said, they were a film company," says Frank Zaffino, who is now Kodak's vice president of equipment manufacturing. "Equipment was okay as long as it drove consumables." If a camera helped sell more film, Kodak would sell it, but there was little concern about what kind of cameras consumers wanted, or how to make them better. Indeed, most corporate power centered around Kodak Park's massive film-making plant. Historically, Kodak's chief executive officers came out of manufacturing jobs at the park.

Executives abhorred anything that looked risky or too innovative, because a mistake in such a massive manufacturing process would cost thousands of dollars. So the company built itself up around procedures and policies intended to maintain the status quo.

The giant Kodak machine churned along with little interruption. Managers who grew up in Kodak manufacturing never really developed broader business skills to help them as they advanced to senior positions. It didn't seem to matter who ran the company; the franchise from the strong Kodak brand kept producing good profits. To manage Kodak meant to keep order and continuity.

With that came paternalism, which had grown even stronger since Eastman's days. The generation that grew up in the Depression was eager for jobs. Lane Riland, who has taken Kodak's pulse as the company psychologist for forty years, has a pretty clear picture of the typical Kodaker. Riland's years of surveys and studies helped him shape his description of what he calls midwestern Gothic. A Kodaker was often a first-born child who left a farm family to attend a state university and then seek lifetime employment at a large manufacturing company. Or he came from generations of blue-collar workers who left high school for Kodak's factories, trading parents' care for the Yellow Father's. Regardless of their job title, Kodakers craved security from a paternalistic company.

In Rochester, Kodak was the place to work if you wanted to be successful. "If you didn't work for Kodak, you didn't have a real job," recalls Streeter, who moved up from assembly-line jobs to work in communications. It was important to behave like a Kodaker. Streeter recalls being commended for his goal statement on his Kodak application: I want to buy a house, have a couple kids, and maybe own two cars. Rochester historian Gerling suggested that getting a job at Kodak required "a few clean shirts, well-kept nails and a Hickey-Freeman suit."

The order of it all extended to every aspect of an employee's life. Nancy Gallagher, who worked as a Kodak secretary from 1968 to 1970, remembers how the company arranged for her to join a carpool when she told the interviewer that she didn't have a way to get to her new job. Besides doing office work, secretaries were encouraged to serve as models in the labs where photographers tested new film. Even Rochester's downtown traffic was regulated by Kodak. "We worked from seven-thirty A.M. until four-twelve P.M. Not four or four-thirty," Gallagher said. That way, Kodak helped the city avoid jams.

There wasn't much that Kodak didn't provide for its employees. The company had indoor golf courses, bowling alleys, movie theaters, and a pistol range. Employees could do their banking at Kodak and buy pies at the in-house bakery. Kodak even offered discount safety shoes at a shoemobile; employees could buy them through payroll deduction. At lunch, employees sat and watched Hollywood movies. Those who went out to eat usually stayed out for a couple of hours. Managers were allowed to play golf in the afternoons.

Leading Kodak in the years after Eastman's death was a string of manufacturing managers who climbed the ladder to become CEO. They were alike in many ways, always following the risk-averse plans of their predecessors. Most of Kodak's senior management went to a sort of finishing academy at M.I.T.'s Sloan School of Business, so they all got the same training. Perhaps the strongest example of the control-oriented CEO was Walter Fallon, who became chief executive in 1972. Sales that year had climbed to more than $3 billion, fueled by Kodak's pocketsized Instamatic cameras. Fallon embodied the organization men of his era, who sat on each other's boards, enjoying the perks that came with their positions. He had been a director at General Motors and copied some of that firm's opulent style back at his Rochester headquarters. He built a private dining room so he didn't have to eat with the rest of the staff. He commissioned a private airport terminal for the company's Gulfstreams. When he flew, he insisted that a bulkhead be installed on the corporate jet to separate him from any others on the plane. Yet his wife once described the Fallons as "just average-living people."

Fallon had joined the company in 1941 as a chemist and was obsessive about controlling film production, even when he was in the executive suite. He would study graphs of a film's composition and ask to see the corresponding sample to analyze it, too. The joke was, "You're nobody if Walt isn't doing your job." His nickname became the the subject of a company memo: "Do not refer to the chief executive officer as the 800-pound gorilla." At community meetings, Fallon was known for that same authoritarian style. "He'd say: Here's what the issue is and here's what we're gonna do. Any comments?" recalls Tom Mooney, head of the Rochester chamber of commerce. "A lot of creative people wouldn't say a word because they were afraid of him."

Fallon wasn't an inspiring leader. Local newspaper stories described his speech demeanor as boring or frightening. He favored pin-striped suits and drove a car provided by his friends at GM. On the weekends, he tended his rhododendrons. He once said that Kodak introduced products in an orderly fashion and that "we sleep well." Trouble was, he was sleeping through the beginnings of a revolution in American business. The leaders of General Motors were guilty of the same thing. Japanese manufacturers were getting their acts together and coming up with better cars, electronics, and film, while U.S. companies took their near-monopoly status for granted.

At Kodak, this arrogance fueled the growth of a nightmarish bureaucracy so entrenched that it could have passed for a government agency. Those asked to give speeches had the text prepared by in-house writing services, which would take a month, maybe more, to produce the speech. There was an emphasis on doing everything according to company rulebooks. Mary-Frances Winters, who worked at Kodak from 1973 to 1984, was assigned to update a manual of market research. There were few changes, but the project "took one and a half years," she says. "It was very frustrating." She was also involved in a program to encourage young women who wanted to pursue secretarial or other office careers. "It took five years to set that up."

Since George Eastman's days, Kodak had followed a calendar that divided the year into thirteen periods, rather than twelve months. The company discontinued the practice in 1990, but only after a task force took more than a year to study whether dropping it was a good idea. Routines were important in Kodak's world. Secretaries typed up daily schedules in advance. If someone asked to see a manager for ten minutes, an entire hour was scheduled. Meetings were held prior to meetings to discuss issues and establish agreement in order to avoid confrontations, which were considered un-Kodak-like.

Evaluating and developing employees wasn't a priority because Kodak was an environment in which you waited until your boss got promoted or died and then you took his job. So the performance appraisal system was a flawed, ineffective management tool that laid the groundwork for a lot of Kodak's problems in the 1990s. For years, everyone was evaluated by a manager and assigned a rating of 1 through 7. If you were promoted, you got a lower ranking in your next performance appraisal, the assumption being that you were new to the job and still learning. Managers who tried to give recently promoted employees higher rankings to reward good work often found that their superiors would refuse to grant approval.

Even worse, the system didn't accurately assess good and bad employees. For decades, that didn't matter at Kodak, because the company could afford to keep legions of workers, regardless of their performance. "The performance evaluation system was so sloppy," says Lee Horschman, a business planner who worked at Kodak until 1990. "It was like Lake Wobegon: everyone was above average. Supervisors are not disciplined enough to say you're not getting the job done." One manager who had been trained in the marines asked about the toughness of Kodak and was told to expect something closer to the Red Cross.

In management circles, the key to getting promoted was to create a kingdom full of layers and layers of people: to have a lot of people in your department produced the illusion that you were powerful. With all those layers, decision-making on any project was an exercise in frustration for anyone with an interest in moving fast. "The whole company was run on 'Let's not make decisions because you could be wrong,' " says Scott Brownstein, a physicist who helped Kodak develop new films and products for more than twenty years. When decisions were finally made, "they often didn't take hold," recalls Kathy Hudson, a former vice president.

There were few checks on spending at any level of the company. Budgets were mere suggestions for spending limits. "You could raise the ceiling by ten percent without justification," said Roger Reisman, who managed Kodak's security department. Indeed, most managers never saw financial reports, even for their own line of business. Only the finance department had access to that information. And all pricing decisions went through a centralized office. No one was really accountable for the financial performance of a department.

Kodak's biggest worry, insiders often joked, was that the government would discover how much of the U.S. market the company controlled. It had a virtual monopoly, with about 80 percent of the film market. The government did impose two consent decrees on Kodak, in the 1920s and 1950s. One decree blocked the company from tying its film sales to processing by Kodak, which competitors saw as fostering a monopoly on the processing business. The other barred Kodak from selling film under any label other than its own. In the 1970s, the Justice Department did investigate Kodak for possible violations of antitrust laws, but closed the case without filing charges against the company.

The emphasis on internal matters, like manufacturing, was so extreme that anyone with an external focus, such as marketing products, was never considered for the CEO's post. Gerald Zornow, a rising star from the marketing side of the business, was passed over in 1972 for the CEO job and given the title of chairman instead. (At the time, Fallon was CEO.) Zornow was one of the few who worried about relations with the outside world; rather than just sit in the office and hold meetings with insiders, he met with customers and traveled frequently to make calls on them. Sometimes he even hosted poker parties at which he'd stay up late and drink beer with customers.

The next management team was led by Colby Chandler, the son of a Maine dairy farmer, who often drove a pickup truck to Kodak headquarters and routinely wore a Mickey Mouse watch. He joined Kodak in 1950 as an engineer at the Park. Like others of his generation, he was influenced by his memories of tough times during the Depression. He said that the experience taught him the "importance of friendships" and how much "we need each other." Fatherly in demeanor, he would often greet employees by their first names.

By the early 1980s, Kodak had $10 billion in annual sales. When he was named chairman and CEO in 1983, Chandler made it clear that as CEO he intended to maintain the staid Kodak culture. "It never is the dawn of a new day when you change CEOs," he said.

The lack of insightful leadership led to one of the first and biggest setbacks in Kodak history. After Kodak passed on Ed

Land's invention of instant photography in the 1940s, Polaroid built the instant camera into a successful consumer product. Kodak supplied some film products to Polaroid, but lost the contract when Polaroid decided to use other sources and do some of its own manufacturing. Kodak officials then decided that they would enter the instant market with their own films and cameras. The company spent more than $90 million to create a peel-apart film like Polaroid's product of the early 1970s. But Polaroid was already working on its next generation of film, which didn't have a peel-off cover. So Kodak had to scrap all that work and start over. Finally, in April 1976, Kodak launched its own instant camera, with much fanfare. Company insiders say the rollout was motivated by a combination of the belief that instant photography was a viable market and injured pride from losing the film contract with Polaroid. "It was sort of retaliation," said one manager.

Six days after announcing the instant camera and film, Kodak was sued by Polaroid for allegedly infringing on numerous patents. Indeed, during the design and manufacturing of the cameras, many insiders had questioned whether Kodak could get away with building a product so similar to Polaroid's. But the bulk of patent litigation until then had favored Kodak. "The attorneys said you'll get sued on day one, but you will prevail," said Edwin Przybylowicz, a Ph.D. chemist who was then Kodak's chief technical officer. According to Gary Van Graafeiland, Kodak's general counsel, "We had views of inside and outside counsel that the instant camera did not infringe. The conclusion was that Kodak designed its way around Polaroid patents or specific Polaroid patents were not valid."

But Kodak eventually lost, after ten years in court. The company withdrew from the instant-camera business in January, 1986, after losing the case. In 1990 it was ordered to pay a final settlement of $925 million—far less than the triple damages that Polaroid, arguing that Kodak willfully infringed its patents, had sought. "The cost is beyond the money we paid," Van Graafeiland says. "It was a blow to our prestige." Perhaps more significantly, Kodak's decision to expand into instant film damaged its relationship with its traditional photofinisher customers. For decades, Kodak had been the biggest supplier to photofinishing stores, which bought tons of Kodak's photographic paper and chemicals. With instant cameras, of course, consumers don't need to spend money at a photofinisher. "At a convention of photofinishers, we announced we were going into the instant business. They booed," recalled one manager who attended the meeting. "These photofinishers had been one hundred percent loyal to Kodak. They bought all their hardware, software, chemicals. Now they began talking to the Japanese companies. The romance was over, because Kodak took them for granted." Now the photofinishers diverted some of their traditional 110 and 35mm photo-processing business to Fuji and others.

Furthermore, Przybylowicz says, the instant program "chewed up a lot of resources" and created a "diversion into areas that ultimately didn't pay." The company had hired several thousand workers for the instant program and other new projects. Giant instant-film machines that cost millions of dollars were eventually dismantled for scrap. "The company was riding on its collective ego," Przybylowicz says. "We were the imaging company of the world. We could produce better instant pictures. No one sat back and said: 'What is the customer looking for? What is it going to cost consumers?' " (The prints cost about a dollar each, and there is a limit to how much an instant photo can be enlarged or duplicated.) "But we literally had no competition for so long, management hadn't become accustomed to it. Historically, if there was a competitor, Kodak would blow them away." Przybylowicz calls it the Monroe County syndrome. "We're an insular place."

Indeed, Kodak's arrogance was becoming apparent to some inside the company. Al Waugh worked as an engineer at the time when Kodak was dismantling the instant-camera program. He often salvaged leftover parts and machinery for use in his research lab, so he was invited to visit the instant-photography building when the company had its version of an internal fire sale. Waugh didn't fully appreciate the magnitude of the decision in the Polaroid lawsuit until he walked through the cavernous building. No one was working, but he could hear noises in each of the giant bays where the instant machinery had churned out film. He walked past more than a dozen of the machines. The workers making the noise were chopping up the machines and culling whatever could be salvaged. Waugh was allowed to take anything useful back to his lab. But he found the scene too depressing. "I didn't want to take any of the stuff. I just felt totally demoralized."

It was a sign that Kodak was doing more than dismantling film machines; it was admitting its first big defeat.

2

Slippery Slope

The arrogance that produced the instant-photography debacle gradually began to weaken Kodak in other areas—most devastatingly in its core business of manufacturing and selling photo film. Like other insular, successful U.S. companies, Kodak somehow ignored the increasing threat of competitors in its home market. In 1976, Fuji Film Company of Japan was the first to introduce 400-speed color film, faster than any made by Kodak. More and more photofinishers were also switching to Fuji's photographic paper and other supplies instead of buying Kodak's, which were about 20 percent more expensive. Some inside the company tried to warn Kodak's senior management about the onslaught, but were unsuccessful. In a case study on Fuji and the Japanese market, Mary-Frances Winters warned of Kodak's eroding market share. When the senior management read the report, they asked who had issued it. The response was "Shoot the messenger," she says. "They didn't believe the American public would buy any other film." The report was ignored.

Kodak officials started to pay attention when Fuji flew its blimp over Rochester. Paranoia increased so much that Kodak management feared that surveillance planes were photographing its manufacturing sites. At the time, Kodak increased security measures, for example requiring ID badges to get into buildings. All speeches were proofed by security officials. Couriers taking Kodak materials were forbidden to put their bag in a plane's overhead compartment. If it was too big to fit under the seat, they were instructed to pay for the adjoining seat and keep the bag at their side.

Perhaps the biggest sign that Fuji was a real threat came when Kodak tried in 1981 to win a coveted sponsorship slot as official film of the 1984 Olympics. Kodak negotiators were insistent on not paying too much. While they balked, Fuji officials basically told the Olympic organizing committee to name its price. The Japanese company paid $7 million for the sponsorship. "This was tantamount to another incursion that occurred offshore," said Peter Palermo, who was Kodak's senior vice president of imaging. "It was December seventh [Pearl Harbor Day] at Kodak."

Another attack from Japan came that same year when the Sony Corporation unveiled its plans for a filmless electronic camera called Mavica, which would display pictures on a television screen; the pictures could then be printed out on paper. Publicly, CEO Chandler said that Kodak could invent its own electronic camera, but contended that people "like color prints." Inside the company, however, senior management began to panic. The Sony camera was seen as a death knell for traditional silver-based film, the mainstay of Kodak. "It sent fear through the company," says Hudson, the former vice president. The reaction was: "Oh, my goodness, photography is dead."

As CEO, Chandler recognized the need to groom his successor and delegate some responsibilities to others. For a time, Chandler ran the company with Kay Whitmore as president and Phil Samper as vice chairman. Whitmore and Samper were opposites in many ways. Whitmore grew up in the Mormon culture of Utah. Samper grew up in California and traveled the world. Samper pushed for change, while Whitmore studied situations for months before acting. The triumvirate set them up as competitors for the CEO's post. From the start, however, Whitmore showed a certain indifference to the job. A colleague once asked him a hypothetical question about his future plans: If he could choose his job, would he prefer to be a disciple in the Church of Latter-Day Saints, or CEO of Kodak? Whitmore didn't hesitate: He would pick the Mormon church. Like Chandler, Whitmore believed the company would just roll along undisturbed. So his leadership emphasized staying the course. Samper, on the other hand, had international experience and approached his job as if he were a country manager watching over all aspects of a company's national business, not just acting like a caretaker.

By the time Chandler, Whitmore, and Samper were running the company, its payroll was bloated with bureaucracy. Kodak's U.S. employment peaked at 93,300 in 1982. Worldwide employment was 136,500 that year. Managers say they had a simple motto: If the job required one person, hire two.

During Chandler's era, there was little oversight by the board of directors, despite strong signs that foreign competition was starting to hurt the company's core business of film making. It was a docile group. In 1984, for instance, the fifteen-member board included eight directors from Kodak's management. And the outside directors, including Charles Duncan, a Washington lawyer, Juanita Kreps, an economist, and John Smale, then CEO of Procter & Gamble, didn't have much of a personal stake in the company's business. Indeed, each held only one hundred shares of Kodak stock. And as a group, the directors held only 85,669 shares, including 48,771 options granted as part of their compensation packages. In addition, in 1984 the directors were each paid $17,000 in retainers, plus fees for each meeting they attended. "The board was a rubber-stamp organization," said one former vice president. These were very clubby times for corporate boards in general. If there was an open chair, the directors simply called on a friend from the business community to fill the seat. For their part, shareholders weren't very vocal, either: This was before big investment funds held giant blocks of stock, which gave them more leverage with a company's management.

In the 1980s, fearing that a competitor would beat the firm in the inevitable switch to digital photography, Kodak began to scale back its investment in traditional color film and search for a way to develop digital products of its own. Rather than using traditional paper and chemicals to develop and print photos, digital photography allows images to be stored on discs. The discs are then used to display the image on a computer or television screen.

John White, who worked in high-ranking Pentagon and other government posts before moving to the software business, was hired to help push Kodak forward into the digital world. Or so he thought at the time. "Kodak wanted to get into the digital business, but they wanted to do it in their own way, from Rochester and largely with their own people," White says. "That meant it wasn't going to work. The difference between their traditional business and digital is so great. The tempo is so different. The kinds of skills you need are different. Kay and Colby would tell you they wanted change, but they didn't want to force the pain on the organization." The company had a split personality. It foresaw the eventual drop in usage of traditional film and cameras and the shift to computers and digital cameras. But its management didn't really want to admit that its core film-making business was in jeopardy.

And this all resulted from the old monopoly mentality. "As in many large old successful companies, people running it never created a business. They presided over the franchise," White says. "That's not a good place to train people to be tough."

Dick Bourns, a senior vice president who now heads part of Kodak's photography division, concedes that Kodak "overreacted to the threat of electronics." In fact, the shift away from chemical-based film would be a long-term evolution, and would not immediately jeopardize Kodak's core products. Many say that one of the casualties of the time was camera development, an area in which Kodak had thrived for decades with products like the 110 and 126 Instamatics. Even the successful 110 camera was being pounded by cheaper competitors. Consumers Union tested pocket cameras and rated Kodak below cheaper models. And many basic problems in manufacturing cameras were masked because no one cared about anything besides making film.

Kodak's internal quality problems became apparent to consumers when the company launched the Disc camera in 1982. It promised "crisp images" from a small disc that contained tiny chips of film for each exposure. The $40 million advertising budget was the biggest in Kodak's history. Actors, including Telly Savalas, were hired as pitchmen for the camera.

In developing the Disc camera, Kodak failed to realize the inroads being made by Japanese camera makers, who were simplifying 35mm cameras, developing convenient point-and-shoot models that didn't require amateurs to do much more than push a button. "The attitude was, 'We are the market. We launch the system and that's the system people will use,' " says Scott Brownstein.

Przybylowicz, the chief technical officer, said the "assumption was people would take more pictures if they got more satisfactory results" from an easy-to-use and compact camera. But the camera didn't create high-quality photos; instead, prints were often grainy and fuzzy. Kodak discontinued the Disc camera in 1988.

"The camera design and the camera itself were outstanding," says Dave Biehn, now vice president of consumer imaging. But Kodak introduced a product "before our film technology was ready for it." The Disc program also added thousands of workers to Kodak's already bloated payroll.

Kodak began to realize that it had too many people to support in an increasingly competitive environment. Mass layoffs were unheard of at Kodak; only a small number of workers had ever been let go. But pressures in the marketplace prompted Kodak in 1983 to offer the Optional Retirement and Separation Plan, an early retirement package, which 5,000 workers decided to take.

However, the cuts didn't lead to cost savings in many cases. Some of those who left were hired back on a contract basis. "Many people came back and sat in the same desk and did the same work for a year or two," said one manager. "The organization didn't develop the capability to do without that person." Kodak was starting to sense that it had a real problem, but it had scarcely begun to imagine a solution.

The advances by Japanese film and camera makers prompted a drive by Kodak to find new businesses to supplement the lost income from its core businesses. For example, Kodak tried for years to expand its imaging business to office copiers. Early attempts weren't fruitful. One engineer recalls how one model was designed with a fire extinguisher inside the copier cabinet because the machine had a tendency to catch fire. "We weren't allowed to use the 'F' word," he says. "In this case, that meant fire." Another enormous copier introduced in the 1970s was dubbed "the Savior." The machine was so big it filled an entire room. It got its nickname because people would open the door and yell, "Jesus Christ!" when they saw it.

Kodak eventually perfected its copier technology, but the development played second fiddle to the simultaneous investment in instant cameras in the early 1970s. "The [copier] technology was terrific," says Horschman, the former business planner. But Kodak wasn't accustomed to this sort of product, which customers rent, making the payback slow. "You dig a deep cash hole . . . and they pay you back a nickel at a time," Horschman says. He believes the company "made the wrong trade-off" choosing to pursue instant cameras instead of focusing on copiers.

Some customers complained about the pricing and service of Kodak copiers. Indeed, even some of Kodak's own subsidiaries leased copiers from Kodak's crosstown rival Xerox instead of using their own brand.

Kodak's copier business was part of its information systems business, which at times posted quarterly losses of $20 million. Compared to Kodak's core film business, copiers never became a big revenue or profit source for the company. Basically, Kodak couldn't figure out how to compete with Xerox.

Meanwhile, Kodak was trying to fix its sagging photographic division. (Growth in that business had stalled at about 4 percent a year—down from about 10 percent, which it had seen in the 1970s.) Management figured a decentralized structure, reorganized into seventeen business units, would make the company more nimble and less bureaucratic. The plan was laid out by McKinsey consultants, but the problem was that few Kodak managers had the skills to run these little kingdoms. Even Whitmore said he had a "high level of nervousness because we've got these very competent but quite inexperienced managers running off in seventeen different directions."

By early 1986, all of the bungled diversification efforts, combined with Kodak's problems with cameras and film sales, meant the company had to make deep cuts. For 1985's fourth quarter, Kodak reported a $194 million net loss, including a charge of $494 million to cover part of the costs associated with discontinuing the instant camera and film business. The company was saddled with too many workers who had been hired to build the instant cameras, which were now being returned by the thousands. To make matters worse, Wall Street watchers speculated that Kodak was a takeover target and that GAF might try to buy it or force a breakup of the company. Kodak was a target because of lousy earnings and a stock price that had tumbled since 1973 from its peak of about $151 a share. Other reports listed Ivan Boesky, the Belzbergs, and Saul Steinberg as buying up Kodak shares.

In 1986, managers were ordered to cut spending by 5 percent and employment by 10 percent. For the first time, thousands of people—nearly 13,000—were fired. The cuts were made throughout the company. A security guard watched employees crying as they left the building when layoff notices were issued. One employee, a father who was expecting his third child, sat in the guard's booth and cried for half an hour. Employees were bitter: "Kodak had opportunities galore," said one engineer. "They blew it because management made decisions that were stupid or wrong." Others found the new pressures too stressful to manage. "I'm just too old for this rah-rah-rah stuff," said James Singleton, fifty, who had worked at Kodak since 1953. Singleton was interviewed about the layoffs in early March 1986 by the local newspaper. He died at Kodak headquarters a few days later, of a heart attack.

There were plenty of other signs to remind employees that times were changing at Kodak. The cafeteria cut its hours. There were no more ten A.M. coffee breaks. And free medical checkups were eliminated. Phil Samper, described as having the subtlety of a Chicago Bears linebacker, once stood on a cafeteria table and told those eating in the cafeteria that they must not be working hard enough if they were sitting around in the lunchroom.

Some employees met with union organizers, a first in Kodak's history. Kodak responded to the pressures with a series of workshops on managing stress, including sessions called "The Time Bomb Within." Employees were invited to wear a "biodot," a patch placed on the skin to measure emotions. The grim times sparked some sick humor. A common joke that made the rounds during Kodak cutbacks: Q: What's the difference between Kodak and the *Titanic*? A: The *Titanic* had an orchestra.

But the pain of Kodak's cutbacks wasn't shared by everyone. While Chandler ordered a 10 percent cut in employment and a 5 percent cut in budgets, the board of directors voted themselves another $1,000-per-year raise and higher meeting fees, $900 per session. They would now receive a retainer of $20,000 per year. Directors also received a $100,000 life insurance policy that continued at a rate of $50,000 after they retired from the board. These were deemed reasonable gestures to keep outside board members. But employees resented the symbolism. No one at the top seemed to be sharing in their pain or offering to make even a slight sacrifice.

At the May 1986 annual meeting, shareholders began to make noise. Earlier that month, Kodak had said its first-quarter results would be lowered by a special charge to pay the expenses incurred in its cost-cutting. Shareholders at the meeting said the board should look for new members, such as the chairman of GAF or T. Boone Pickens, Jr. The directors seemed oblivious to the criticism. Indeed, some board members left the meeting early.

Chandler tried to reassure his workforce that the layoffs were behind them. In an August 1986 interview, he assured Rochester residents that Kodak wouldn't use any more company-wide job-cutting programs. Instead, Kodak would be more careful about hiring and would drop unprofitable businesses.

As the pressure on Kodak grew, management decided on more aggressive diversification efforts, despite earlier setbacks. Kodak looked to the pharmaceuticals business, which it figured could grow from its own chemical research and provide generous margins similar to those found in film. The company's interest in health-care products had started when George Eastman sold photographic plates to Wilhelm Röntgen, who had discovered

X rays in the 1895. Now Kodak began looking for ways to apply its vast chemical expertise in related products. One outgrowth of that search was a prepackaged test to analyze blood for cholesterol and other components. That led to other research, including work on enzymes produced through fermentation of such things as zucchini peels. "The joke in the development stage was that people in the research-lab cafeteria got sick of eating zucchini," said one Kodaker.

Kodak built a large fermentation vat in Cedar Rapids, Iowa, and ventured into joint projects with seed and pesticide companies to explore ways to make plants resistant to fungi. But Kodak didn't spend a huge amount of money and employed fewer than a dozen people in the business. That wasn't much when competing against the likes of Monsanto, DuPont, and Dow Chemical. Kodak exited the business after only a couple of years.

Back in Rochester, the company also pulled the plug on some animal nutrition experimentation. Since 1985, Kodak had been working on research programs with small pharmaceutical companies and individual scientists. The company recruited outside scientists and 200 other staff people to run the new pharmaceutical program.

Meanwhile, it was also launching its efforts to foster new businesses and inventions throughout its empire. Henry Gottfried was one of the outsiders, recruited to develop his idea of selling training programs to outside companies or government agencies. His product became the core of a company called Discus, one of Kodak's ventures under a program called New Opportunities Development, NOD. Other entrepreneurial companies developed products that didn't quite fit within Kodak's traditional businesses.

Gottfried discovered how hard it was to be an entrepreneur inside the Kodak culture. Once one of these ventures became a Kodak business, there were problems. For starters, Kodak insisted that its ventures group adhere to its corporate policies, which drove up the fledgling companies' costs. NOD set up separate offices in an old building on Commercial Street to serve as an incubator site for new companies. "It was a real exciting time," says Robert Tuite, who headed up the venture program. Over spaghetti dinners, entrepreneurs who had started their own companies would sit and talk to Kodak's managers. The idea was to create entrepreneurs and an environment that was much more take-charge than the bureaucratic Kodak culture.

But Gottfried's first meeting as a Kodak manager in the executive offices on the eighteenth floor of the State Street headquarters showed how hard it was to defy the parent company's culture. In a dark-paneled room, George Eastman's picture watched over the meeting, which lasted two hours, involved about twenty people, and concerned bulletin boards.

Kodak officials were eager for the new companies to grow fast. The goal was for each to reach $50 million in sales within five years. Discus reached $2 million in about eighteen months. And, says Gottfried, the ventures got "a bottomless checkbook from Kodak. . . . It allowed everybody to go crazy. We all felt like we were running big companies."

Discus was eventually one of the casualties of the ill-fated ventures program. "They were not prepared for the long-term development," Gottfried says. He didn't fully appreciate the Kodak bureaucracy until he tried to take home the large carved mahogany cat that hung on his office wall. He had bought it on a trip and used the cat as his company's logo. But Kodak officials claimed the carving belonged to the company. "I had to threaten a lawsuit over a cat that I owned and had a receipt for."

Another business that grew out of the innovation efforts was batteries. In May 1986, Kodak introduced a line of lithium batteries to be used in both the Disc and instant cameras. (Battery failure was a major cause of lousy photos.) Kodak had built a pilot lithium-battery plant and "we convinced ourselves we could build a business around it," Tuite says.

One reason was the belief that lithium batteries would last for ten years, perform at low temperatures, and provide more power than traditional alkaline batteries. That made them appealing for use in products like smoke alarms and flashlights. And batteries had the same distribution channels as film.

Kodak set up a joint venture with Matsushita of Japan to build a battery-production plant in Georgia. But the batteries didn't work as well as expected, and customers complained when they didn't deliver on the promise of durability. In 1988, Black & Decker removed thousands of its flashlights from retail shelves and stopped shipment of some smoke detectors that carried the batteries.

Most of Kodak's new ventures were closed or sold, often at a deep discount, and a few were merged into the parent company. It was disappointing, especially as other parts of the company were under siege. "You've got to have a robust deal flow to generate products to offset the ones that are maturing," Tuite says. "This is how you generate employment." It wasn't happening at Kodak.

Another factor driving Kodak's frenzy to diversify was an outside consultants' review of the company in the 1980s. The results showed that Kodak was worth a lot to corporate raiders, who looked for companies with low debt. At the same time, Chandler had been warned by his investment-banking friends that Kodak would be a takeover target.

One way to dissuade a bidder was to take on some debt through an acquisition. Besides, Kodak was realizing by 1987 that it couldn't develop its own pharmaceutical business without outside help. Kodak had ruled out joining the hostile takeover world of the 1980s, but did become the white knight when Hoffmann–La Roche made an unwelcome bid for Sterling Drug in early 1988. Kodak and its investment bankers had already studied Sterling as part of their research into possible acquisition targets.

The bidding on Sterling drove the share price up from $72 (Hoffman's offer) to a hefty $89.50, the price eventually paid by Kodak. The total cost was $5.1 billion, twenty-two times Sterling's 1988 earnings. Kodak also built a large research facility on a one hundred-acre site outside Philadelphia with the help of a $14.7 million grant from the state of Pennsylvania.

Within the first couple of years, nearly all of Sterling's senior management left. The purchase also angered Kodak employees, even those in management who saw how Chandler and Whitmore were swept away by the idea of buying a drug company, regardless of the steep price. "There was a panicky feeling that the drug industry was consolidating too fast and [Sterling] was the last pharmaceutical company available. Kodak got into a bidding frenzy and was poorly advised by investment bankers," says Horschman, the business planner. "The company paid $5.1 billion for a company that was worth $3.5 billion before the takeover. In order for that to be reasonable, you have to bring $1.6 billion worth of value to it, through the ability to manage it better or take costs out. None of those plans were in place." And there wasn't much pressure from Kodak's board, which now had sixteen members, including eight inside directors. Their fees had risen to $33,000 a year, plus fees for each meeting they actually attended. Part of the fee was in Kodak stock, but most was in cash.

The acquisition meant that, for the first time in its history, Kodak had massive debt, requiring hefty interest payments that would cut into its usual freewheeling attitude toward spending. The debt left the company little financial room to manuever. For instance, Kodak was interested in late 1987 and early 1988 in buying Duracell, one of the most successful battery lines in the United States. But Kodak dropped out of the bidding, choosing instead to focus on buying Sterling. Some insiders say that buying Duracell would have made more sense for Kodak than trying to become a pharmaceutical company.

It was a bad year on many fronts. The company also disclosed in the spring of 1988 that it was the target of FBI and New York State investigations regarding chemical leaks at its Kodak Park facilities. Neighbors of the massive plant now learned that chemicals had been leaking out of the plant into the surrounding soil and water. Tests indicated that the groundwater was contaminated with methylene chloride, a suspected carcinogen used in Kodak's film-making process. Inspections by the Environmental Protection Agency showed extensive leaks in Kodak's ancient thirty-one-mile sewer system.

It was a frightening time for Rochester residents. Their Yellow Father was not only losing their respect as an employer, but also, perhaps, poisoning them as well.

Despite Colby Chandler's assurances that the 1986 cutbacks would be Kodak's last, the company was forced in 1989 to downsize again. Chandler's credibility with the rank and file was shot. And this time, the layoffs were more expensive because a benefits package, including up to seventy-eight weeks of pay, was used to attract volunteers to leave. About 5,000 people did go, many of them voluntarily. Fear was sweeping the company. One man was so afraid that he would lose his job that he came to work every day despite a broken back. He stood at his job at the Elmgrove equipment-manufacturing plant in a brace. "You didn't want to take any chances at all. I was scared," he said. Absenteeism fell to less than half the 1986 level at Elmgrove, and the plant was dubbed "Elmgrave" because of the layoffs.

Frank Zaffino, who heads Elmgrove, recalls how hard it was to keep going back to workers with more bad news. He had already cut 4,500 jobs at the plant in 1986 and 1987. But senior management continued to see it as a place for cuts because it isn't part of the key film-making process at Kodak Park, located across town. "Even if we excelled, we never felt like a strategic player," Zaffino says. The Elmgrove team called themselves "stepchildren."

Employee anger was evident in a spoof of the latest management memo. Its author predicted that by 1996 headquarters would be a rented mobile home. Kodak Park would be called "Kodak-Fuji Park." Worldwide employment would be thirty-seven, and research-and-development spending would be $27.55. Mocking the reshuffling that was going on instead of real change, the satire said that personnel at headquarters would simply "move over one desk." (Insiders referred to the restructurings as the bird-cage game: everyone flutters around the same cage, then lands on a different perch.) The spoof memo noted that senior staff would still get raises. (Indeed, in 1989, the directors' compensation climbed to $38,000, including some stock, but mostly cash payments.)

Meanwhile, Kodak was taking more hits in its basic business. Senior management was so preoccupied with diversifying that it was missing some major advances by Japanese competitors. In 1986, Fuji began selling a disposable camera, which became a big hit in Japan. Fuji was first to introduce the camera, but Kodak researchers say they had actually developed similar products in the lab earlier in the 1980s and failed to patent them. Some say it was internal fighting that slowed the patenting process. One problem was disagreement about whether such cameras were a worthwhile alternative to selling film, which didn't involve the additional expense of making the camera. Besides, Kodak had not had a winning camera since the 110 and 126 models of the 1960s and 1970s. And the 35mm cameras made by Japanese competitors were increasingly popular with U.S. consumers. So inventions such as the disposable camera often languished in the labs.

Kodak had a tough time figuring out how to read the disposable camera's success in Japan. For decades, the company didn't have its own sales force there, which put it at a disadvantage against entrenched competitors like Fuji and Konica. One manager recalls going into Kodak's stores in Japan and seeing signs for Fuji film. Kodak film was stacked on shelves, while Fuji's was refrigerated. The Fuji film was cheaper and was featured in newspaper ads. When he asked the store manager about all this, he was told: "We make more money on Fuji."

Kodak did recognize the importance of research in the Japanese market, and in the mid-1980s built a lab to study developments in electronics, such as digital cameras. "There was a gut feeling that we ought to have a lab in the heartland of the consumer electronics revolution," says Przybylowicz. But there was no vision of how that lab should operate. Shortly after it was established, it was put on a pay-as-you-go basis, meaning that it had to find support from individual business units rather than be funded as part of an overall corporate strategy. Consequently the scientists constantly had to market their own research to several different managers to prove that it should continue. If one manager didn't see value in their ideas, the scientists would have to move on to another department to try and find money to finance the lab. "That's an impossible situation," Przybylowicz points out.

By late 1989, Chandler was adamant about controlling costs. To emphasize that he was serious about making drastic cuts, he walked into one senior management meeting carrying a machete and started chopping up a wooden crate. But Chandler was dubbed "the leader of the gang that can't shoot straight." He became obsessed with short-term concerns and couldn't seem to focus on the long view. He formed a group called Sector 7 that met two or three times a year to discuss the company's future. "The group was supposed to do strategic thinking. How should we move forward?" Przybylowicz says. "But often it ended up as discussion of financial matters. I used to ask to be excused. . . . There weren't any precipitous decisions made."

By December 1989, Kodak's board announced that Chandler would retire in June 1990. It had been another disappointing year. Kodak's net income had fallen to $1.63 a share, from $4.31 the previous year. Chandler's two lieutenants, Whitmore and Samper, were contending for his job. Whitmore was more like Chandler: cautious to a fault. They were both friendly with the troops. Chandler liked to spend his spare time on his farm; Whitmore spent his with the church. Neither one was aggressive or eager to make bold decisions. But Chandler, seemingly oblivious to Whitmore's shortcomings, endorsed him, and the board picked him to take all three top posts, dissolving the triumvirate. Samper quit upon learning that he wouldn't have control over the photographic division. "On the surface, they seemed to get along, but if you were in a room with the two of them, you could feel the tension," said one Kodak manager. "Samper couldn't accept being number two."

That put entirely too much control at one desk, with a CEO who didn't even seem terribly interested in the job. Or in addressing the urgent need for change. At times, Whitmore's lack of enthusiasm was quite apparent. He would often fall asleep at business meetings. "He'd call a meeting and then doze off," former vice president Kathy Hudson recalled. Whitmore vowed to continue in Chandler's tradition. "Don't expect huge announcements. The changes will be incremental," he said.

The message was all too clear: Kodak's gradual downward drift would be allowed to continue. No one had a plan to stop it.

3

Hitting the Wall

Kay Whitmore's weakness was frustrating for Kodak's management around the world, who wanted to see the company move beyond its troubles. "There was a lot of indecision at the top . . . about how the company was going to be led into the 1990s," said Ziggy Switkowski, chairman of Kodak Australia. It seemed as if one thing after another went wrong during the final days of Chandler's term—and for Whitmore, too. For starters, the ongoing environmental investigations led to Kodak's guilty plea for violations of New York's environmental laws. In April 1990, Kodak was fined $2 million in civil and criminal penalties for its contamination of Kodak Park. One charge hinged on Kodak's failure to report promptly a 5,100-gallon spill of methylene chloride from tanks at the park. The spills had occasionally released solvents into the Genesee River.

The Sterling Drug acquisition, which had been championed by Kay Whitmore and his lieutenant Leo "Jack" Thomas, was turning into a nightmare. Operating earnings for the health group declined nearly 18 percent, which Kodak linked to the cost of closing some Sterling plants. One of its flagship brands, Bayer Aspirin, was getting hammered by Tylenol and Advil. Indeed, Bayer's sales had dropped by 25 percent since Kodak acquired Sterling. And the company wasn't having any luck getting other drugs approved by the U.S. Food and Drug Administration.

Meanwhile, the debt undertaken to acquire Sterling was costing Kodak millions of dollars each quarter in interest alone.

Still, Kodak management forged ahead with its diversification efforts. In 1991, Kodak introduced a product called Photo CD, with the promise that "The future of memories is here." Photo CD starts as a blank compact disc. A photographer's roll of film is developed by a photofinisher, and the images are then transferred to the disk rather than being printed as paper pictures. Storing images on a CD gives users the ability to preserve a large number of pictures on a single disk. Besides, the images can be viewed on a television screen with a special Photo CD player, or on a computer screen with a CD-ROM. The product was one of Kodak's first attempts to bridge traditional photography and the more advanced world of digital technology.

Many were uneasy about the project, considering that Kodak was at that same time shelling out over more than $900 million to Polaroid for its last big blunder, the instant camera. And besides the fine, Kodak had lost about $675 million on the project during its ten years in the business.

Managers on the Photo CD project said they took the idea to the board of directors, some of whom questioned whether it was a good idea, considering Kodak's financial problems. The project was projected to be a $600 million business by 1997 with $100 million earnings from operations—this although there was little evidence that average film buyers would invest in a new piece of equipment to view photos on their home television, or that they would pay the premium required to put the pictures on the disks. But the board of directors approved the launch.

But changes had begun brewing inside the boardroom. Slowly, Kodak was getting more outsiders, who were not complacent. A handful of directors were emerging as strong voices asking tough questions. For instance, John Phelan, the former head of the New York Stock Exchange, and Roberto Goizueta, the CEO of Coca-Cola, actually talked about various company plans, rather than just rubber-stamping whatever the CEO wanted. The others still took their role less seriously, and considering their post an honor rather than a pressing business commitment.

So Kodak proceeded to announce Photo CD. While some worked on the consumer end of the market, the invention team, including Scott Brownstein, knew the real potential was in the commercial market, including publishers, advertising agencies, and others who need to store and use a lot of images. But inside Kodak, the developers had to get funding, so Photo CD was launched through the consumer business. While the press conference focused on consumer uses, Brownstein and his group worked on alliances with computer companies, which had to be convinced to make their CD-ROMs compatible with Photo CD. He made friends with the likes of Apple Computer's John Sculley, who supported the program.

Brownstein says senior Kodak management at the time wanted a quick hit with Photo CD and "would never understand our real vision or strategy." The biggest problem was getting tradition-bound Kodakers to understand the fast-paced world of Silicon Valley. Many in senior management had never even used a PC, so it was extremely difficult to get them to understand how to negotiate deals with the likes of Microsoft. "They don't understand how the whole infrastructure works," Brownstein says.

The group did manage to get an audience with Microsoft's founder, Bill Gates. But Brownstein and others on the Photo CD team weren't even invited to the first Rochester meeting. Eventually, senior management figured out that they needed "some interpreters."

Perhaps the worst meeting was the one during which Whitmore fell asleep. "Here we are, sitting with Bill Gates, and Whitmore is sleeping," Brownstein says. Gates began to rock in his chair. And no deal was struck at this time, because Kodak wanted royalties from Microsoft even though Microsoft would have to redesign its CD-ROMs to be compatible with Photo CD. Later, when Brownstein and his team did manage to win over computer companies, they still had problems explaining the deals to Whitmore. He would ponder the terms for a month and then want to change them.

The Photo CD players were another problem. They didn't generate much consumer interest, and prices tumbled from the original $399. Television advertising for the players didn't hit the air until December, too late to convince many consumers that they'd make good Christmas gifts. Another problem was that clerks in consumer electronics stores didn't know much about the technology of Photo CDs versus audio CD players, so they showed little interest in demonstrating them or explaining the differences to consumers.

Meanwhile, other parts of Kodak's empire were under siege. And there was still little discipline in drawing up budgets or making forecasts. For instance, in the film business, Kodak decided to bolster its standing with professional photographers by opening an "Imaging Center" in Camden, Maine. It was envisioned as a place for seminars and other events. The project ran way over budget, and the opulent center was eventually sold.

And more and more customers were switching to Fuji film and paper. John White recalls a meeting in Berlin shortly after the Wall was torn down. The hosts gave their Kodak guests a photograph of the Wall coming down, and an actual chunk of the Wall. As the group admired the photograph, one of the Kodak officials turned the picture over to see the words "Fuji Film" on the back of the print.

Consumers were finding that they could save a couple of dollars per roll of film if they bought brands other than Kodak's yellow box. Private-label brands, such as those sold under the K Mart label, or 3M's Scotch brand, were getting more shelf display at retailers, who earn a bigger margin on their own products than on big national brands like Kodak. By 1985, Fuji's share of the U.S. market had grown to 11 percent, while 3M had 3.7 percent. Kodak's share started to fall as the others moved in, from about 80 percent of U.S. retail sales to about 70 percent. As point-and-shoot cameras made it easier for amateurs to take pictures, they learned that they could get cheaper, decent-quality pictures with something other than Kodak film.

But inside Kodak, managers continued to present rosy sales predictions, which insiders called hockey-stick forecasts because they showed a rise in business, curving up at a sharp angle, just like a hockey stick at a conveniently distant future date. The sunny projections would be relayed to the board of directors. Vice president Hudson got so disgusted with these forecasts that she once showed up to a meeting wearing a goalie's mask and carrying a hockey stick, vowing not to make such predictions. Managers would frequently present the numbers and then spend the next several meetings figuring out "how do we catch up," she says. As one manager remarks, "there were no public hangings"—or, indeed, consequences of any kind—for missing a forecast. That was because senior management rarely asked questions. "It was very hard to get Kay to ask penetrating questions in a business review," Horschman says.

The board seemed uninterested in hearing details on the business. "In my five years as an officer, I spent thirty-eight minutes with the board on substantive issues," Hudson says. When asked what went right during those years, she replies: "I'm hard pressed to think of something that went well."

Those who worked with Whitmore saw that he was now preoccupied with getting Wall Street off his back. All the Street wanted was an accurate assessment of the business. Instead, the rosy forecasts delivered to the board were also dished out to the investment analysts who predicted Kodak's earnings. The company was rarely right or candid in its projections. Insiders found it increasingly difficult to get Whitmore to listen to ideas for implementing a strategic plan rather than just announcing one restructuring or downsizing after another.

Senior managers from various parts of the company had spent three years on a strategic plan and were discussing it at a July 1991 meeting at Niagara-on-the-Lake that included the company's top thirty officers. It seemed that everyone was unanimous about the need for a detailed strategic plan that focused on evaluating the company's core imaging technologies and how they could be expanded. Pryzbylowicz thought "everybody was getting in line" behind the plan. But then Whitmore told the group that Kodak would have to have another round of about 3,000 cuts.

"Several of us tried to dissuade him from that position," says Przybylowicz. "Our argument for that was, if we implement the strategic plan first, it will become a lot more obvious where to target reductions." The past three reductions in force had been unstructured. For instance, Kodak lost some managers and factory workers who were specialists on the various product lines. In other cases, it simply lost too many people in one department, forcing it to hire temporary workers to fill in so work could be done. "They left us decimated in certain areas and skill bases," says Przybylowicz. In many cases, "we had to offer them a contract to come back to cover the transition period. What we proposed was another [reduction]." Alex Henderson at Prudential Securities had coined the term "bulimic management": Kodak would feed, then purge, then feed and purge again.

Instead of dissecting the problems behind its ailing financial health, Kodak once again seized the option of reducing its payrolls in 1991 and 1992. "It was death by a thousand cuts," Horschman says. In August 1991, Kodak unveiled its Resource Redeployment and Retirement Plan (Triple R). This voluntary plan, open to anyone in the company, offered a $5,000 retraining allowance and a "bridge" payment equal to the Social Security payments the employee would get at age 62. Those who left also got a full pension and a year's pay. It was one of the most generous buyouts in the history of corporate America. Even insiders were astonished that Whitmore would agree to such a lavish package.

Przybylowicz struggled with his own future over the Labor Day holiday. He asked himself: "Could I live through another one? You get into a credibility problem with your own people." He wrote Whitmore a letter that weekend and said he, too, would take the early retirement package in November 1991. Others were equally frustrated. "You can't shrink your way to success, but basically, that's the way we've managed many of our operations," Switkowski says.

Not only was Triple R expensive, but Kodak lost some people that it wanted to keep. "The baby went out with the bathwater," says Van Graafeiland, the general counsel. For instance, Kodak once again hired some people back as consultants to fill in the gaps. In other cases, people had to be promoted more quickly than expected, leaving them unprepared for their new jobs. All four of the supervisors who managed one department in Kodak Park took the plan. That meant that the four most skilled people who supervised this twenty-four-hour operation wanted to retire at the same time. Instead, Kodak officials asked two of them to stay on and extended the Triple R benefits until they could train their replacements.

In all, about 8,300 people took the Triple R package, instead of the 3,000 that Kodak had hoped would leave. The eventual cost: about $900 million. Moreover, the departure of so many employees meant it was nearly impossible to implement the company's strategic plan.

The buyout infuriated many retirees, who had been encouraged to leave or been forced out of jobs just before the generous 1991 buyout. Indeed, they had good reason to be angry: the senior management team that had bungled so many times was now parachuting out safely with a hefty retirement plan. And investors had reason to be angry, too. All the restructuring and special buyout costs meant Kodak posted net income of just 5 cents a share for 1991, down from $2.17 a share in 1990.

By 1992, investor dissatisfaction became louder and more apparent to Whitmore and the board of directors. Unlike earlier rumblings, this round got their attention, because the nineties were an era of change among senior management and boards. More and more CEOs were being fired for poor performance. And directors were seeing themselves labeled villains, which was not their idea of the good time that used to come with being a corporate director. So Kodak investors were starting to get noticed as they prodded Whitmore and the board to make some changes to reverse the erosion in the company's market and financial positions.

Robert A. G. Monks and other principals in LENS, Inc., a Washington, D.C., firm that buys stakes in underperforming companies, bought about $2 million worth of Kodak shares in July 1992. Monks wrote to Whitmore and asked for a meeting, at which he offered some very specific suggestions on how to fix Kodak and reverse the low shareholder returns during the last decade. His group deemed Kodak's empire-building a failure. And management had thrown larger and larger amounts of money at the core problem of dwindling film market share, without a strategy.

Nell Minnow, another principal at LENS, likens Kodak's

empire-building to an addiction: "Robin Williams used to say that cocaine is God's way of telling you that you're making too much money. What we call promiscuous conglomeratization is God's way of telling you that you don't have a good governance. . . . You don't have some kind of direction and focus."

And Kodak's hefty debt caused LENS to suggest selling off some businesses and spinning off others to shareholders. It suggested selling the health division assets, then selling half of the chemical business through an initial public offering, with the other shares distributed to Kodak shareholders. Monks also cited Kodak's sagging $4 billion information division, which included copiers. The division had no strategy and sometimes wasn't even mentioned in management reports to shareholders.

Monks urged Whitmore to address some governance issues, such as annual election of directors. "Director accountability on an annual basis is an essential component of credibility with shareholders."

He also chastised the company for having a high proportion of company employees and former CEO Chandler sitting on the board. "Where the need for change from past decisions seems so clear, the imperative for a board largely composed of 'independents' and without the complications caused by the presence of a former CEO seems compelling." He also suggested separating the chairman and CEO posts to "demonstrate change" and the willingness to create a "new accountability."

Finally, LENS wanted shareholders to adopt new bylaws that would make management more accountable so that it would consider such proposals more carefully.

What LENS didn't ask for was more layoffs. "The pressure [Whitmore] was under was everybody calling for layoffs," Minnow says. "We never thought that was the answer."

Some investors questioned the fact that board members owned so few shares. "I once asked why not compensate the board with stock rather than cash until they have a meaningful stake," Horschman says. He was told that some board members relied on the fees as part of their income. That's a questionable arrangement: directors should have independence so they will question a CEO, rather than feeling beholden to the company for a paycheck.

By early 1993, Whitmore seemed to be getting the message. On January 11, he hired an outsider to be his new chief financial officer. News that Christopher J. Steffen, a cost-cutter who had worked at Chrysler and Honeywell, would join Kodak sent the company's stock up $3.25 a share to close at $45. Steffen would be the first outsider in two decades to join the stodgy company's management. Whitmore, facing the daunting task of what to do with a company that had $10.3 billion in debt, pledged that Kodak would now act on its plans, rather than just talk about them.

Within days, Kodak also announced that it would link more of management's pay to performance and require that executives invest one to four times their salaries in Kodak stock. For Whitmore, that meant he had to buy $3.8 million in stock within five years.

Still, Kodak management believed they had to cut even more jobs. This time, layoffs hit the once-sacred research staffs. About 2,000 people were let go in Rochester in January 1993.

Kodak's layoff policies continued to be ill advised and randomly planned, at best. The company suffered a huge embarrassment—and expense—when it tried to cut back its Japanese staff. Job offers to eight engineering and science graduates recruited from Tokyo University and other schools were revoked. The universities' job placement departments complained: because of the rescindments, the students had missed other job offers. Eventually, Kodak offered each student a payment of 2.5 million yen as compensation.

The Japanese research center also asked seventy of its 110 researchers to take early retirement. Others wanted to go, too, and the company had to convince them to stay. Japanese press reports suggested that the personnel moves would hurt the company's standing in Japan, both in future recruiting and in sales of the company's film, which already lagged way behind Fuji's 72 percent share and Konica's 17 percent share.

In Rochester, there were signs that the board was beginning to understand that changes must come from them, too. Whitmore announced a new corporate directions committee of board members, including John Phelan; John Burlingame, former vice chairman of General Electric; Alice Emerson, a fellow at the Andrew W. Mellon Foundation; and Paul Gray, chairman of MIT. They would work with senior management on major issues.

Wall Street was responding. Even before Steffen arrived in Rochester, *The Wall Street Journal* dubbed him "the $2.2 billion man." That was how much Kodak stock market value had climbed since he was named to the CFO's job. But once he took office, Steffen quickly showed that he was interested in cost-cutting and little else. He sent fear throughout the organization. At Kodak's Eastman Chemical division in Kingsport, Tennessee, employees were nervous when Steffen came to visit. He wore gold jewelry, Trafalgar suspenders, and matching tie-and-handkerchief sets, so he stood out, especially among the home-spun managers of the chemical division. They had read about his mecenarylike career, which featured stints at many companies— quite a difference from the lifetime careers of most Kodakers. "The financial wizard came in here and paid us a visit," says Harold Corn, who works in personnel at Eastman Chemical. "There was a pretty high anxiety level about him because the feeling was that this guy doesn't care about people. He cares about himself. He's trying to make a name for himself and con-tinue to add to his status as a financial wizard in the Wall Street area, and all the benefits that come with that." Word spread quickly that Steffen, the "cutter and slasher," was in town. "The people know his reputation."

The big question throughout Kodak was "What's going to happen to us?" Indeed, Steffen's frequent references to his days at Chrysler Corporation, which went through drastic cost-cutting, showed his emphasis on the numbers rather than the people. When half of a workforce gets laid off, "the other half buy in pretty quickly," he said. In a speech to a management group, Steffen said that, in any restructuring, inflicting pain is a given.

In Rochester, Steffen focused on the numbers and spent little time mingling with the masses. "All he wanted to do was look at spreadsheets," Hudson says. This didn't fit with Whitmore's col-legial style. And Steffen quickly realized how reluctant Whitmore and others were to make substantial changes. Certainly he was a hit on Wall Street. His meetings with analysts were met with support. But he wasn't getting along with Whitmore, who still wanted to call the shots. "If Chris Steffen comes in here assuming he's the Lone Ranger, he will not last very long," Whitmore told *The Wall Street Journal* in April 1993. "He can't do it all by himself."

The day after that quote appeared on page one of the newspaper, Kodak announced that Steffen had resigned following a confrontation with Whitmore. The two had disagreed on a plan for how to sell off pieces of the company and introduce other cost-cutting measures. Whitmore reminded Steffen that he was the boss. Steffen was supposed to host an analysts' meeting in New York City that same week, but Whitmore showed up in his place, telling the analysts that the two had disagreed about how to make changes. Whitmore wanted to consider issues other than just the numbers. To soothe the disappointed analysts, Whitmore pledged to have a new financial plan ready in five months and said he had hired investment bankers to help guide him.

But the market wasn't impressed. News of Steffen's resignation sent the stock down $5.125 to $47.25, taking $1.7 billion of the company's market value with it. (Ironically, IBM's stock climbed $1.50 a share the day Steffen resigned, because the rumor mill suggested that he might move on to that company.)

Kodak watchers had been encouraged by Steffen's comments that more layoffs would follow. "The market thinks the wrong guy resigned," said Ralph Whitworth, president of the United Shareholders Association, a shareholders' activist group. The Steffen departure wasn't the only bad news for Kodak: the company also reported a first-quarter loss of $1.88 billion.

Whitmore took off to visit major shareholders and explain that the company wasn't going to stand still just because Steffen had left. CALPERS, the influential California pension fund, one of the country's largest institutional investors, said it might vote against management's slate of directors. Investors who attended the meeting said Whitmore "saw his own mortality" there. One investor suggested that Whitmore should have quit instead of

Steffen. Whitmore blushed and said that that would have been a mistake.

At a management meeting, back in Rochester, Whitmore got a warmer reception. "The man was going at a hundred miles an hour," recalls Jane Lanphear, who was Whitmore's assistant at the time. "He told me to gather every overhead in the world. . . . I had no idea what the man was going to talk about." Whitmore went to the ninth-floor auditorium and delivered an emotional speech, telling his managers that he believed in them. "We will make this work," he said. He didn't believe that Kodak's problems would be solved by "removing all the management people." The entire group stood up and cheered him. "If you could have, you would have gone and put him on your shoulders because he was open," Lanphear said. "He was honest."

It became increasingly clear to those inside the company that Whitmore realized that the end was near for him. Lanphear recalls that he said: "I could leave, but we're gonna see this through together. . . . But if it becomes necessary for me to leave, I will."

Lanphear was so impressed by his speech that she told him, "Kay, you know, you should get really tired more often": he hadn't sugar-coated his remarks as he did in official CEO presentations. This time, he spoke from the heart. It wasn't a matter of offering earth-shattering plans to change the company in the speech, which was long on cheerleading and short on specifics; he just seemed to strike a chord with his faithful followers, who wanted to believe that somehow Whitmore could still figure out how to save Kodak. And some cheered simply because they were glad that Steffen had left. His ideas for cost-cutting were too severe for many in the genteel world of Kodak, so they were endorsing their familiar leader over the outsider who had frightened them.

Likewise, the board of directors seemed to return to coddling Whitmore, at least publicly. Despite increasing pressure on the CEO by Wall Street, the nine outside directors soon issued a statement that they fully supported Whitmore's efforts to solve the company's problems. But they did warn that performance "must be improved significantly." And CALPERS met with Kodak's management, while the United Shareholders Association solicited proxies to push for annual election of directors.

By the May 1993 annual meeting, held in Florida, Whitmore was facing a no-win situation. Shareholders, including John Ragusa, were angry over the lack of progress in fixing the problems. Instead of offering rosy forecasts as in the past, Whitmore finally acknowledged that Kodak had a lousy track record of keeping its promises. "For a long time, major corporations in this country have made talk and claims about change and shareholder value," he said. "But in many cases, including this company, we have in fact delivered relatively little against those expectations. We are driving for change in Kodak today."

Monks, Ragusa, and others stood up and prodded Whitmore about his plans. Because of the previous investor meetings, some of his critics didn't even bother to attend the Florida meeting. Whitmore assured shareholders that Kodak would shrink some more and that it was his "personal mission" to answer demands for change. Whitmore also announced that he and his successors would no longer stay on the board after leaving the company. Chandler planned to retire that same year. And, Whitmore promised, a major divestiture would be announced by the end of the year.

Still, 42 percent of shareholders voted against Kodak's staggered board-election system. Whitmore and his party were losing support in some important circles inside the company, too. Kodak's troubles were increasingly frustrating for its managers, including the Photo CD team, led by Brownstein and Georgia McCabe. "We were always externally focused, while the guys at home were campaigning for their jobs. That convinced us to leave. And we couldn't lie publicly much more," Brownstein says.

Kodak's continual restructuring meant musical chairs and new managers who had "little knowledge of our vision, history, or accomplishment," says Brownstein. "It became increasingly difficult to publicly represent Kodak and maintain our own reputations in the computer world." Brownstein and McCabe left with thirteen of their colleagues from Photo CD to form a digital imaging division for Applied Graphics Technologies, a pre-press and printing company owned by Mort Zuckerman and Fred Drasner.

The summer of 1993 was stressful at Kodak. It was clear to managers that some members of the board were starting to push Whitmore to move faster. Lanphear and others saw factions within the group. "Some relished the opportunity to make a difference," she said. "Some said: 'Oh boy, I don't know how this is all gonna work out.'" Watching all this as Whitmore's assistant was "like getting an MBA in real time."

In June, Whitmore announced that Kodak would spin off its Eastman Chemical Company in Kingsport. Shares of the company would be distributed to Kodak shareholders on a one-for-four basis. The chemical business had been consistently providing cash to the parent company to patch up other areas that were bleeding. And Eastman Chemical had really flourished, despite the parent company's woes. Only about 8 percent of its sales came from supplying chemicals and other materials for film and other products to Kodak. "That fact alone is a good indicator that Eastman is not strategic to the Kodak portfolio," says Earnest Deavenport, Jr., who headed the division and became its CEO after the spin-off. Besides, the deal meant Kodak could shift $2 billion of its debt and 17,500 employees off its own books and into a separate company.

By July, however, the directors decided that Whitmore had had enough opportunity to make changes. It was time for him to go. Another meeting with investors prompted another chorus of calling for his head. The investors had lost patience with his pledge to deliver a turnaround plan in September.

Board members were supposed to attend, but Whitmore went alone to face the angry investors. He opened the meeting by asking them how to fight off advances by private-label film, which continued to eat up Kodak's market share among amateur photographers. By 1993, 3M had carved out 5 percent of the market, and Fuji had 13 percent. Whitmore's question was proof that he was struggling with the major issues hurting the film business. But some in the group were angry that a CEO had to ask outsiders for advice on his core business. The meeting turned into a lecture on how Whitmore should get serious about finally cutting jobs and selling Sterling. The investors asked for deeper cuts this time: another 20,000 workers.

Despite the sharp criticism of his performance, Whitmore seemed to remain firm about sticking to his own plan. His approach wouldn't be so aggressive. To many, that was the final signal that Whitmore simply couldn't make the deep changes needed to save Kodak.

After the investors' meeting, the board of directors voted to ask Whitmore to step down as chairman and CEO. The board gave him time to tell his family and others before the directors announced the news.

By then, Lanphear, Whitmore's assistant, was about to start her own new job, as vice president of health sciences. She was on vacation in Maine in early August when Whitmore called to tell her he'd been fired. He planned a special management meeting before the news broke. Lanphear could hear the emotion in Whitmore's voice. Several times in the past, he'd told her that he wouldn't question the board if it voted to take away his job. But now that he had lost the fight, he wasn't so dispassionate. Trying to mask his own feelings, he simply said: "The family is quite upset."

Wall Street investors cheered the news of Whitmore's departure. The next day, the announcement sent Kodak shares up $3.25 a share to close at $58.625, raising the company's market value by $1 billion. The following day's Rochester *Democrat & Chronicle* carried the headline "Overhaul Starts" over a picture of Whitmore driving away from his Kodak office.

The outside directors issued a statement saying: "We believe there is a clear need to move faster and further on operating cost efficiencies and enhanced earnings." Some directors, including Goizueta and Phelan, finally acknowledged that they had been frustrated for two years, but had given Whitmore that time to try and fix Kodak's problems. That was difficult for employees to understand. The company had bungled its many attempts to solve its problems, using unstructured and random layoffs as a quick fix that never addressed underlying issues. Workers were losing their jobs, while Whitmore was still allowed to coast.

Insiders were angered by the directors' sudden admission that they were critical of Whitmore's tenure, given that in prior years they had showed little interest in really pushing him to change. Only when investor pressures were made public did the directors say they were ready to kick Whitmore out.

A search committee of board directors, who would recruit a new CEO, met with Kodak's senior management to explain the firing. The meeting left many even more ticked off with the board. "They treated us like, '*We're* the board and you're a bunch of jerks,' " Hudson says. Despite the board's proclamations that it had pushed for change, Hudson believes the group is still "very much a club."

Whitmore's top officers say the rest of the summer was dreadful because the lame-duck CEO was ineffective. Besides, despite their problems with Whitmore's management of the company, they were sorry to see their friend get the ax. In some ways, he had become the scapegoat for problems that began long before his tenure and were apparent to the board long before it stepped in.

Later that month, Whitmore delivered more news on the company's restructuring plan—which wasn't easy to do, considering that he had resisted making massive cuts through layoffs and now wasn't going to be around to carry out his own plan. Kodak announced that it would eliminate 10,000 more jobs by the end of 1995. This time, there weren't any special buyout packages, just layoffs. Once again, Kodak was slicing jobs but "not addressing the fundamental problems," one manager says. Indeed, director Phelan told investors that Kodak has "got to learn to solve their problems and not just throw money and time at each of those problems." He said cost-cutting was improving, but "really doesn't fundamentally exist today and it must start at the top."

Other budget cuts stalled successful programs that looked promising. Morale bottomed out as rank-and-file employees openly expressed their rage, even in the employee newsletter. "They get rid of workers. They have to get rid of some managers," wrote one employee. Adolf DaCosta, a technician, wrote: "We've lost some very good people with past reductions. You can only cut people so much, and then less people will have to do more work and quality may suffer." The local newspaper carried a cartoon of Whitmore's head resting on a platter and uttering: "Only 9,999 to go."

Amid this turmoil, managers in the photography division—seemingly oblivious to the need to conserve cash—decided to move their headquarters to Washington, D.C., under the guise of being closer to their customers. The move would cost about $10 million. Jack Thomas, Whitmore's second in command, defended it because of the need for Kodak to get some of its people out of the Rochester mind-set. "We spend too much time with each other looking inward. . . . Our culture seems to tie us up in endless meetings," he said in a memo to employees. Indeed, Kodak's market share in Rochester is more than 15 points above that in the rest of the United States, so it made a lot of sense to argue that managers based there might have unrealistic perceptions of the company's standing. But it didn't resonate with the rank and file, who were losing jobs while their bosses were moving to fancier digs in Washington.

The move was led by Bob Hamilton, vice president and general manager for the United States and Canada. He and Thomas contended that many trips by Kodak management were canceled at the last minute because of meetings in Rochester. Thomas told employees he was concerned that they were not receptive to change: "We say we want it. But we don't really like it when it happens."

Besides the outrage sparked by the move's $10 million price tag, many inside the company saw how the senior management was vacillating about basic decisions now that Whitmore was a lame duck. He became more withdrawn about day-to-day business, and seemed to be grieving over the fact that Kodak was falling apart. Indeed, Whitmore had once told some of his managers that he didn't want to be "the guy to turn the lights out around here," Horschman recalled. What Whitmore didn't understand was that it "may be necessary to turn the lights off in a lot of rooms to keep it going."

Besides, the relocation was symbolic of the uncertainty that faced everyone. About a hundred jobs would be affected, and only about a third of those employees would be relocated to the new office. Employees were left in suspense over whether they would be invited to move or would lose their jobs, such as administrative positions, which would then be filled by local hires. The impact was felt throughout the company; managers found it more and more difficult to motivate employees who were waiting to hear who was losing his or her job and who was staying behind. Even the managers saw little promise that improved results would make a difference. "Incentives tied to achievement were virtually nonexistent," Switkowski of Kodak Australia says. The joke was that "your reward is you get to keep your job."

Van Graafeiland, the general counsel, says the summer of 1993 was "by far the most difficult" experience in his twenty years in law practice: "operating the company for four to five months in late summer–early fall 1993 [was] just about as close to impossible as you can imagine."

There was a lot of concern about who would take over as CEO. Many feared that a harsh cost-cutter like Steffen would be appointed to hack away thousands and thousands of jobs. Goizueta said that the new leader would need "exceptional drive and energy to do what must be done." Meanwhile, for their efforts to find a new CEO, the search committee members received $1,500 per meeting.

The choice, made in late 1993, was Motorola's CEO, George M. C. Fisher. It was a surprise to many. Fisher would be leaving a hugely successful company to come to one in absolute chaos. Goizueta called him energetic and "a man of vision."

To attract him, the board offered a multimillion-dollar compensation package, which infuriated people throughout Rochester. The pay package was especially annoying to those who were looking over their shoulders, fearing they would be among the 10,000 employees laid off. And here was a new CEO getting, among other things, a $5 million signing bonus. "I am really appalled and angered," said George M. Schuttee, a Fairport, New York, resident, in a letter to the *Democrat & Chronicle*. "I find this ridiculous, offensive, obscene and a clear slap in the face of every working man and woman in our community and especially the unemployed workers in Monroe County."

Inside Kodak, there was both optimism and fear as employees waited for Fisher to take his post. Most had become quite realistic after years of disappointments following previous management promises to really change Kodak's culture and solve its many problems. "Most of the problems arise from the big decisions by management," Switkowski says. "The casualties become the rest of the organization."

Observers on Wall Street and in the media applauded Fisher's appointment as a sign that, finally, something would change inside Kodak. *Business Week*'s story on the new CEO offered him some advice and a simple "Good luck. You'll need it."

PART TWO

The Morning After

4

Downscaling the American Dream

The drive into Scottsville, New York, just west of Rochester, is like a trip through picture postcards from the American dream. White houses fly flags for Memorial Day. A Little League team plays ball on a dusty field at sunset; a boy wearing orange jersey number 8 waits for his turn at bat. The main street still has a tailor, a diner, and a bowling alley. Norman Rockwell would have felt at home here. He could have pulled out his brushes and filled a canvas with front porches, white wicker rockers, and pots of red geraniums at the ends of lanes. The American Legion Hall sits at the edge of town, where pavement gives way to cornfields and weathered gray barns.

Beyond the stone fences and tall weeds, Bob and Meredith Couture live in a blue colonial house with an affectionate and lumbering Newfoundland called Rosie. Theirs was once a comfortable life, thanks to the dual Kodak paychecks for their jobs as a mechanical engineer and a systems analyst. Continuous raises ensured the usual trappings of success: a spacious house on a five-acre lot and a driveway with three status symbols—a BMW, a Volvo, and a Saab.

The Coutures could afford to eat out every weekend at their favorite restaurants, such as The King & I for Thai food. They could indulge in new stereo equipment for the living room. Bob took up woodworking as a hobby; Meredith wove colorful tapestries on looms he built for her.

They earned their lifestyle. Bob spent long days designing

Kodak's signature cameras and copiers during his twenty-two years on the job. Meredith, trained as an industrial engineer, worked as a systems analyst, keeping the computer network inside Kodak updated with new records.

But Kodak changed their lives forever when scores of engineers were laid off in one of the company's restructurings. Bob lost his job in the January 1993 layoff. More than a year later, the couple worried that 10,000 more job cuts and a new CEO would bring even more upheaval to their lives. Meredith, whose department had been restructured several times, constantly feared that she would be in the next round of cutbacks. Bob was still searching for a new job. Most days, he sent out résumés and cover letters, pursuing leads. Or he attended various support groups and visited outplacement centers with other unemployed Kodakers. Meanwhile, Meredith went to work, bitter that Bob was let go after more than two decades of service. "It's hard to go in without him," she said.

They considered relocating to another city, if Bob could find a new job. So he spent days fixing up their house, hoping to increase its sales value. He installed a new toilet and sink and painted the trim and the gray horse barn out back. Household chores fill his days. Most days, Meredith came home at 5:30 P.M. to a home-cooked meal on the table.

One evening, Bob experimented with a new cheese fondue recipe. He tried wine in the fondue, but that wasn't too good. So today's batch had a touch of beer stirred in with the melted cheddar cheese. Fresh bread was neatly cubed and ready for dipping. His homemade dressing topped a salad of mixed greens. For dessert, he used the red Kitchen Aid mixer to add Amaretto to the fresh whipping cream that would top the raspberry short-cake: "My special recipe."

His engineering background occasionally sneaked into his discussion of recipes. "It was about six months before I started cooking seriously. It was a matter of getting enough knowledge of why things like roux and emulsifiers work," he said. A *Better Homes and Gardens* cookbook sat ready on the counter. Bob was proud of his meal, but he noted that his new role as suburban stay-at-home husband had one big drawback: "The pay sucks."

White-collar unemployment is shaking suburbia. What was once a plight of factory workers in blue-collar households has moved up to the middle-class homes like the Coutures'. At the very least, the unemployed find their self-esteem shaken. A lost job often takes the person's identity with it. Those once accustomed to the nine-to-five world are now adrift, losing the weekday routines that once anchored their lives. They are downscaling their part of the American dream.

Joblessness is especially wrenching for men, because their identity traditionally has been shaped by their work. After years of working at one company, they feel betrayed. So the generation that grew up seeing the tranquil lives of Ozzie and Harriet Nelson or June and Ward Cleaver now find their own lives are more like the modern sitcom *Roseanne,* in which Dad drifts in and out of jobs and the family has trouble paying the electric bill.

"Americans as a group have historically believed in the system," says Dr. Ernesto Michelucci, a psychologist who counsels the unemployed. "What's happening now says you can't trust the system. People are losing faith."

The Coutures were part of an era when an engineering degree equaled a secure job inside corporate America. A graduate of the University of New Haven, Bob joined Kodak in the early 1970s because he wanted to design cameras. He'd been an amateur photographer in college. Meredith followed a similar path, joining Kodak through a college co-op program. "A lot of people didn't bother putting résumés out to other companies," she said. "Kodak had a big pipeline of people coming in."

They married in 1983, following a courtship that started when friends convinced them both to enroll in a cooking class, where they met. Both spent the early eighties advancing to new jobs, riding a wave of expansion inside Kodak. They bought a new BMW, their trip car for excursions to the Rocky Mountains or to visit Meredith's family in the Midwest. And they had money to spare, even though Bob was supporting a son from a previous marriage.

As Kodak began to cut costs in the late 1980s, the Coutures worried most that Meredith's job would be eliminated. As a systems analyst, she was considered part of the support staff, whereas Bob helped design products and get them to market, so they figured he was secure. Meredith pondered quitting Kodak to start her own weaving business. The couple even got engineering plans to add on a large studio for her looms. But something told them to put off the addition.

By late 1992, Bob knew there was trouble. The project he was working on was suddenly canceled, and rumors flew that 500 to 1,000 jobs in the copier division would be cut. "At the same time, they cut twenty-five percent of my department," Meredith said. At Kodak's Building 20, many of her colleagues were given sixty days to find a new job inside the company. Others were told to leave immediately. "We didn't know if we'd have jobs or not. It was really tough not knowing."

In Bob's department, his colleagues were scrambling to find transfers to new jobs. "They looked for a job that was safest from the cuts. Some took pay cuts just to hang on to a job." Kodak shut down its internal job-posting system, so transfers became impossible. Seeing what was happening around him, Bob focused on cleaning up his projects. It was something he could control, unlike the unpredictable process of trying to transfer to another job inside Kodak. He inventoried equipment left over from the copier and printer projects. And he trained people on computer-aided engineering while he waited to see whether he would get a new project or lose his job. Most staffers couldn't believe the company would resort to layoffs. The company had just finished the massive Triple R early-retirement buyout a year earlier, and contractors had been hired to fill vacancies created by the retirements.

But just before Christmas 1992, Kodak's chief executive officer, Kay Whitmore, announced that cost-cutting plans would include layoffs of at least 2,000 people from the Kodak imaging business, including new product development, where Bob worked. Officially, he was given sixty days to find a new job. "I knew there was nothing to be found. There weren't enough jobs, and I knew I'd lose at musical chairs," Bob said. Instead, he helped several other people find jobs. Two other Kodak veterans—Paul Langlois, a programmer analyst, and John Wise, a physicist—were caught in the layoffs, too.

They each remember when the news was delivered: January 20. "I remember that it was Inauguration Day," Wise said. "Black Tuesday for us. It was hard for everybody to go in to work that day. Nobody knew the criteria they were gonna use."

Paul's wife, Ruth, his high school sweetheart from their hometown of Springfield, Massachusetts, also worked at Kodak, so they were both told to wait for news that morning. Learning that he'd been laid off, Paul called Ruth, who worked in distribution at Kodak Park. Fortunately, she hadn't lost her job. But she felt as if she had. Ruth's usual soft speaking voice became louder when she talked about her reaction to the news, and about how others who weren't laid off felt a sense of relief. "People called themselves survivors. But of course, I didn't feel like I was a survivor. I was a victim because Paul was a victim."

As they learned the names of other layoff victims, a pattern began to emerge. It was hard to believe, but Kodak was firing those who had been recently promoted—that is, tossing out its best performers. The procedure, they learned, was to add up the scores from the employee's past three performance appraisals. At Kodak, employees received a ranking of 1 through 7, or a D for "developmental" if they'd recently moved into a new job, where they were expected to learn new tasks. Thus, each time an employee got a bump up in wages, he or she also got a lower ranking. Many of those fired had been promoted in recent years, so they had lower scores in the formula. When Wise and others questioned the layoff system, they were told by human resource managers that they were "victims of circumstance." Others complained more strenuously, prompting a memo in which senior management explained that the company didn't want to give the impression that it was discouraging people from taking on new jobs for fear of getting lower rankings. Kodak officials said they would review the system and improve it. "That's nice," Langlois said. "But it's like using videotape to review bad rules in football and saying, 'We'll change the rules next year.'"

Bob Couture was skeptical about whether other companies would offer him security, either. He had become rather cynical and averse to taking chances. Professionally, he was afraid that a new employer would simply cut him loose at the first downturn; and that time, he wouldn't have the two decades of security that should have helped him keep a job at Kodak.

His pessimism surfaced in many aspects of his life, which was now based on daily rituals rather than long-term plans. He didn't stock up on groceries to last for the week; instead, he shopped each day for that evening's meal. He puttered around the house, doing odd jobs and writing more cover letters on his personal computer. Instead of work clothes, he now favored wrinkled shorts and shirts. His black beard was streaked with gray. He was troubled by his new status as a business statistic and by how he and thousands of others were part of the bloodletting that feeds Wall Street. "There is a small group at Kodak who believe the people forced out are somehow inferior. Some have been foolish enough to say so publicly," he says.

But in fact, it simply isn't true that those laid off were poor workers. They were caught in a numbers game that punished those who moved up the ladder. Al Waugh was another one who got caught. "This was a product of marketing and bean counters," Waugh said. "A lot of people they let go were highly trained and highly skilled." He took the layoffs personally because they contradicted Kodak's historically paternalistic ways. "If somebody had known how I felt about my line of work, I think things would've turned out differently. It was done very impersonally. I felt let down by the company. I would've done that job for whatever they would pay me, wherever they want to put me." Waugh no longer believed in the old adage that if you work hard, you'll succeed. "That's what's really bothering me. One of my beliefs has been dashed to pieces. People worked hard, got a decent living, and made a good enough wage to raise a family. The whole thing came tumbling down. In my lifetime, I haven't seen that. People were always hired back. But there's no doubt in my mind that I'll never work for Eastman Kodak again. Having that work ethic chopped out and the fact that I won't work where I put in twenty years, those are the tough things to take."

The trauma of being laid off can be especially intense for someone whose job represented a move up the ladder from blue-collar work to white-collar success. Consider Patty Minisce, who started her Kodak career as a factory worker making $7 an hour. She'd earned a college degree in music education, but found no jobs for teachers in the early 1980s. So she went back to school. As part of Kodak's Special Opportunities Undergraduate Program, or SOUP, she could work twenty-four hours a week and attend classes, while still being paid for forty hours. Minisce earned a bachelor's degree in computer science in 1991, and moved from factory work to data entry to assistant programmer to systems analyst. "That was my downfall," she relates. "I was promoted to a new status and moved to the bottom of the stack" in the ratings.

Minisce gave birth to a son in December 1992 and was on maternity leave when rumors of layoffs were rampant inside Kodak. She had lunch with some friends in late December. "They were all worried about layoffs. They were told it would be based on performance appraisals, so I thought I didn't have anything to worry about. I had nice performance appraisals." She'd even worked some weekends when necessary.

But in January, her managers came to her house to give her the news of the layoff. "I didn't know what to do, so I made them coffee. They were just the messengers." She had sixty days to find another job within Kodak, but found nothing.

In 1994, as her severance and unemployment dwindled, she was looking for a waitressing job to help pay the bills. "Even if I got another clerical position, it would take years to be promoted again." It was difficult for Minisce to understand why a company would "spend thousands on my education and then lay me off."

By nature, Minisce is an optimist. As she talked about her job search, she found a way to feel good about an otherwise bad situation: she had time to be with her son, Zachary. "I never would've taken that time. This is a luxury," she said. "A lot of people who are laid off have no reason to get out of bed. He's my reason to get out of bed. He fills my days with a lot of happy times."

The layoff was especially frustrating for Patty's husband, Skip, who worked as a toolmaker at Kodak from 1976 to 1989 and was among those who chose to leave during a buyout. One reason he left was to avoid the "stress and frustration of wondering who was going to be laid off." After he took the money, he moved to Florida to work with his brother at a fabrication company. Eventually, he returned to the Rochester area and a company that made countertops and other surfaces. As project coordinator, he processed purchase orders and scheduled installations at customers' homes.

Skip grew angry when he talked about Kodak, a company that he once respected as the best employer in town. He tried to look at the bigger picture, at how the fear in the company was hurting his friends, not just his family. He spent a lot of time on the phone with friends still inside the company, offering them words of support. Many of those friends were just marking time until they either got laid off or found another job and could leave Kodak. "Will anyone try hard to get promoted if they see everyone around them get fired after they've advanced?" Skip asked. One of his friends put it quite simply: "I don't aspire to do anything better. I'm a fly on the wall. I do my job. I don't want to go to school. All the people who advance are then out the door."

Skip's compassion for the anxieties of those still working did run short when he considered how the lost Kodak paycheck was hurting his family. He had a lot to worry about because he was paying support for his children from a previous marriage. Besides, he was still getting used to his new job, and was often preoccupied with the pressure of work and keeping two households ahead of their bills. He looked tired. Patty looked as if she might cry at any moment.

"What frustrates me the most is having to cut back in what I could do for all the kids," he said. "I just can't give them things. It's very frustrating when they ask for stuff. But they are good about it." All vacation plans were on hold until Patty could find another job. Even home repairs were put off.

For the Wises, losing John's paycheck was especially difficult because he was the sole provider for the family. His Kodak pay had supported his wife, Janet, and their three children, who grew up in a nine-room farmhouse in nearby Holley, New York. The old house needed remodeling, and John had been putting on an addition and siding with a home equity loan.

Janet's medical problems made the layoff even tougher. She had worked as a librarian at an elementary school, but developed problems with her wrists, which were diagnosed as multiple sclerosis. She had lost feeling in one arm and also suffered occasional attacks in her legs. On many days, she looked fine, giving no clue that she has MS. On other days, she had trouble moving around. When asked how she was feeling, she said she was just fine.

Wise received two weeks' salary for every year he worked at Kodak, so there was money coming in for thirty-eight weeks. He got a temporary job building transmitters for military radio systems, but that lasted just nine months. He also worked part-time at Dick's Clothing and Sporting Goods, but had to quit once he started collecting unemployment. Benefits for the unemployed are divided into four days, so if he worked even one hour one day a week, he'd lose a quarter of his unemployment check. That was frustrating, because he wanted to work somewhere, but he couldn't afford to lose his unemployment money in exchange for a $6-an-hour store job.

Now the Wises lived on about a third of John's old Kodak income and Janet's disability check. "I had a vision of retiring from Kodak at fifty-five or fifty-seven. That's changed. When I get another job, I'll have to spend another ten or fifteen years at least with that company. Or companies."

Others laid off discovered that they suddenly had lots of free time to, for example, take a vacation, something they couldn't squeeze into the forty-plus-hour workweek. But now they felt guilty when they did relax.

In some ways, Bob Couture was luckier than others in the ranks of the unemployed. Kodak's severance package was generous—two weeks' pay for every year at the company and several months of outplacement services at the Career Resource Center. For two months prior to the layoff, the Coutures had talked about what to do if he lost his job. They decided to save as much of the separation package as possible, less the money needed to fix up the house. "We're spending carefully on things to make it more valuable," Meredith said.

The Coutures still had Meredith's salary, but they had cut out every bit of extra spending. They no longer went to shopping malls to look around for books or new compact discs. "We didn't do a lot for Christmas beginning in 1992," Meredith recalled. They had become so frugal that Bob now feared spending for anything—even an interview suit, an investment in his future. (He finally bought one on sale at JCPenney.) "It's interesting because you have to psych yourself up to spend money again," he said. "We used to come to Christmas and say, 'I don't need anything. I bought it all last week.' "

They're glad their cars are paid for and their mortgage is low. "We don't go to bars and we don't gamble," Meredith said.

"Well, we did gamble with Kodak," remarked Bob. "And we lost."

If he couldn't find another job, the Coutures would dip into their lifetime of savings. "I can't hope to get back on track," Bob pointed out.

For many unemployed workers, the financial pressures are even worse because they don't have a cushion from savings accounts once unemployment runs out. The national savings rate declined from 8.7 percent of income for the period from 1947 to 1973, to just 4.9 percent for 1986 to 1990. Patty and Skip Minisce used her unemployment to pay down bills. "But now that it's gone, it's become a juggling game. I look at the bills and say, 'Who can wait?' Rochester Gas & Electric can't wait. The mortgage can't wait," Patty said. "Maybe life insurance and the cable bill. If they cancel cable, what's it gonna do? It won't matter." The Minisces now relied on credit cards for emergencies. She used her severance to pay off some credit card debt and for Christmas gifts. "They're rising again with me out of work," she admitted.

The problem for many families is that they lived beyond their means even when they were employed. Some were one paycheck from disaster. "Some come in and have not planned well," said Deb Koen, director of the Career Resource Center in Rochester. "Sometimes they need to learn basic budgeting."

Some resort to food stamps and welfare to get by. As of December 1993, more than 1 in 10 Americans were using food stamps, an all-time high. The report on this increase was released just one day after the U.S. Census Bureau reported a sharp rise in the number of people deemed the "working poor." In 1992, about 18 percent of the country's 81 million full-time workers earned less than $13,091, the poverty line for a family of four. That represented a 50 percent increase from 1979.

Financial worries mean another blow to a person's sense of self-worth, especially when he or she has been firmly entrenched in the middle class. Blue-collar workers are more accustomed to the boom-and-bust times of basic industries like coal or steel, and to strikes that sent them away from work. So, for the most part, they plan ahead with savings and thrifty behavior. "The other group [middle-class] says, 'I can still do anything.' To admit they have to save money [for such emergencies] is to admit failure," says Dr. Michelucci, the psychologist.

The news of layoff comes as a shock, even to those who have heard rumors that their company is downsizing. "They think, 'It will never be me. I'm better,' " says Dr. Michelucci. His caseload has been increasing as Kodak, Xerox, and others in Rochester purge their payrolls. As a former plant manager at Mobil, Michelucci had to lay off 200 of his plant's 450 workers in 1985. "We worked on developing team spirit. Then all of a sudden, you have to tell two hundred people they have to go." Mobil was consolidating plants to reduce costs, responding to increasing pressures such as environmental worries about plastics, one of its big businesses. Michelucci didn't want to continue in the plant-manager role, especially after the layoffs. "It was sobering. I never considered myself indispensable. The next one in line might be me," he says.

So he returned to college to get his Ph.D. in psychology and now counsels people who have lost their jobs. Some of his patients are still employed, but fear they will lose their jobs: "People are developing depression because of talk of layoffs. So much emotional energy is going into worrying about what's going on. They can't focus on their usual jobs."

Michelucci finds a difference between blue-collar and white-collar employees. "The blue-collar workers tend to worry, but they're more in touch with what's going on than those in white-collar jobs, who have talked themselves into being blind. Blue-collar workers in a sense might not be as sophisticated, but they know how to deal with it. And they're more likely to ask for help. The higher up you go, the harder it is to ask for help."

He has seen a rise in the number of people suffering from depression. Clinical depression, a neurochemical imbalance, can be triggered by an event. Symptoms include loss of interest in everyday activities, or even in leaving the house. Depressed people withdraw and become irritable. They often sleep poorly, and wake up early in the morning. Decisions become difficult. In severe cases that don't respond to medication, patients require electroshock therapy, he says.

One exercise Michelucci recommends to his patients is to rethink their definition of self-esteem. "It's no longer, 'I'm as good as my job.' It's, 'I'm as good as I am a good father' or husband or other roles. You have to take them away from 'I'm what I do.' If they feel like they're a failure at work, they feel like they're a failure as a husband and provider, too."

Roger Reisman, a former marine sergeant in the military police, was manager of corporate security until 1991, when he retired. He saw how people reacted to Kodak's layoffs: "Anytime there's downsizing, employees become restless. Morale is affected. And it becomes more competitive among employees. . . . In the 1980s, we saw more acts of violence and threats of violence."

On days when layoffs were announced, Reisman's department had plenty to keep it busy. Sometimes they confiscated handguns and knives that were brought into work. "Someone who was fearful of layoffs brought in a rifle," which was confiscated by security.

In another episode, a worker was called into his supervisor's office late one afternoon to hear the news that he'd lost his job. "He jumped over the desk and assaulted the division leader and his supervisor. There were black eyes and cut lips."

In other cases, the workers simply vowed: "I'll kill you." If a manager believed someone to be laid off was prone to violence, security would have a plainclothes officer in the vicinity when the notice was issued. Sometimes, corporate security would go so far as to do "some profiling on people," interviewing friends and associates to see if a person owned guns or had ever been violent. Sometimes, Kodak would just contact the police for information, Reisman said. "We told the police if a supervisor was threatened, and asked that they give special attention to patrol of their home."

Counselors often aren't sure if the newly unemployed are joking when they vow to get even. "We've encountered people who say: 'I'm a gun collector. Maybe I ought to show them my collection.' You can't take it as a lighthearted comment," says one counselor.

Many laid-off workers referred to the movie *Falling Down* when talking about what could happen one of these days at Kodak or Xerox. In the movie, Michael Douglas portrays a laid-off defense worker, who must resort to lining his shoes with newspaper to cover the holes in the worn soles. He pulls out a gun when a fast-food restaurant won't serve him breakfast. Indeed, violence among workers is a problem. From July 1984 to July 1993, there were 125 cases where a killer had a link to a company where the violence occurred. The episodes resulted in 393 deaths and 214 wounded people. The U.S. Postal Service saw several episodes of former employees killing their coworkers.

The fear of violence, of somebody "going postal," was a common topic of conversation in Rochester, especially among Kodakers. "People inside the company say Kodak better watch out. . . ." said one laid-off worker. "Somebody will go in there with an automatic weapon one of these days. They've got people at the breaking point."

Indeed, the congregation at Gates Presbyterian Church in Rochester was concerned about family violence and the apparent increase in problems following job losses. "We have a violence task force," explained Bob Kaiser, pastor of the church. "Economics creates stress on families. Violence and economics are related." One response was to sell gun locks as Father's Day gifts.

In some households, friction arises because one spouse is now stuck at home while the other goes off to bring in a paycheck. It was a blessing that families like the Coutures could still keep up with basic needs, but Bob sometimes wished he weren't depending on his wife for money. He often said that time would help him put aside his pride and anger: "There will be a day when my feelings are different." His bitterness, though, ran deep. The discussion of layoffs made him think about his first marriage, and the trauma of going through a breakup. "When I got divorced, I had twenty-seven thousand dollars in horses. It was a serious part of our assets, so it had to be liquidated. It really bothered me that I had to get rid of the horses. I'm still nostalgic, particularly in the spring when the foals are out." That was in 1981, but in 1994 his memory of the events was still fresh and detailed. He seemed sad when he looked out the window to the tall weeds that now fill the empty pasture.

Job loss can also create tension when a formerly stay-at-home mother is forced to return to the workforce to help pay the bills. This is especially troubling in a Kodak family, where generations have worked and retired without problems—the life Al and Mary Waugh expected for their family. Both come from a long line of Kodakers. Indeed, Al's grandmother Bessie Waugh worked as a secretary to George Eastman. "She used to tell stories about being in the steno pool for Eastman. They wore white, long-sleeved shirts and some matronly lady would walk up and down the aisles, watching them work. It's interesting to think that she met him," Al said.

"He's probably turning over in his grave a hundred times a day," Mary added. Her grandparents were toolmakers from Germany, hired to help build cameras at Kodak. Each generation since had worked at the company. "My grandfather was a Kodak man. My father was a Kodak man. It was a very secure place to work, so I applied for a job as a secretary." Mary was one of the first employees at the Elmgrove plant when it opened in the late 1960s. Al and Mary met in high school and married in 1969. She worked as a secretary for seven years so he could go to college. Eventually, he was hired at Kodak. And both families were happy the young couple would have security. They bought Kodak gifts for relatives at Christmas, all from the company store. "Everyone said, 'Work hard, be good to your company. Don't cheat them. Give them forty hours of work for forty hours of pay. Live the Kodak lifestyle and you'll make it like I did," Al said.

He did just that, often giving many more than forty hours without extra pay. "I would work until ten or eleven at night, four or five nights a week to get something completed." His backlog of projects was enough to convince him that he wouldn't be among those cut.

But a year after the layoff, he joined the Class of '93. One morning about eleven, the department secretary called him: "Al, they want to see you in the department head's office." Inside, he heard the news. At first, he figured he'd have the sixty days to find another job. "No Al. You're one of the people with three days to clear out. It's not an option to look for another job here."

He called Mary around noon.

"You won't believe this, Mary," he said. "I lost my job."

"They can't be serious," she said.

Al says now: "She knew how hard I'd been working and the kind of things I'd given the company. Mary took it worse than I did."

With his severance, Al decided to take a few months off to think about what came next. He spent a lot of time teaching sailing on the Finger Lakes and Lake Ontario. By midsummer of 1993, he became "Mr. Mom," doing the household chores. Mary decided to go back to work to help make ends meet and pay for health insurance. She had been home for about two decades, ever since the Waughs' oldest, Katie, was born. Katie was now attending business school and had recently moved back home. A son, Rob, was in high school.

Returning to the workforce was difficult for Mary. She took a job at Kaufmann's, a department store, where she often worked until ten at night, constantly on her feet, selling women's clothing. Al believed that for her, having to work such long hours was more of a strain than the loss of his job. He hated to see her stay out so late, and to see how tired she looked when she got home.

Indeed, Mary's fatigue was evident when she described her new life as a salesclerk. "I have no free time now. The hours are ridiculous. I'm not a happy person. I work nights. The breaking point is when the store stays open till ten on Saturday, and then I have to work Sunday eleven to seven." Mary was happy because the next day was a day off, her first in a long time. But her joy was temporary; the day after that she would return for another six-day stretch. The paycheck was little comfort: she made slightly more than minimum wage, and so far, her wages had climbed just 35 cents an hour. Raises were scarce, and there was increasing pressure to sell more. "If you don't open enough charge accounts, you get a lecture," she said. It was plain that she didn't like to peddle credit cards to people like her. "Who needs more debt?" is how she looked at it.

Al sent out dozens of résumés and letters, but got few interviews. A year after the layoff, he was considering taking any job, just to help pay the bills. "It's a matter of watching your savings going down at a faster and faster rate." Instead of focusing on jobs that would build on his career, Al applied for a night janitor's job at a local school. "It would not have caught my eye, but the hours were eleven P.M. to seven A.M.," which would allow him time during the day to keep searching for an engineering job.

The stress affected Al physically as well as emotionally. One day, all the muscles in his neck and back cramped. He needed painkillers to ease them. And, with his wife and children at work and school, he had learned to appreciate what it means to be a housekeeper. "I understand what my wife was going through for twenty years when I yell, 'Pick up those dirty clothes and put them in the wash!' or ask why they didn't put their dishes in the dishwasher."

Mary had more to adjust to than the loss of her husband's paycheck. She considered Kodak a part of the family. The Waughs rattled off a list of Kodak shirts, bags, even shoes that were stashed in their closets. The familiar red block letters were as familiar to this family as their own last name. It would've been heretical to buy a competing brand of film. Now Mary didn't hesitate. In fact, she had launched her own boycott of the company: "I'm from a Kodak family and this wasn't supposed to happen this way."

For some, a job loss can lead to divorce or complicate one that's in the works. Rochester attorneys said they were seeing more clients who were losing both their marriage and jobs. "I've seen a lot with Kodak and Xerox families," said Michael T. Hagelberg, a local divorce attorney. "It seems to be an epidemic."

He recalled one client, the wife in a twenty-year marriage, who had worked at Kodak for twenty-three years when she was laid off in the January 1993 round of cuts. She and her husband were already having marital problems by then, and were proceeding with a divorce. "His attorney said she wasn't trying to get another job, so she could milk him for more money," according to Hagelberg. But in October 1993, her husband lost his job, too.

Hagelberg contended that marital strife makes someone a target for layoff when companies are looking for people to cut. "The mentality is: 'Why not get rid of her? She's having problems anyway.' "

Job losses in the middle of divorce proceedings can be devastating. "I see people get divorced because they've spent too much time at work. They've run away from their marriage to the place where we get our strokes. So this is a second blow to their ego. And it's painful."

Settlements are affected because of lost jobs. More clients are forced to settle quickly, with less discussion about division of assets, because their money is running out. But resolution of issues like child support and maintenance can be delayed because it's harder to establish net worth and income when someone leaves a big company job for self-employment or a smaller company. "Everyone you know becomes a consultant. That's a small business based on cash, and he's sure not gonna tell the wife what he's got. It really affects establishing what proper support should be," Hagelberg said.

Some couples can no longer afford to divorce. In one such case, of a couple who had been married for years, the husband was the sole breadwinner, and his wife stayed home to raise their four children. Her parents helped by sending them extra money to supplement his Kodak salary. A couple of weeks before their divorce was final, he lost his job. "Now there's no money coming in, so they're still living together in a shell of a dead marriage. The effect on both of them is negative. And the effect on their children is even worse."

Explaining the impact of a job loss to parents can be a nightmare. Their generation did well, and they believed in the system of working for a big company for forty years and then collecting your pension. It was that easy for many. Now they worry about how their fortyish children will cope with getting laid off.

Meredith Couture's parents called every so often to check on Bob's job search. "They're worried about us," she said. Her father was an accountant, laid off when Firestone closed regional offices back in the 1970s. "But he walked out on a Friday and had a new job on Monday," so he and Meredith's mother felt that Bob should've found something by now.

"When I tell them nothing good has happened, there's fifteen seconds of silence while they figure out what to say," Bob said. "It's hard for them to realize that we could be better off financially to stay here [in Rochester] right now."

Koen at the Career Resource Center said that just 12 percent of the center's clients relocated to another town in 1993. "A lot of people feel anchored here. In many cases, they grew up here. Going through another traumatic experience like moving is to go through another loss."

The Waughs wouldn't even consider relocating to another city: both sets of parents were in their eighties. Besides, they figured they'd never be able to sell their house for what it was worth. Or match their lifestyle in another town.

Using 1982 figures, the Career Resource Center calculated that of its clients, about 67 percent of professionals who found jobs earned at least as much as they did in their last job. "If anything, the picture is not quite as good now," Koen conceded. Among hourly workers, 47 percent of those who found jobs earned at least as much as they did in their old jobs. And "it's taking people longer to find jobs," Koen said.

Many laid-off workers encounter age discrimination. Older

workers cost more because they expect to be compensated for their experience—a reasonable notion, considering they bring value to the workplace. "The irony is, when we look at what we want in the future workforce and the characteristics of those that are exiting, it makes no sense," says Helen Dennis, a consultant on aging and employment who has worked with Fortune 500 companies. Chris Leavitt, a career counselor, tells her clients to remind future employers that "you're living on unemployment; then they will begin to identify with you." Some former Kodakers with a Ph.D. left the doctorate off their resumes in hopes they would get a job at a smaller company. Likewise, some older applicants learned to only list their last few jobs, rather than those of the last few decades, a sure tipoff to a manager of someone's age.

Statistics show that older workers have reason to worry. An average of 667,000 people aged 55 and older were unemployed in 1993, a 31% increase over 1988. This comes as the number of workers over 55 increases. The Labor Department says that figure will rise 38 percent by 2005, reflecting the aging of the baby boomers. All of this comes as quite a shock for the generation that was used to prosperity and the security of long-term employment at companies like Kodak. Katherine Newman, a professor of anthropology at Columbia University, says: "Nothing in the boomers' upbringing, schooling, or early experience in the labor market prepared them for what we must all confront now: the U.S. economy cannot provide the kind of job opportunities or personal security that the country took for granted only a generation ago."

Certainly nothing in Michael Donnelly's career prepared him for a layoff. After graduating from Kent State University in 1963, he worked as a broadcaster and for United Press International, then moved to DuPont in corporate communications. In 1970, he joined Kodak, where he worked at various jobs in advertising and communications. Kodak's CEO once invited the head of the International Olympic Committee to visit company headquarters in Rochester. Donnelly was asked to plan the entire visit and escort the guest around town. "I always made sure everything was buttoned up," he said. His itineraries for such events were so specific that senior managers were instructed as to "what we do at 12:06," he said.

Planning events like Kodak's sponsorship of the Special Olympics entailed a grueling travel schedule. Donnelly often traveled six months a year. "When I was in Rochester, I'd eat lunch at my desk or in the cafeteria. I very rarely went out," he said. His only luxury was membership in a country club in Rochester. A divorced father of two, he focused most of his time at the office.

All along, he figured he'd be secure at Kodak. His record was picture perfect. "My ideal thing was if I could work until I was fifty-seven or fifty-eight, take a good retirement package, then go back into broadcasting or become a publisher of a weekly newspaper," he said.

When Donnelly got the news that he was losing his job, he immediately began to collect letters of recommendation and references, especially from senior management. Both Colby Chandler and Kay Whitmore, former chief executive officers, offered their support. "Colby came up to me and said: 'Here's my private phone number. If anyone would like to talk to me about you, tell them to call me.' " Whitmore wrote a letter of recommendation for him.

And he sought the help of outplacement services. "I never had a résumé in my life. Within a week, I had one." After years of helping others do business with Kodak, he started to call "everybody I knew through the years. I probably contacted four hundred to five hundred people.

"I thought I'd be able to just go back out and get a job, just like that. But I learned how it is to be fifty-two years old and seeking a job."

Leads on jobs, such as director of corporate communications for a Michigan company, seemed to dry up. Sometimes, Donnelly was picked as a finalist, but wouldn't get the job. "A lot of people come back and say, 'You've got great skills. You have great qualifications.' I think what they're basically saying is that your age is against you and that you're overqualified. My response is, 'If I'm overqualified, at least you know you got somebody who knows what they're doing.' "

Age discrimination was a problem, even if employers "don't come right out and tell you that you're too old." But the feedback indicated: " 'We want someone who is twenty-nine for half what they were paying you.' "

The network of people who once called on him seemed to dry up, too. "I found that a lot of people didn't want to talk to good old Michael anymore. Michael wasn't as important to us as he was at Eastman Kodak. All of a sudden, they forgot the Michael Donnellys of the world. They forget the people that were very good to their cause." Many phone calls went unanswered, even when the message made it through the layers of secretaries and voicemail boxes that greet job seekers like him.

By the end of his first year of unemployment, Donnelly had used up the outplacement service allotted by Kodak. So he spent most days in a friend's basement office, where he could borrow a desk and a phone. "This gives me some structure," he said. Each day, he still dressed in a suit and tie. "But there are no more plane tickets, no more planning trips."

He started packing his lunch and cut back on other living expenses to conserve cash for his mortgage and health insurance payments. He took in a boarder, who rented the upstairs of his house. "I have to decide: do I keep the house or sell it?" he said. Retirement planning had changed: the question was no longer when to stop working, but whether Donnelly would ever be able to stop looking for work. "It's taken a toll on me financially. I walk around sometimes with two dollars in my pocket. I'm afraid to cash a check sometimes. It's day to day."

No one was immune from the cutbacks at Kodak. Even those who once did the company's hiring got the ax. Tom Walker, a director of human resources, was also among the Class of '93. Walker joined Kodak as an industrial engineer, right after his military service ended in 1968. By 1974, he had moved into human resources as a plant recruiter and was visiting college campuses for new engineers. Kodak's policy was to hire more of the same: "They taught us to hire unto your own image." Walker would do sixteen interviews a day, hiring one or two people a day, during Kodak's boom times of the 1970s. "But over time, we lost credibility on campus because we were down to zero hiring, even though we were showing up to try and save our name," he said. "Eventually, we just didn't go to some campuses."

In 1981, he had been promoted to manager in charge of the corporate succession planning process. In that job, he worked with senior management to select employees qualified for the fast track. One program tapped managers to attend the MBA program at the Sloan School of Management at M.I.T.

Walker's last job was as director of human resources in the government systems division, where Kodak makes special products such as lenses for space telescopes. Cutbacks made him consider taking early retirement under the Triple R program in 1992. "If I'm not gonna be safe in '93, I'm out of here," Walker told his boss. Like dozens of others, he was reassured that he was immune. "There would always be an HR job somewhere in the works," he said. But not for him. "I was notified February ninth that a layoff would take place on the tenth. We had a briefing in the morning with all the HR managers. We were told how it would be handled. My boss called me that afternoon to say he needed to talk to me, leaving the impression he was bringing me my list of names who I was gonna lay off the next day."

At four P.M. that day, Walker was given sixty days to search for another Kodak job. His boss added: "You can take tomorrow off. We'll take care of doing the duty that you would've had to do."

He left work without telling his secretary the news. When he got home, his wife, Gerry, a schoolteacher, wanted to talk about her day at work. She was upset: her boss had told her she might not have a job the following year because of consolidations in the school system. Tom just sat in the corner chair in the living room, silent for a few minutes, before saying: "Well, have I got a bombshell for you." After hearing his news, she said: "It figures."

Initially, Walker was optimistic that he could apply for a variety of management jobs in other companies. "My first reaction was to go out and get a vice president's job as an HR director somewhere. If I have to relocate, I will. Then we suddenly realized: Do we really want to do that?"

Some of those who believed Kodak had cheated them out of proper retirement benefits or a generous buyout went to see Rochester lawyer Donna Marianetti, who had built much of her practice on the increasing number of unhappy Kodak and Xerox employees. In her small office in downtown Rochester, Marianetti was swamped with calls and visits from people who had lost their jobs. "My practice has tripled over the last several years," she said. "And it's growing.

"In 1989, people would come in and see me. Growing up in Kodak town, and having a lot of relatives working for the company, it was a very paternalistic atmosphere. Employees were still fiercely loyal. They thought Kodak could do no wrong." She estimated that only ten of 150 prospective clients actually retained her in 1989. "Now you can't keep the Kodak people out of the office. They are being treated so shabbily. I get them in here while they're still working, asking: 'What should I do?' " About 85 percent to 90 percent retained her. It used to be difficult to be the lawyer suing the Big Yellow Box. "I took a lot of heat." Even though she was now more popular among some, Marianetti still practiced under her own family name, not her husband's, because he "has to work in this town."

Marianetti believed that employers were often guilty of age discrimination, but that they had become more subtle. "We used to see a pattern emerge where you were a good performer, then, a year before you were terminated, you got the worst performance review. Then some saw harassment. In the last eighteen months, the policy companies use to decide who will be reduced, while it may appear neutral on the face, has a disproportionate impact" on older workers.

During some layoffs at Kodak, managers used performance review scores to determine who stayed and who left. "That looks like an objective criterion that didn't take age into account. But performance appraisals are ranked one through seven, with seven as the highest. Historically, when you were hired, it was easy to move through the ranks. They were free with performance ratings." Employees often received 5s or 6s and then a promotion, after which ratings dropped back to a 4, or to a D for "developmental." "There comes a point when a person worked for the company and based on experience and education, reaches a plateau. And you reach the job you retire from. [High] performance ratings are harder to get and they tend to level off at average, while younger workers are still easily attaining the higher ratings." But older workers "come out on the lower end." Some of her clients lost jobs that paid $60,000 or $90,000 a year.

Beyond the individual costs, Marianetti said, "People don't realize the devastating impact to society. Some have no medical insurance. They can't find another job. They retire with a pittance. It will tax our system. This is a big problem."

The biggest source of outrage among those forced out of their Kodak jobs was the various buyouts that preceded 1991's hefty Triple R. Early in 1991, employees whose age plus their years of service totaled 75 were eligible to retire with 50 percent of their pension. Those with 85 points received full retirement. "At the time, people heard rumors that Kodak was coming out with a major buyout," Marianetti said. "When groups of individuals were considering retiring, they went to benefit counselors to see if another package was coming. They were told the rumors were false. So they began to retire in January 1991, through July and the beginning of August."

On August 12, 1991, Kodak announced the Triple R, Resource Redeployment and Retirement Plan. "It upset people, especially those who retired the first week of August or in July or June." Marianetti contended that Kodak benefits counselors knew the program was coming, yet didn't tell those who were leaving earlier that year. "You couldn't put together a package like this in one week." About 135 people who received reduced benefits had sued. And those who retired after the Triple R ended were bitter, because they got a much less generous package.

Suing on the basis of age discrimination can be a difficult ordeal. At the Equal Employment Opportunity Commission (EEOC), the backlog of cases nationwide stood at 97,000 by the end of 1994, up 24,000 from a year earlier and double what it was in 1990. Even the agency's chairman, Gilbert F. Casellas, admits that "the agency has essentially lost credibility with the public."

Sam Marcosson, an attorney who works at the EEOC, has seen a pattern of older workers getting laid off, for some obvious reasons: They tend to make more money, so a company saves more when older employees are cut. And younger workers can advance through the ranks if older ones are dismissed. The other reasons are based on stereotypes about older workers—that they are set in their ways, less likely to adapt to changing times. "Ironically," Marcosson said, "a lot of people doing the selecting are themselves older workers."

One of the EEOC's problems is the conservative nature of the courts. "The federal courts are largely populated at this point by appointees of Reagan and Bush. They tend to be more conservative. They tend to read the statutes more narrowly." And they are also more willing to dismiss a case before it ever gets to a jury. Judges "don't have the perspective of somebody who was a worker on a factory assembly line for twenty-five years and who thought he or she had something valuable in their seniority and in their investment to that company. These workers, rightly in my view, see that company as part theirs. The judge who sits on their case sees it as the stockholders' company. Legally, that's true. But the plaintiffs feel they invested something through their years and their work and their efforts in that company. And they're cut loose."

So they face the prospect of suing, waiting for years, and dealing with the stigma of being a disgruntled ex-employee as well as the usual problems of trying to find a job when they're over fifty. Besides the bitterness those laid off feel toward their former employers, they also must now compete for jobs with those early retirees who took the generous buyouts but still want to work.

Bob Couture went back and forth about starting his own engineering consulting business or moving out of Rochester. "I'm really very lucky. I'm able to take time and go through the entire assessment process and decide what I want to do. I considered teaching, but I'm not sure I want to start a new career of teaching at age forty-five. I decided I want to continue being an engineer.

But there aren't a lot of senior positions out there. It's tough to get people to consider you for less. They assume you'll take it and continue to look. That puts people like me in a bind."

The Coutures were relieved that they hadn't jumped into starting a weaving business. But Bob wondered out loud whether he would ever be able to trust and believe. "Am I forever going to be unwilling to do things?"

He was interviewing around the country, but debated the wisdom of uprooting Meredith from her job, pension, and benefits. She said, "We don't want to leave and go through this again. What if we sell the house with a low mortgage and find out another company has problems and lays him off? Or what if it's an area that you can't live with long term? I weigh that against the risk of my losing my job, too. Nothing says we're done with layoffs at Kodak."

Bob found himself odd man out in job interviews when managers talked about getting the "right fit." "They want a particular personality. Few people are making efforts to get diversity. They're unwilling to take on people who don't think like they do or have the same set of social skills. I am disturbed enough that I keep going back to the idea that maybe I ought to go deeper into the woods or run a canoe shop in the boundary waters. Or a general store in the Adirondacks. It wastes what I've learned in twenty-two years. I have something to offer. It's a societal problem that gives me deep concern."

He paused and added: "If I were single, I would've counted out money for Chris to finish his fourth year of college and I would've gone away. Almost without a doubt. For six months. Or for the rest of my life."

5

White Knight

On a warm summer morning in June 1995, a couple of hundred Kodak workers gathered inside the gymnasium at the Elmgrove plant for a chance to question their boss, George M. C. Fisher. The chief executive officer had invited forklift operators, secretaries, and middle managers together for a "town meeting," where employees could stand up and ask him anything.

Just stepping inside this plant could be risky for anybody wearing pinstripes and a corporate title. Employees here figured that any visit from the CEO meant more bad news. The Elmgrove plant had been decimated by continual layoffs in the 1980s and early 1990s, as previous Kodak management pared manufacturing lines. So the workers had every right to be skeptical of guys in ties.

Fisher knew how to win over this audience. He talked about jobs and why every employee in the building should care about the brewing U.S. trade war with Fuji and Japan. A professor at heart, Fisher dissected the Trade Act of 1974 into easily digested pieces. "We're basically locked out of the Japan market," he said, showing giant pie charts of Fuji's 75 percent share of the Japanese market and Kodak's 6.9 percent, compared with the rest of the world, where Kodak had a commanding 44 percent versus Fuji's 25 percent. Fisher offered a quick history lesson on post–World War II Japan and how the rebuilding of the country was fueled by interlocking conglomerates like Mitsui and

Sumitomo. "You might ask what the impact of all this is. Basically, it allows Fuji to use Japan as a profit sanctuary . . . and make horrendous profits. And guess what they do with their profits?" he asked the group.

"They basically bring it to this country and to Europe to try to buy our market share. . . . They've amassed ten billion dollars. . . . And guess what they want to do with that cash?" he asked the silent crowd. "They basically want to kill Kodak."

He drove home the point with a message they all understood: $6 billion in lost sales in Japan meant thousands of lost jobs right here in Rochester. "That," he emphasized, "should mean a lot to you." Employees lined up at microphones to ask him questions. Others scribbled Fisher's comments into notebooks.

Portraying Fuji as the enemy to Kodak employees was hardly a stroke of genius for Fisher. What did qualify as a management breakthrough was the fact that a Kodak CEO had bothered to show up at the plant and share trade information with the workforce, to give them a dose of reality that they really needed to hear. Earlier Kodak CEOs rarely left their offices, making only occasional plant visits that were full of pomp and lacking in substance. Since Fisher took over in late 1993, his performance in the trenches of Kodak, as well as in Japan and Washington, had marked a new era for the troubled company. He had ditched grand diversification plans and focused instead on improving the basics, like selling more yellow boxes in Japan and the United States. He decried the excesses of the 1980s empire building, even griping to some insiders that he wished the company didn't own its downtown Rochester office tower because it's too corporate and isolated. Many said he'd prefer an office at a manufacturing plant, and would use it only as a pit stop between calls on employees and customers.

At five foot nine, Fisher is a compact and fit Midwesterner. He wears glasses and favors navy blue or gray suits. He is rarely without a red tie under his collar and a pager on his belt. He says "That's neat," when he hears good news. But he is just as likely to mutter, "Bullshit," if he thinks someone is . . . well, feeding him some BS.

From his first week on the job in 1993, Fisher took the

heretical step of telling the Wall Street stock watchers to be patient. Rebuilding Eastman Kodak would come from growth, and it would take three to five years before the Street could expect to see solid results that reflected real change. Taking restructuring charges in nine out of the past eleven years was no way to run a company. And the passing out of round after round of pink slips—an action typically applauded by Wall Street—he deemed "mindless number crunching."

To be sure, Fisher didn't hesitate to cut jobs when necessary. He knew that he had to cut some of Kodak's bureaucracy if the company was to survive. What he didn't endorse was the previous CEO's approach: announcing that 10,000 jobs will be cut, then figuring out where to cut them. Instead, he decided each department should constantly monitor its staff, trimming as needed to deliver results. That approach would enable the company to move beyond cutting jobs by using poorly designed formulas that in essence assigned every employee a numerical ranking but incorporated little thought about who is needed to do what job.

The first outsider to take on the CEO post, Fisher brought hope, relief, and some fear to Kodak employees battered by a decade of upheaval. They weren't used to the likes of him. While past chieftains had found solace in the wood-paneled executive dining room, Fisher held court over cereal or salad during his regular breakfasts and lunches in the employee cafeteria. He invited employees to join him, asking simple questions like "Where are we missing the boat?" A scientist and engineer by training, Fisher wandered the hallways of the research labs, quizzing fellow Ph.D.s about obscure technical details that would make most folks doze off. Even his wife popped up in various offices and plants, introducing herself simply as Ann, without emphasizing that she is the chairman's wife. She was sometimes mistaken for just another employee. "I asked her where she worked," recalled one Kodaker who met her when she was roaming around.

Fisher talked a lot about a return to core values, often sounding like a preacher of the Golden Rule and prompting some Wall Street analysts to scoff that he should worry more about cutting Kodak's costs and less about mushy subjects like values. Fisher's approach emphasized accountability at all levels of the company, and urgency to get things done. That sounds simple enough, but at Kodak it was practically rocket science, after the years of drifting. Fisher also knew how to fit in quickly—he often quoted founder Eastman, referring to him as "the first George." A new Kodak, he believed, should first look backward if it wanted to move forward. Fisher cited Eastman's key values, such as the importance of product leadership and of making cameras that were easy for consumers to use—basic principles, Fisher said, that "people have lost sight of today."

It is helpful to look backward to understand George Fisher if you want to understand him and his vision of a new Kodak. Born in Anna, Illinois, in 1940, George Myles Cordell Fisher was the third of nine children. His parents both tended nurseries: Ralph, a horticulturalist, raised trees; Catherine, a sociologist, raised their passel of children. George's middle name, Cordell, was borrowed from Cordell Hull, secretary of state under Franklin D. Roosevelt. Family members dubbed him Corky, a nickname that Fisher's family and friends still use today. He calls his parents his role models; they instilled in him a combined interest in the hard science of chemistry and the soft science of a sociologist trying to see what makes people tick.

As in most big families, in the Fisher clan it was every kid for himself. "You get very independent because there's not gonna be somebody there to do everything for everybody," Fisher recalled. "It was a great way to grow up." When reflecting on his youth, Fisher quoted Eisenhower's line about never knowing he was poor until he left his hometown. But he tempered it a bit: "We weren't poor. My father always earned a good income, but we also were not wealthy enough." The Fisher children knew they would have to pay for their own college educations. "You were on your own."

The Fisher siblings scattered as they pursued varied careers: pharmacy, microbiology, teaching, the navy, farming, and nursing. George's first career ambition came from his first love: baseball. He excelled in Little League and even made it to the college team at the University of Illinois, his parents' alma mater. "I would have loved to have been able to play professional baseball," he says. But the shortstop's dream was short-lived: he hurt his knee while wrestling during his sophomore year. He tried pitching. "I probably could have knocked around in the minor leagues for a lot of years" and ended up "very frustrated. It's a good thing that end came because I really wasn't as good as I thought I was, and I would have kept trying and it would have been a mistake."

When he wasn't on the ballfield, Fisher studied engineering. A professor encouraged him to continue his education, so he attended graduate school at Brown University, where he earned his master's degree in engineering and a Ph.D. in applied mathematics. His goal was to teach at a university. But his thesis adviser "really thought that I would love working at Bell Labs and I should try that for a couple years."

Just before finishing his degree, he found another love: Ann Wallace. The daughter of a preacher, Ann had recently graduated from Brown with a degree in English literature. She'd planned to join the Peace Corps in Ethiopia after graduation, but instead took a secretarial job in the university's athletic department, making $52 a week. The two met when Ann was assigning students their gym lockers. They agree that George came in for a locker combination, but the story has different twists, depending on which spouse you ask. Ann says that George came back three times to say his locker wouldn't open. "He says I gave him three combinations that wouldn't open, so that he had to come back." After the third try, he asked her out on a date. She liked his smile, so she gave him her phone number. George didn't waste any time. "He told me that he was gonna marry me on our first date," Ann says. "It sounded okay to me. . . . He seemed really nice."

Less than a year later, Ann sewed her wedding gown, and one for her bridesmaid, and the couple were married in her father's church. The next year, they moved to New Jersey for his job at Bell Labs. George calls Ann "the smartest part of the family" and a "great mother" to their three children, Jennifer, Barcy, and Bill, who were born during his tenure at Bell. He found time to coach

Little League and to take camping and ski trips with his family. The scientist and teacher in him tried to turn almost everything into lessons for his children. "It's a family joke. . . . We ask him to please not give us a lecture, just the short version," Ann says. "But he was always teaching them something." Often it was a point about being good to others. Often it was science or math. When George had to travel, he'd give the family his schedule so the children could call him for help with their homework. "He'd work on their math problems at night," Ann says.

Indeed, one of Fisher's favorite vacation hobbies is to sit with a yellow legal pad and work out a complicated math problem. "He'll go, 'Ooohhh, you know, I think I solved this,' " Ann says. George likens math to playing golf. "It's a total distraction." Reflecting on this unusual hobby, he conceded: "I'm the only one that doesn't think it's strange."

Appropriately, Fisher's time at Bell Labs focused on exploring what others sometimes deemed strange. There was work on a two-way video telephone back in the early 1970s. Scientist figured every home would have one by the mid-1990s. He considered himself a "young idealist" who would spend his life helping people communicate in new ways. As part of a crew of about 700 researchers, Fisher was allowed to wander and wonder. "It was truly Camelot for those of us that were there," he says. "It was just unbelievable." Foreshadowing his arrival at Kodak, he did some work related to photography, such as conveying and compressing images.

He also found mentors who looked out for his career. One of them moved to Motorola and convinced Fisher that he would enjoy the experience of being "a broad-based businessperson" rather than just a scientist. So he left for Motorola's Schaumburg, Illinois, headquarters in 1976 to work as director of manufacturing systems.

Paul Galvin founded Motorola in 1928 as Galvin Manufacturing Corporation, to make battery eliminators. That market quickly dried up, so Galvin switched to making car radios, which he called Motorolas, from "motor" and "Victrola." The company also made two-way police radios and televisions. During World

War II, U.S. troops communicated with Motorola's "Handie-Talkie" radios. In 1947, Galvin renamed the company Motorola. The company eventually produced semiconductors; by the 1970s, it had sold off its television business after getting battered by cheaper Japanese products and was focusing on high-tech ways to communicate information.

Motorola learned the benefits of unconventional management practices long before it was chic to seek the opinions of the masses or push decision-making down from the CEO's office. In the 1950s, Paul Galvin's son, Robert, questioned why so many problems were still being handled by senior management rather than by those closest to the action on the factory floor or in the lab. And early participative programs, such as BREAD—for "Better Results Earn Additional Dollars"—shaped the company's belief that everyone has a stake in its future.

Fisher worked his way up quickly. About a year after joining the company, he was named the number two manager in the startup of a new police-radio plant in Fort Worth, Texas. It was an ambitious project that taught him a valuable lesson. "We tried to do everything new," ranging from a new product line to new computerized warehousing, assembly, and test systems. The result? "We just fell on our face." Everything seemed to go wrong. In the most ludicrous episode, a back-up generator contained no diesel fuel, so the plant didn't have a working generator during a power outage.

"We thought we could do a lot of things all at once. These were all the right things to do, any one of them, but when you tried to put them all together, the probability of going belly-up was very high." The experience taught Fisher that "it's not the grand ideas that shut you down or make you successful, it's the little things."

Eventually, Fisher became a vice president and general manager of the communications sector's paging division in Fort Lauderdale; in 1984 he was named senior vice president of the communications sector. It was a time of rapid change in the electronics industry, and Motorola and Fisher often found themselves on the front lines of the battle to preserve the U.S. industry from powerful Asian manufacturers. From his earliest days in the

Fort Lauderdale plant, he got a lesson on how tough the Japanese competition can be. Motorola was pushing its semiconductor and wireless communications products, such as pagers, and management decided that Motorola had to crack open Japan, a profit sanctuary for Japanese manufacturers. Fisher remembers how many were skeptical. "Some people thought we were crazy, and maybe we were." When he tells the story, he makes his point by quoting comedienne Gracie Allen, who once quipped: "They laughed at Joan of Arc, too, but she went ahead and built it anyway."

Motorola was the world's top producer of pagers, so it had reason to feel confident of its quality and market position. But the Japanese market was dominated by its own manufacturers, and U.S. companies were excluded. The key to breaking open the market was to sell to Nippon Telephone and Telegraph, the country's phone company. NTT had previously bought only from closely related companies, so Motorola had to go through a lot of formal and informal tests to see "whether or not we could be considered a family member," recalls Merle Gilmore, president of Motorola's Land Mobile Products Sector, who worked for Fisher. The process was one of the cornerstones of the corporation's strategy and was headed by Fisher.

One of the biggest hurdles was to surpass the Japanese standards for quality. A test of competing Japanese pagers showed a failure rate of about .5 percent per month. Motorola, meanwhile, was "operating significantly worse than that," Fisher says. So the company reviewed all of its manufacturing and design practices, and in time qualified as a supplier, winning a major chunk of the Japanese market. "We went from nowhere in Japan to being a preferred supplier to one of the toughest customers," Gilmore says. The company has now sold more than a million pagers to NTT.

Gilmore recalls how Fisher took a personal interest in projects throughout the company. The two first met when Gilmore was a second-level manager on a project to develop a pen-sized pager, code-named Leprechaun. "It hadn't gotten support," Gilmore says. When Fisher came in as head of operations, he made the rounds to talk to engineers about what was in the works. "He put his feet up on the desk and we had a heart-to-heart about the project," Gilmore says. "The thing that impressed me was how George asked: 'Merle, do you have everything you need to get this project done?' " And then he delivered, so the project could finally be finished. It was a first, Gilmore says: during his tenure, no one at Fisher's level or higher had ever visited his office.

Gilmore and Fisher continued their respective rises through the company management; Fisher always stayed in touch with those he met along the way. "I used to consider myself one of George's inner circle," Gilmore says. "As I moved along in the corporation, it was amazing to me that hundreds or thousands considered themselves part of the inner circle."

The two fought a second battle with the Japanese in the early 1980s. The pager industry had become the target of the Japanese manufacturers; wanting a piece of the U.S. market, they halved their prices. "I've always believed that it was in retaliation for our being successful" in Japan, Fisher says.

A few big customers accounted for half of Motorola's paging business. The Japanese "were going in making offers to these few big customers that really would break the bank for us if we matched them." The business went from profitability to the brink of collapse, almost overnight. It was a tough time for Fisher. "I remember lying awake all one night and thinking, 'Oh, my God. I'm running this business and we're goin' out of business.' That's very scary."

Fisher and others launched the dumping case through the U.S. government. "I didn't even know what a dumping case was at that time," he said. Gilmore remembered how Fisher and others pulled together a team of experts on trade law and began to round up allies in Washington. "It was a real uphill battle. Industries were falling one after another" because of Japanese tactics.

Eventually, Motorola won the case, and the United States applied duties to the Japanese products. "It saved the U.S. paging industry," Gilmore said. Motorola became a case study for other U.S. companies in battles with the Japanese manufacturers. Robert Galvin, son of the founder, who eventually became CEO, even helped write a series of newspaper and magazine ads called

"Meeting Japan's Challenge," which ran from 1981 to 1985, to reinforce the company's belief that U.S. industries can compete.

The paging episode also reinforced Motorola leaders' earlier efforts to improve quality. And it revealed a lot of problems in the company's cost structure. "We were still in denial on cost," Fisher says. One project that addressed both issues was launched in 1986, when Fisher and others convinced the board of directors to invest in a new pager project, dubbed Bandit. The name was selected because it suggested stealing every good idea they could find. Fisher personally asked the board for funding and made regular trips to the plant to keep close tabs on the project. Within eighteen months, spending $10 million, the Bandit group simplified the pager so it could be produced in an automated factory in Boynton Beach, Florida. Bandit was "aimed at doing a quantum leap in manufacturing technology," Gilmore says.

Pagers' cycle time—how long it takes to get a product finished—was cut to two hours from two weeks. Pagers could be custom built in orders as small as one. "It was George's visible sponsorship within the organization, as well as in the corporation, to establish it as a model factory," Gilmore says. Today, Motorola's best plants have "roots in what we created in the Bandit days," Gilmore says. That project was part of the reason that Motorola won one of the first Malcolm Baldrige National Quality Awards in 1988.

Throughout the company, Galvin pushed people to cut out extra steps and look for hidden defects in processes. They looked for ways to reach "six sigma," a term that means practically zero defects in manufacturing. Employees were issued pocket cards bearing the slogan "Total Customer Satisfaction." This was billed as the company's fundamental objective and everyone's overriding responsibility. On the reverse, the card lists Motorolans' key beliefs: constant respect for people and uncompromising integrity; three key goals of best in class, increased global market share, and superior financial results; and key initiatives to accomplish those goals. The backbone of that was the push for six sigma and cycle-time reduction.

In 1987, Galvin set two specific goals: to reduce manufacturing defects by 90 percent every two years and to improve cycle

time 90 percent every five years. The results have shown in cru-
cial products. For instance, in 1985, it took three years to get cellular phones from design to production. That time was cut down
to fifteen months by 1989, with plans to cut it even more. And
newer models of phones contained a fraction of the parts found
in earlier models.

Galvin also pushed his senior managers to visit more customers. The CEO himself went to see a customer about once a
month, and wrote a report on the visit for others to read. The drive
for customer satisfaction and quality filtered down through the
company. One of Galvin's ideas that had a big impact on Fisher
was his belief in an orderly and early transition in senior management. Fisher's efforts in paging and other company operations got
the attention of Galvin, who wanted a "graceful leapfrogging from
a vintage team of sixty-year-olds to a youthful chief executive
office team," Galvin says. The succession process included a transition and training program that ran from July 1986 to January
1988. As of July 1986, when he was forty-five, Fisher was named a
senior executive vice president and deputy to the CEO; he was set
to become president and CEO as of 1988 and chairman in 1990.

Fisher calls Galvin one of his mentors and remembers that
appointment as a highlight of his Motorola career. Was the challenge daunting? "I didn't know it was supposed to be daunting.
I'm sort of like Magoo. I just keep bouncing off one wall after
another."

Much of George Fisher's success at Motorola must be credited to his predecessors. He inherited the Galvin family's track
record and a stable of successful products to launch his tenure as
CEO. But insiders note that Fisher brought even more attention
to improving the basics in products and people. Like those before
him, he pushed training and basic education for plant and office
workers. "The fundamental directions were in place," recalls
Keith Bane, now an executive vice president at Motorola, who
has known Fisher for nearly twenty years. What Fisher added
was a new level of hands-off management.

Motorola has a culture of dissent. Employees at all levels of
the company are encouraged to express their opinions, no matter

how contrary. Bane recalls meetings in which division presidents were yelling at one another as they defended their points of view. "We argued like cats and dogs," Fisher says. "Loudly, sometimes." Indeed, if employees disagree with a manager's decision to, say, cancel a project, they can file minority reports with the next level of management for review and possible reversal. That process has saved some of Motorola's biggest projects, such as Iridium, a planned network of satellites to ease around-the-world communications.

At times, Motorola has been described as a pressure cooker because of the constant push for more, better, faster. But there are signs that senior management at least acknowledge that people have lives outside of work. For example, all the employees received a booklet called "The Role of the Adult in the Life of a Child," intended to make them more aware of the need to invest time in the next generation.

Motorola officials also instill a belief in renewal on the job. Training begins with the basics for those who are illiterate. In one Motorola plant, only 40 percent of the workers passed a test with questions such as "10 is what percent of 100?" Training also helped move workers beyond the old supervisor-worker environment to teams that are self-managed. Even senior management had to take training. From 1985 to 1987, the senior executives spent seventeen days each in classes on topics ranging from manufacturing and global competition to cycle-time managment.

As CEO, Fisher pushed the training center to have more autonomy and grander visions for the future, even suggesting that it become Motorola University. One of the university's courses is on managing change. Bill Weize, a former CEO and vice chairman of the board, says he teaches lessons based on this idea: "I built this bureaucracy, and if I was twenty-five years old, here's how I'd blow it up and build what we need for the next ten years." Retirees from other companies also serve as guest lecturers.

Fisher also promoted math and science programs for children, such as the "university's" summer camps. He gave unusual attention to his managers' needs to balance home and office.

Gilmore recalls how Fisher sent him a note congratulating him on the birth of his son, Kevin. He told the Gilmores that the baby would be "a treasure" in their lives. "There was a cautionary note at the end," Gilmore says. "He knew I gave a lot to my job and career," and he reminded the new father to "give even more energy to my family." The Gilmores framed the CEO's note and hung it in the baby's nursery.

Fisher showed the same attention in the workplace, and rewarded those who worked hard. Bane recalls how Fisher invited him and his wife, Kathy, to spend a weekend with the Fishers at Disney World to celebrate Motorola's venture with IBM and Apple on the PowerPC project, which Bane led. "We spent an entire day wandering around Disney like lifelong school buddies," Bane says, noting that Fisher seemed to like Futureland the best.

Motorola continued to grow under Fisher's leadership. It was especially strong overseas: in 1993, it sold more than 4 million pagers in China, four times as many as it did in 1992. And the company had 85 percent of the world pager market. Motorola has also been awarded more than 140 cellular infrastructure contracts in twenty-three of China's twenty-seven provinces. The company's quality continued to improve. During 1993, Motorola saved more than $1.4 billion in manufacturing costs as a direct result of quality improvement efforts started since 1986. Many of the gains come from nonmanufacturing areas, as quality efforts seep into more mundane matters such as paperwork. For instance, Motorola gave a gold award to a satisfaction team called Da Patentabulls for the group's efforts to simplify the process of filing patent applications.

A team of "Flexperts" continues to improve the Boynton Beach plant. The team has reduced manufacturing-line conversion time from eight hours to about thirty minutes, allowing a line to be converted during a lunch break or team meeting. The company hasn't hit six sigma yet—Motorola officials say that will depend on raising the quality of materials coming from outside suppliers—but it is close. The company counted 6,000 defects per million parts in 1987. As of 1995, it was about 20 to 30 parts per million.

Fisher's track record at Motorola got noticed, especially by headhunters who in 1993 were busy trying to fill the increasing number of empty CEO chairs as more boards of directors gave entrenched leaders the boot. That year, Fisher was approached by headhunters looking for a replacement to head IBM. Telling people that it was the wrong time for him to leave Motorola, Fisher asked the IBM search committee to remove his name from the list of candidates.

But the overture did make Fisher think about his future, an exercise he says he had avoided before because "I was just going to stay at Motorola forever." Both Ann and George thought about "how we're gonna spend the next ten to twenty years." Motorola was "on a great course and it wasn't gonna stop. . . . We had in place really good people running all the businesses. They were as good as I was and they didn't need a lot of help." Fisher figured he could "sort of ride herd on that and be Solomon in a lot of disputes between businesses." But the IBM job opening made him realize there were other choices.

In the spring and summer of 1993, the Fishers read about the management upheaval at Kodak as it unfolded, culminating in the ouster of Kay Whitmore in August and the immediate speculation about who would take over the job. They read the list of candidates in the press reports. "My wife and I were amused because we had just been through the IBM thing and said: 'Aren't you glad we're not in this one? . . . Those poor guys, what they're going through.' "

Then he got a phone call about taking the Kodak job. "Unlike the IBM time, I had given a lot of thought to what I might want to do with the rest of my life. But I never consciously said if the right opportunity came up, I would take it," George says. But negotiations moved quickly. And Ann realized that her husband wasn't going to pass on this one. "There was a look on his face and in his eyes that told me that he wanted to do this, and I would have never stopped him," she says.

A self-described "lousy" picture taker who hates cold weather, Fisher still found the job in Rochester impossible to resist. "Kodak is like apple pie and, you know, motherhood. You couldn't get much more wholesome or rewarding than that. . . . It had this great ring of goodness to me and it was in great trouble. And somehow they convinced me that I could probably turn it around. I mean, I wasn't so sure of that, but they seemed convinced, and they knew more about it than I did." That belief was coupled with the "fact that I didn't want to coast the rest of my life."

He reflected on what he calls the serendipity of the IBM and Kodak jobs. "Had the order been reversed, I probably would have turned down Kodak and done IBM. . . . Whichever one came first I would have turned down, because I hadn't thought about it."

One of the toughest aspects of the decision was leaving behind a $2.5 million home. "We had just bought our dream house. It was beautiful. I still love it." More important, it was hard to leave his friends at Motorola. "I grew up with some of those people. . . . It's like leaving your family. I was the first non-Galvin to be chairman. There's a lot of heavy stuff there that really made it very, very personally difficult to do that."

Initially, the news was kept quiet. Indeed, some Kodak board members didn't know about it until the day before the public announcement in October 1993. On the morning of the official news release, Bane called Fisher's office about eight A.M. to talk business. "You're a dear friend," Fisher told him. "Come up to my office." When Fisher told him that he'd resigned the night before, Bane cursed a bit but thought Fisher must be joking. "I was shocked."

Reflecting on his friend's decision, Bane concluded that Fisher wanted the chance to really build something. "I think he felt that he had an opportunity to take a company and put his own personal mark of accomplishment or leadership on a particular situation, as opposed to continuing the direction Motorola was already on. That's a big difference. Kodak was in a period of transition, where it had to have a leader come in and give it a new direction. George has the opportunity to be the individual to really change Kodak. At Motorola . . . to individually stand out in terms of putting your mark on things is a difficult challenge."

Besides, Fisher was going to make a fortune just by signing up at Kodak. The board of directors made him an offer that even

exceeded what he might have made had he become a professional baseball player. For starters, he received a $5 million
signing bonus and a base salary of $2 million a year for the life of
the five-year employment contract. In addition, he was guaranteed an incentive bonus of $1 million in both 1994 and 1995.
After that, his bonus would be tied to the company's financial
performance. Kodak also lent him $8.3 million, to be forgiven at a
rate of 20 percent a year if he stayed for the length of his contract.
Fisher used most of the loan to buy 107,400 shares of Kodak
stock. He also received a grant of 20,000 shares of the stock,
which he was obliged to hold for five years, and options on 1.323
million shares, which could be exercised in equal parts during the
length of his contract. A long-term incentive plan would give him
up to 65,214 additional shares if he reached certain financial
goals. The company also bought his $2.5 million house and paid
the closing costs on the sale of an earlier home. At the very least,
Fisher would get about $25 million in salary, bonus, and loans,
before adding in the value of stock, options, and other bonuses. If
Kodak's stock price rose high enough, Fisher could net more than
$100 million.

Regardless of its eventual worth, the face value of the package
shocked many inside and outside Kodak, who were used to the
smaller wages paid to earlier CEOs; Whitmore, for instance, had
been paid $930,769 in salary and $374,255 in bonuses. Kathy
Hudson, who had left her job as a Kodak vice president before
Fisher arrived, deemed it an insult to other Kodak employees.
"The people who left [in early retirement programs] left with a
lot of money. The people who stay get low raises. And the people
who are hired guns come in with $25 million." Hudson, who is
now CEO of the sign-making, label, and printing company W. H.
Brady, said: "If he saves the company, people won't begrudge
him the money." But, she added: "I'm a little irked."

It is impossible to justify why anyone should be paid millions
of dollars for running a company. Compared to other titans of
industry, Fisher was getting his fair share. Michael Eisner of
Disney got $203 million in 1993, while his employees at Disney
World were lucky to get 3 percent raises. The pay system in U.S.
business reflects, among other factors, how boards of directors

don't do enough to link pay and performance at all levels of the company. But companies practically have to get into bidding wars to make sure they get executives like Fisher to leave cushy surroundings at profitable firms like Motorola to lead salvage missions at places like Kodak. Other companies would gladly cough up the same amount, maybe more, to have Fisher as their chief. Companies in worse shape than Kodak have paid even heftier wages to hired guns. For instance, Westinghouse Electric Corporation paid $10 million to Robert A. Watson for just eighteen months of work. His chore? Liquidating the company's financial services business, which was suffering losses. (Those inside Westinghouse called him Rich Bob.) Richard Koppes, general counsel for CALPERS, the California Public Employees Retirement System, which invests in many major companies, was quick to offer his reaction to such an outrageous paycheck: "For the record, I'm choking, gagging," he told *The Wall Street Journal.*

Public sentiment concerning such paychecks has soured as more companies use layoffs to cut their costs, while rewarding the CEOs whose mismanagement forced the cutbacks. Robert Allen, CEO of AT&T, cut 40,000 jobs. His salary? $3.36 million. (Some inside the company say AT&T now stands for Allen & Two Temps.) Yet it was Allen who, as CEO, overpaid for the buyout of NCR in Dayton, then failed to effectively merge the company with AT&T, leading the company to sell the business. Allan Sloan of *Newsweek* put it well when he wrote: "What really matters is that although unemployment is relatively low and the economy is cranking out new jobs, millions of Americans believe they're being screwed by corporate America and Wall Street."

In Rochester, many agreed that Kodak had overpaid for Fisher. No wonder, considering that the town had seen round after round of layoffs. Even if Kodak could no longer be the Yellow Father, Fisher's salary did set him up as the new king of the town, an image that didn't quite fit with his efforts to be seen as "one of the guys." He ate in the cafeteria with other employees, answered every piece of mail, and urged his colleagues to tell him when he was wrong. But it was impossible for others inside the company to treat him as an ordinary coworker when he was being paid such an outrageous sum.

It was especially hard to take for Kodak's Class of '93, which got the ax without the cushy retirement packages offered in earlier rounds of cuts. Patty Minisce heard the news when she was looking for work as a systems analyst and waiting tables on weekends to make ends meet. She had to work on Mother's Day, rather than be home with her young son. She was trying to juggle bills and the everyday demands of raising kids, so multimillion-dollar executive compensation packages didn't win points with her. "It makes me sick." Her father was so outraged by her job loss that he wrote to the new CEO, asking why a company would pay for his daughter's education, only to lay her off from her job. Minisce was angry, but she did concede that if Fisher could improve Kodak, that could only help Rochester. That was one of her biggest concerns, because she wanted to stay in Rochester, rather than relocate to find work.

Even those who still had jobs inside Kodak had mixed feelings about Fisher's paycheck, a topic of many lengthy discussions. "I would've preferred if he took the Lee Iacocca approach and took a dollar," along with stock, as his pay, said Bob Kalita, a Kodak engineer. "It would've been nice to take a little more personal sacrifice."

Erich Bloch, a former IBM executive who then became a senior fellow at the Council on Competitiveness, knew Fisher from his work with the council and in his role as a director of Motorola. His comments summed up what many felt was a system out of whack: "If anybody is worth that money, he certainly is." But "Is anyone worth that much money? Personally, I don't think so. I think some of the executive salaries are exaggerated."

What did Fisher have to say about his pay? "I never dreamed of making this much money." He couldn't defend it in the context of those who were unemployed or hadn't seen a raise in years. "How do you justify that? It's very hard." But he noted that his package at Motorola had been worth more, when his stock options were included in the tab, and that he had the potential to save Kodak far more than he would be paid during his tenure. "Other people have to be the judge as to whether it's worth it or not, but I'm not embarrassed by it." Ann Fisher said, "Money means nothing to me. . . . I don't ever think about it. But I can say that because I have it. . . . We've been incredibly lucky."

To their credit, the Fishers gave away millions to various charities. But in the end, George Fisher's tenure at Kodak—including his compensation—would be judged by a single standard: Could he and his team save and rejuvenate one of the world's largest yet most badly mismanaged companies? If so, the furor over his pay would recede in the face of an acclaimed triumph of executive leadership. If not, Fisher would be remembered as merely the last well-paid, well-intentioned captain of a doomed vessel—an industrial *Titanic* lost among the icebergs of late-twentieth-century capitalism.

6

Wake-up Call

CEO George Fisher started working on Kodak before his official starting date. One of his first requests was for a copy of the biography of George Eastman. Fisher thinks Eastman was a genius ahead of his time because he understood the consumer market and the benefits of mass production even before these principles were used by the auto industry. "You can't help but have great respect for founders in general. He was just an incredible man." One of the first things Fisher concluded was that Kodak needed to return to some of Eastman's commonsense business principles.

To understand every aspect of Kodak, Fisher also asked for detailed reports on everything from market-share in Japan to employee morale, which was in bad shape. The period after Whitmore's ouster was one of uncertainty inside Kodak, largely because everyone expected the board to hire someone who was a "slash-and-burn type of CEO," said Dave Swift, who worked as Whitmore's assistant at the time of his departure. "So the morale was awful, all the way up to the seniormost people in the company. It was not a pleasant time to be at Kodak." Jack Thomas, the second-highest executive in Whitmore's team and an inside director, was even more blunt: "There was some fear among my colleagues in Kodak that the board would hire Attila the Hun."

But when Fisher was named, even Whitmore was pleased by the news. The two executives had worked together in various CEO groups, and their wives knew each other. "As disheartened as he was to be in that position, seeing the selection of George was like a dream come true," Swift said. "If he had to lose his job, this is the way to have it happen."

Swift sent Fisher reams of documents before the new CEO's arrival. "He was sucking in information as fast as we could feed it to him. Before he made any kind of decisions at all, he wanted to absorb as much information as possible." That "instilled immediate confidence" among Kodak managers.

After Whitmore's lackluster performance, it was easy for Fisher to make a strong debut as CEO. At his first press conference, Fisher told reporters, as well as employees watching via video hookup, that he looked forward to being on the front line in the information revolution: "Kodak has a great franchise. My hope is that we can build on that and really get out some exciting growth and make all our publics much happier than they've been."

The meeting was the first clear indication of how Fisher viewed his role as CEO. His immediate goal was to clean up Kodak's financial house, he assured investors—but for the long-term good of the company, he would rank customers and employees ahead of shareholders. "I really focus on five publics in Motorola. . . . You cannot have total customer satisfaction that we strive for at Motorola without having total employee satisfaction. So I think those go hand in hand." The third constituency was shareholders. "The owners deserve a fair return." Next came suppliers, who "have to be an integral part of our success or feel our failure so they help us." Fifth were the communities where Kodak operated. "The company has a responsibility to the communities because it does affect the welfare of the people that live there."

Fisher's approach to ranking the various publics differed from his predecessors' in several ways. The old Kodak clearly put employees' interests ahead of shareholders. For instance, the company used to make such fiscally irresponsible moves as borrowing money to pay bonuses during years when it didn't have enough earnings to justify a bonus for anybody. Fisher wanted to put employees first, but without such generosity and with more accountability. He linked pay to performance at all levels of the company, and believed in measuring performance carefully. If that was done, Fisher believed, the employees would deliver results that would satisfy investors, customers, and the rest of the company's publics.

Fisher also made it clear that Kodak would no longer indulge in a Rochester-centric view of the world, and would not take a backseat to any foreign competitor, especially those from Japan. He also said he wouldn't rule out selling off some parts of the company, once he figured out the best strategy for Kodak. Initially, he figured that Kodak's growth would be based on two pillars—health care and imaging. He told the group that he had already had sleepless nights as he thought about the possibilities. "Ninety percent of my ideas may never work. But there are ten percent that will be killers."

Fisher was a hit with the board. Roberto Goizueta, Coca-Cola's CEO and a member of the Kodak search committee, praised Fisher's track record, including creating shareholder value at Motorola at a rate of 26 percent annual returns. "When we started this search, our number one candidate was God, and we stepped down from that," Goizueta said, demonstrating the size of CEOs' egos.

Fisher immediately began to get advice from all corners of the company. The company newsletter, *Kodakery,* published employees' thoughts on why the new guy had better be different from Whitmore. These staffers worked on the front lines, where they saw the incredible waste and mismanagement, so they weren't as easily charmed by the mere arrival of an outsider. Instead, they urged Fisher to get busy reducing Kodak's massive debt and figure out how to increase employees' enthusiasm for their work. Even retirees—Ray Romeiser, for one—said Fisher should tour Kodak Park and talk to workers, rather than rely on his handlers to interpret the feedback. "Find out for yourself," Romeiser said. Some employees just wanted Fisher to give them a "reason to trust management again." Others wisely advised him to get out and meet customers and ask a simple question: Why do you buy competing products instead of Kodak?

In response, Fisher sent clear messages from the start, especially to local officials who were eager for the new CEO to get to

Rochester. He made it clear that he wasn't going to be another George Eastman, in terms of being the town's Yellow Father. His first priority was to fix Kodak, not to try to solve Rochester's myriad social and economic problems by serving on countless boards and committees. Indeed, he was cautious about his every move once he got to Rochester. When he was asked to join the Oak Hill Country Club, the hangout for Rochester's upper crust, Fisher asked several questions: How many minority members belonged to the club? Were women equal members? How were the club's finances? Fisher got positive answers to his questions, so he joined. (Oak Hill Country Club's general manager, Eric Rule, said the club didn't have a deficit at the time Fisher asked, but did expect to incur some debt for renovations. When asked about the number and treatment of women and minority members, Rule replied that the club treats all members equally, but he wouldn't disclose how many of its 915 members were minorities or women.)

The Fishers kept a relatively low profile in Rochester. He turned down most requests to speak, making an exception for the Sisters of St. Joseph at Nazareth High School Academy, who asked him to speak at a fund-raising dinner. When asked why he agreed, he said he was afraid the nuns wouldn't send him any more cookies, a gesture they made when the Fishers moved into a nearby house on East Avenue in Pittsford. It's the same street where the other George had built his mansion.

The Fishers' choice of houses made headlines, much to their chagrin. Not because of the East Avenue address, but because of the price tag: they paid $2.35 million for the fifteen-room house, which had previously belonged to car dealer John Holtz. The *Democrat & Chronicle* reported that this might be the highest price ever paid for an existing single-family house in Monroe County. The 7,200-square-foot home is surrounded by fourteen acres of land and 200-year-old oak trees.

Ann Fisher didn't fully appreciate the town's obsession with Kodak and its CEO until she read the local newspaper. On the same day when many newspapers focused coverage on a bloody massacre on the Long Island Rail Road, the Fishers' search for a house made bigger headlines. "So that just gives you kind of an idea of what this town is all about," Ann said. "Why are people interested?" She was bothered by the coverage of the house, because reading about massive kitchens and green marble bathrooms might make the Fishers "appear snooty" and give people "the wrong impression."

Despite living in a mansion, the Fishers tried to dispel the notion that they are snobby millionaires. Fisher didn't act like a stereotypical CEO, which came as a real shock to locals. He often ran at the YMCA, prompting some gee-whiz reactions on the track. And the first time he was spotted pushing a cart in K Mart, it became the talk of the factory floors. The fact that he was buying a toaster was noted in the local newspaper. He was a regular visitor to McDonald's, but his normally quick stops now required more time because he was often recognized. Ordinary trips to the grocery store also took a lot of extra time when he stopped to talk to several people. "But it also provides the biggest reward," Ann said. "People generally have been very happy when they see him." Even those who didn't know his name would stop and ask: "Should I know you?" "There's no place to hide in this town," George added. When Ann needed to run a quick errand, she left George at home.

But, Fisher noted, a certain amount of seclusion came with his job. "It's hard to have close friends because people shy away from you or you just don't have the time, more than anything else, so you don't really have personal friends. Our social circle has been family."

On the job, Fisher spent his time making the rounds with the troops, customers, and wherever he figured he could help spread the news about his ideas to fix Kodak. From the start, he worked on getting to know the people he'd be working with inside the company. He liked to visit labs, where he got his start, and talk to researchers. Jim Meyer, a senior vice president and director of research and development, recalled a visit when Fisher trailed behind during the tour to talk to one scientist. Meyer found the two "holding this conversation like I would expect two bench-level scientists to discuss" their research.

Swift, who continued in the CEO's assistant post after Fisher arrived, noticed how Fisher wanted to get acquainted with individuals, not just issues. That was a change from past CEOs, who kept their work relationships strictly business. After one week on the job, Fisher called Swift at home and invited him and his wife, Martha, to join the Fishers for dinner. "He was really interested in knowing the people he was going to be working with, and really making sure that the personal side was gonna work," Swift said.

Fisher prefers small group sessions or getting out to see people, rather than inviting them to his office: "I make a point of not spending a lot of time in my office." When he does sit in meetings, he fidgets a bit, opening and closing the clasp on his watch. "I hate meetings. Just hate meetings with a vengeance." He often includes Ann in meetings; she attends "town meetings," his twice-a-year ask-me-anything sessions at the company's main plant and office sites. She also travels with him, often going on plant tours or visiting employees while he attends to business. "He really used Ann as an ambassador," Swift said. "It's a really interesting relationship that has spoken volumes to the employees." (Ann Fisher even had a Kodak business card, with "Ambassador" as her title.) Her favorite unofficial duty is to visit Kodak people at factories around the world: "They're the hard workers. The ones that don't get much notice."

Unlike some CEOs, who have climbed the career ladder with little regard for their wives, Fisher gives Ann a lot of credit for helping him professionally, as well as being his best friend. "She understands the basic business issues that I'm dealing with almost as well as I do. And since I spend the most time with her, it's good that I have a sounding board. But also it's important because of the amount of time I have to work that she's understanding of why the hell I work so hard. So I think it's just good common sense and good for the relationship." She calculated that because she traveled with him, they had spent more time together since he took the Kodak job than they did when he worked at Motorola.

The biggest difference Swift noted in the new CEO was his approach to dealing with his subordinates at Kodak. Swift was in a position to know: the assistant-to-the-CEO job had traditionally been a soak-it-up year for a junior manager like Swift. But the junior employee would rarely participate in decision-making. Under Whitmore, for instance, the assistant was supposed to sit in a chair in the corner of the CEO's conference room, rather than take a seat with the execs, even if there was a free seat at the large table. "I called it the dunce chair," said Swift, a Harvard MBA. Out of habit, he took that chair during his first conference-room meeting with Fisher.

"So George kind of turns around, looks at me and says, 'Well, what are you sitting over there for?' "

Swift answered: "This is where I was told I was supposed to sit."

"Well, with me, if you're gonna be on my team, you sit at the table where you're gonna be a contributor," Fisher replied.

The change made some senior managers a bit uncomfortable. "It took a little while for them to get used to that," Swift said. Fisher also changed the assistant's job, assigning Swift major projects, such as analyzing which aspects of Kodak's business should be kept and which should be sold. Swift was also given the unpleasant task of being Fisher's point man on the previously announced plan to cut 10,000 jobs during the next three years.

By the time Fisher arrived in late 1993, between 3,000 and 4,000 jobs had already been eliminated. He wasn't happy about inheriting the rest, but he had pledged that he would carry them out. ("He was not too pleased to have to deal with it, but he's a man of his word," Swift said.) However, Fisher would handle future cuts differently. There would be no more mass announcements; instead, each department would be in charge of continually monitoring its staffing. If the department had too many people, there would be cuts. Once he took over, Fisher avoided big announcements about cuts; now they were done quietly and in smaller numbers. In other words, he avoided a lot of the public outcry by simply being discreet. He didn't promise people jobs for life, and he realized that layoffs have to occur when a business no longer fit with the company's strategy. What he preferred was a workplace where staffers were constantly training for new opportunities that were created as some parts of the business grew and

replaced failed ones. In some cases, people were rehired as contractors, especially at peak times when Kodak needed extra help.

Fisher spent a lot of time talking to employees, trying to
convey the message that Kodak must trim its costs. At the same
time, he tried to reassure employees that he did believe that "the
single most important asset that a company has is something
that doesn't show up on its balance sheet," Swift said.

Fisher never had to make massive cutbacks at Motorola, so he
got his first real dose of wrath and frustration from those hit by
the cuts at Kodak. It was a painful experience. "You know, you
don't cease being a human being because you have these jobs. . . .
You care and it hurts, just like it would hurt anybody else, especially when you're the person that is really ultimately calling the
shots that makes those things happen. The way you have to
understand it is that what we're trying to do here is to end up
with a much healthier company." He got dozens of letters, phone
calls, and E-mail notes from employees and retirees each day,
and he answered all of them, usually within a day. Every night,
he took home a stack of mail and E-mail print-outs. If he was
traveling, he had his mail forwarded by Federal Express so he
could keep up with it. Managers learned very quickly that he
expected prompt turnaround with them, too. One employee
recalled getting a note from Fisher asking why it took four days
for a memo to be forwarded to his office.

Fisher saw the fear among Kodak employees firsthand when
he toured various parts of the company. Such fear remained
long after the announcements of who was affected by the latest
cutbacks. Many employees were still looking over their shoulders, wondering if their jobs would be the next to go. Fisher also
found a lot of lingering resentment from some people who stayed
at Kodak instead of taking the generous buyout of 1991, the
Triple R, and now were afraid of losing their jobs. Fisher didn't
mince words about his disdain for how cuts and buyouts have
been administered in the past. "It's easy to second-guess people,
but I think it was, number one, extremely expensive. Number
two, we lost a lot of really good, experienced people, and now I
think we're making up for it."

Still, he reminded people that there is never a guarantee in today's uncertain world. More cuts could come down the road, if a business was floundering. But he vowed to avoid making major cutback announcements, because they put the entire company on edge. "That is terrible on morale. Just terrible," Fisher said. "We have to get out of that mode and have to handle that much more effectively in the future."

Likewise, he told Wall Street analysts to be patient, not to make unreasonable demands for quick fixes at Kodak. After just a few days on the job, he issued a news release saying that analysts' forecasts for 1994 were "well above what I believe we will be able to deliver." One of his first financial landmarks as CEO was seeing the stock drop by about $7 a share in response to those comments. The share price had been pumped up by a belief that Fisher would make deep cuts in payroll and other costs. Wall Street reacted so negatively because it was far too early in his tenure for investors to see tangible results from his pledges. Fisher could either let Wall Street be surprised when the actual quarterly report was announced, or disclose the problem as soon as possible and get the shock over with. The markets had overvalued the stock on the basis of his arrival, rather than on substantive changes. Disappointed analysts downgraded Kodak stock and cut their estimates by $1 a share for 1994.

That was one of the first reality checks for Fisher and his management team; it was viewed as a temporary setback, and he moved on to address the underlying issues that led to Kodak's long-standing financial problems.

Another of Fisher's earliest moves was a memo to all Kodak employees. Just as he had set the record straight with the analysts, he wanted to settle some immediate worries among workers. He had joined the company in the midst of talks about moving a chunk of the core imaging business from Rochester to Washington, D.C. Just a week after he arrived, he told employees that he was putting the move on "indefinite hold." Those inside the company say he took one look at the proposal and called it off. Why would a company in financial distress spend millions to move a handful of people to a more expensive location? Fisher agreed that Kodak needs to get closer to customers, but moving to Washington, D.C., wasn't the answer. Any move would come only after Kodak evaluated its entire structure and figured out how to grow.

Fisher made the decision for business reasons, but won points among employees because he also offered his apologies for the disruption the planned move had caused employees and their families. Packaging a message is one of his strengths. He is candid and doesn't hesitate to share information—a big change from his Kodak predecessors.

Fisher soon began to issue regular statements to employees about building the basics, a value system. One memo described "Fundamentals for Kodak Renewal" that would provide focus and satisfy Kodak's five publics: customers, employees, shareholders, suppliers, and the communities where the company operates.

The company's finances must be improved, Fisher said, both by reducing debt and by generating better earnings. Greater sales would have to come through serving emerging markets around the world, as well as Kodak's home market. And Kodak would build on its technology base in film, digital imaging, and health care.

But to satisfy shareholders, Fisher—taking a page from his Motorola days—stressed his intent to focus first on customers and employees. "These do, in fact, go hand in hand. For if we pursue total customer satisfaction as an objective, then I am absolutely convinced that we must concurrently achieve a much higher level of employee satisfaction. Unfortunately, today we have some serious problems in both respects."

To improve employee satisfaction, Fisher said, the company had to restore five defining values. First, respect for the dignity of the individual. Under this heading he included issues like diversity of the workplace and respect for long service. Second, uncompromising integrity. Third, trust. Fourth, credibility. And fifth, continual improvement.

Fisher began to repeat this message everywhere he went, inside and outside the company. Others at Kodak began to repeat it, too. Whenever he was asked to contribute an article to an outside publication, Fisher took the opportunity to drive home his message. In the summer 1994 issue of *SimonBusiness,* the magazine of the William E. Simon Graduate School of Business Administration at the University of Rochester, Fisher offered some advice to all U.S. managers: Throw out business books, cut the jargon, and focus on one goal—to learn what makes your customers value your work. Then figure out how to do it even better.

Fisher encountered skepticism about the impact of talking about "mushy" things like dignity, credibility, and trust when people believe that "leanness, meanness, and ninety-hour workweeks are the measures people use to separate the real players from the herd," he said. He admired the fact that Japanese companies consider the human resources director second to the CEO, while U.S. firms relegate the job to "a kind of twilight zone." Hoping to rebuild trust between management and employees, he quickly made personnel changes at the top of Kodak's human resources department. He appointed Mike Morley, whom he calls a "star manager" from the consumer film business, as head. Early on, the change in the human resources department produced more changes throughout the company, including a reduction in paperwork and bureaucracy. Fisher was eager to make a change in that key role because so many of his plans depended on studying each part of the company—how it rewards people, how fast products are made, and other key issues. A new human resources manager was central to those changes, but Fisher had a lot of work to do as he plodded through Kodak's longstanding bureaucracy.

Others in senior management retired, making room for new blood. Fisher went outside Kodak to fill key posts. For instance, he hired Harry Kavetas, former president and CEO of the IBM Credit Corporation, as chief financial officer, an area where Kodak really needed help. Indeed, Fisher has sometimes referred to Kodak's bookkeeping as something out of the Dark Ages. Fisher also hired a new treasurer, Jesse Greene, and controller, Dave FitzPatrick.

Fisher was determined to build up Kodak's ailing digital business, which had been neglected because the traditional-film business managers had typically viewed it as a threat. Kodak had made some strides in digital products—for instance, developing a digital camera with Apple Computer. But many digital programs languished in the labs because they weren't a priority compared with film. By the mid-1990s, however, digital cameras were becoming increasingly popular with commercial users of photography, such as insurance company inspectors documenting claims, and real-estate agents taking pictures of houses. The home photography market hadn't really been disrupted by digital cameras because they were still too expensive for most families. However, the price of the cameras will eventually fall and the quality will improve, so average consumers will start to trade their old cameras for the digital products. Kodak already has competition in all sorts of digital products, ranging from Sony to Nikon, which have historically done a better job of making and selling consumer electronic goods.

Fisher had a lot of ties to the computer world from his days at Motorola, so he called on former Apple chairman John Sculley to be a marketing adviser to Kodak. Sculley was self-employed after a brief tenure as head of Spectrum Information Technologies, which ended in a dispute with the company president.

To head up the digital business, Fisher hired Carl Gustin, who used to work for Sculley at Apple before going to Digital Equipment. To join Gustin, Fisher promoted Dave Swift from the assistant-to-the-CEO post, making him general manager, operations, and vice president for Kodak's digital and applied imaging business. In so doing, Fisher went against the typical Kodak notion that managers needed a certain amount of gray hair before they could become vice presidents. Fisher often spoke of the importance of diversity in gender, race, and age. When he joined Kodak, there were very few people left over the age of fifty-five or under twenty-five, because the company had no credibility on college campuses and so many people had been laid off or had taken early retirement. Fisher believed that would change as the company proved it could grow: "The fact is that you've gotta establish a belief in the future and you've gotta establish a belief in people for themselves and for the company."

A key change was holding people accountable for their forecasts and for meeting tougher financial standards. In the past, it hadn't been a big deal to miss a financial forecast. But Fisher preached the benefits of having everyone in the company looking at return on net assets, or RONA, which measures how much a company is making in relation to the cost of the capital it invests. "If a company is really returning more than its cost of capital, it is more than generating value for the company."

The importance of RONA is most effectively conveyed by showing people throughout the organization how they can affect it and how that in turn will affect their paychecks. That was never a concern at the old Kodak. "You gotta put your money where your mouth is," Fisher said. "Over time, what you find is people begin to understand what drives RONA."

But before he could really press the issue of return on investment, Fisher had to make some tough decisions about what businesses Kodak had already invested in and what returns were coming back from them. Swift and others produced a report, "Kodak 2000," to show Fisher the scope of the company and what it might look like under various scenarios.

Many of Kodak's investors, along with the Wall Street analysts who followed the company, had been pushing the company's senior management to finally give up on the health care business and to divest itself of the chemical company; the latter took place as Fisher came on board. The "Kodak 2000" report showed that "we weren't gonna be able to focus on two businesses, that we had to do one or the other," health or imaging, Swift said. After studying it, Fisher agreed: Kodak didn't have the resources to be a pharmaceutical, household products, and imaging company. That strategy had been approved by the board in the mid-1980s, because of fear that the core photography business would eventually fade. Fisher said that diversification was a "decent strategy" for the time, but that Kodak simply could no longer afford to be in so many different businesses. As a result, he orchestrated the sale of Sterling Drug and several other non-imaging businesses in less than eight months, getting $7.9 billion. He was fortunate that the sale came at a time when companies were being sold at a premium. Kodak immediately used the proceeds to pay off more than $7 billion in debt, perhaps the greatest financial milestone of the new CEO's early days. He thus got rid of a burden that had been crushing the company.

Much of Fisher's approach to running Kodak involved taking action on things that previous CEOs had only talked about doing, such as selling off pieces of the company. That once again made Kodak a company built on imaging—a notion that frightened earlier CEOs, who were certain that traditional photography would fade as digital technologies allowed consumers to stop using film.

Part of Swift's assignment was to look at Kodak's cost structure and key growth opportunities, including traditional photography. Along with three financial gurus, he worked on a plan, covering the walls of an office with pages of notes and numbers. Fisher encouraged the team to study 3M, where he had once been a director. They analyzed 3M's growth rates, sales per employee, and all other publicly available data, and compared them with Kodak. Then they devised a list of 130 actions that could help Kodak get closer to 3M's performance. That list was divided among ten RONA teams, focused on topics like cost of quality, cycle-time improvement, and reengineering. One team looked at "layers," because "we still had too many layers of management," Swift said. A senior person was assigned to champion each team. Fisher headed two, partially to emphasize that he was serious about changing Kodak.

The teams began to tackle problems such as too many levels of management. Morley, head of human resources, took on the task of figuring out how to make cuts. In some parts of Kodak he found eleven layers of management from top to bottom. In human resources, he cut 27 percent of the staff. He also started to address situations where there was too much work for too few people. For instance, he cut the traditional vacation status report issued for each of Kodak's employees. This annual update reminded employees how many days off they had left, a largely useless exercise considering that most people already know how many days off they can take. But cutting out layers of paperwork isn't easy, he found. For instance, Kodak used to issue a fifteen-page alcohol policy statement. It outlined the obvious: don't keep a bottle of gin in your desk or come to work drunk, for instance. Morley told his staff to cut it to one page.

For his part, Fisher became the unofficial champion to reverse a decade of pessimism about the company's core business, film. He believed that his predecessors had been far too pessimistic about the future of traditional photography and felt too threatened by the emerging digital technologies. "People began to think electronics was gonna take over the photography business. And if you're looking at the world from within the photography business, that would be a very scary event. But the fact of the matter is, I grew up in the electronics business and I looked at the photography and imaging business from the electronics side and it's not such a scary event. Electronics will *add* a lot to photography and a lot to imaging."

Fisher did see considerable potential for future products inside Kodak's electronic-imaging patent portfolio. The company had long been criticized for investing billions in research while turning out few blockbuster products. But Fisher said that although the launch of Photo CD as a consumer product wasn't handled well, it had more than recovered as a commercial product. Kodak's film business was now helped by digital technology that made it easier for consumers to buy more reprints and enlargements of their favorite photos. Kodak's Digital Print Station, launched in 1994, allowed consumers to digitize, crop, and alter photos, then use them in various ways. In a matter of minutes, old photos could be used to personalize a calendar, mug, or T-shirt. Fisher considered the process of getting consumers to use such machines to duplicate or change their photos into gifts a huge opportunity for Kodak: "I think it could be the biggest growth driver the company, or the industry, has ever seen."

Kodak made some progress in the digital business, especially with its cameras. The company introduced the DC40 in 1995, expecting to sell 3,500; it sold ten times as many. But it faced intense competition that was growing every week. At the time of the launch, there were two other digital cameras aimed at the consumer market and priced under $1,000. By 1996, there were twenty-five different brands in that category. Kodak also cranked up its sales of supporting products, such as the thermal printers and paper used to make prints from digital cameras once the images are loaded into a personal computer. As of 1996, the digital business wasn't profitable, but Fisher had pledged in 1994 that it would make a profit by 1997.

Another growth opportunity that Fisher believed had been overlooked was film sales in developing countries once closed to U.S. companies. The growing number of households with purchasing power meant more film sales. Specifically, he saw promise in China, India, and Eastern Europe. In China, for instance, about 20 percent of the households had incomes of more than $10,000 in 1996. "I think maybe people didn't properly understand that the world is a lot bigger than the United States and that something fundamental had changed in the last five years. . . . About four billion people in the world are now accessible as a market." What remained to be seen, though, was how fast U.S. companies like Kodak could really crack the Chinese market, or how the rocky relations between the U.S. and Chinese governments would slow down Fisher's goal to invest in that country.

This is the same company that took years and wasted millions to get inside Japan—so before Fisher got Kodak into the world's less-developed regions, he had to fix Kodak's long-standing problems in that nation. Kodak won the right to sponsor the Olympics in Nagano in 1998. And the company also filed a dumping complaint with the U.S. government regarding Fuji's sale of photographic paper in this country. The government agreed. Fuji agreed to stop the practice and charge higher prices. But the issue would become moot when Fuji's U.S. photographic paper plant reached full production.

The bigger push Fisher orchestrated was a filing under U.S. trade laws to get the government to investigate Fuji's efforts, and those of the Japanese government, to keep Kodak out of Japan. This had been his pet project from the minute he became CEO. "I have spent many a waking hour studying how Kodak can become more competitive and how it can best pursue growth for the future," Fisher said. "Key to those thoughts have been how we must compete in Japan."

The problem, Kodak contended, was a highly controlled distribution system that kept its products off store shelves. Fisher had accused Fuji of price-fixing and orchestrating boycotts. Thanks to the interlocking ownership of manufacturers and distributors in Japan, wholesalers and retailers got cash payments from Fuji to help maintain prices and exclude outsiders, Fisher said.

And there was evidence that the Japanese government helped block Kodak from Japan. Reports out of Japan's photo trade groups seemed to support that claim. One published report said, "There is a fear that Kodak will control the Japanese market when the country undergoes 100% capital liberalization; MITI [the Ministry of International Trade and Industry] thus plans to prepare with the members of this industry a system which can counteract Kodak's global strategy." Fisher maintained that Japan's own antimonopoly laws were being broken. "I want them to live by their laws. If they break up the system that protects seventy percent of the market, then Kodak's gonna get a big hunk of that seventy percent, as we would in open competition in Europe or anywhere else."

The situation in Japan enabled Fuji to amass huge profits, with which it underwrote its U.S. and other foreign sales, hurting Kodak. Indeed, one Japanese retailer told a trade association meeting that "domestic products cover the cost of selling goods cheaply abroad." But Fuji officials contend that Kodak faces just what Fuji does in the United States, where it trails Kodak in market share.

Shortly after Kodak's petition was filed, the U.S. government agreed to investigate. The filing coincided with a skirmish over U.S. auto sales in Japan, which resulted in a settlement expected to open up the Japanese market to more U.S. autos and parts. Fisher denies that Kodak's filing was intentionally lobbed into the middle of the ongoing trade battle, though it offered ideal timing in terms of playing to the hard-line sentiments in Washington. "I would have filed that case if war had just been declared. . . . It just doesn't matter what else is going on."

Fisher's aggressive moves were quite a shock to even Kodak people, who had been pretty tame when it came to trying to open the Japanese market. "Kodak people are very polite, very colle-gial, nonconfrontational generally. All very nice aspects. It's an absolute delight to work here. The problem is, though, that I think maybe the company was mistaken in taking the position that being nice in Japan, not being confrontational, would somehow benefit us in the marketplace. What really has hap-pened is by being nice in the marketplace, we have been enslaved by the system that relegates us to beat our brains out with the others in this thirty percent that Fuji doesn't have," Fisher said. "And really, the people we're being nice to end up to be Fuji, not the consumers in Japan."

But Fisher had his work cut out for him when trying to deal with Kodak's blunders in Japan, which couldn't be blamed on the Japanese government or Fuji. For starters, insiders pointed out the missteps during Kodak's many downsizings—for instance, the revocation of job offers to college graduates, an action that created ill will toward the company. Some of Kodak's own retail stores operated under a compensation plan that rewarded man-agers for volume of film sold, regardless of the brand. As a result, Fuji film actually got better display and more attention from the manager, who would take home a bigger paycheck from Kodak if he sold the competing brand. Another blunder was Kodak's scaling back of its commitment to research and development in Japan. "The Japanese have long memories," remarked Ira Wolf, who was hired by Fisher to head Kodak's Japanese office.

When asked about such episodes, Fisher shook his head with annoyance, especially at the fact that job offers were revoked. "I just cringe when I hear that because that is something we should never have done. We made a mistake."

Fisher is optimistic, believing that Kodak could solve its internal problems as well as the ones created by the closed Japanese marketplace. The company is also becoming much more aggressive in its marketing efforts. For instance, it began to sell a private-label film in Japan's CO-OP stores, which also agreed to take more of Kodak's branded film.

Fisher is also pushing hard in both Tokyo and Washington. It was easy to find help. Wolf, who worked at the U.S. trade repre-sentative's office in Washington, had previously been at Motorola with Fisher. When Fisher became head of Kodak, Wolf called to ask whether the new CEO needed some help in Japan. He knew from past experience that Fisher took international markets very seriously. Motorola held quarterly trade policy meetings—a habit practiced by "very few companies," according to Wolf. He likened Kodak's situation in the mid-1990s to what Motorola faced about fifteen years earlier. "The difference is that we have a much bigger presence in Japan as a company today than Motorola did."

Besides hiring Wolf, Kodak formed a political action committee called KodaPAC shortly after Fisher arrived. "If we're going to run an aggressive worldwide company, we're going to have to be heard in Washington," Fisher said. "And if we're heard in Washington, we're heard in Tokyo, Bonn, and London. If you're not heard in Washington, the rest of the world's capitals don't care about you."

Fisher and the Kodak trade filing made some good points about the closed nature of the Japanese market. But so did Fuji. In its hefty written response to Kodak's filing, Fuji even quoted a former Kodak official to help it make its case. Albert Sieg, the former president of Kodak's Japan business, was quoted in a 1988 interview as saying: "We really aren't saddled with any barriers [to trade in Japan]. . . . If you have a good product and you persevere, and you have a head office that is not looking for results week by week but is willing to support you through the long term, you can succeed." Sieg also acknowledged that Kodak waited too long to take "aggressive action" in Japan. Furthermore, Fuji noted, it outspent Kodak on advertising in Japan ten to one from 1986 to 1988. Konica spent eight times what Kodak spent.

All American companies have stumbled, to some degree, when they tried to sell products in Japan. It is a tough place to do business. But at least half the blame for Kodak's problems belonged in Rochester, not Tokyo. Even the company's own employees admitted that Kodak missed opportunities in Japan. Moves such as the job-offer revocations were foolish and sent a strongly negative message to consumers in a country where appearances count. Only after Fisher arrived did Kodak start to pick apart the problem.

Some in Washington criticized Fisher's efforts to get the U.S. government to help fix its problems. For a business leader who wanted to compete around the globe and claimed to want free trade, they argued, his petition was too close to a request for protection. One White House official said that Kodak's case didn't hold up to close examination. Much of the evidence dated from the 1960s and 1970s. Furthermore, government officials were reluctant to impose sanctions, because the Polaroid Corporation sold Fuji-made film under the Polaroid label, and Polaroid had 70 percent of the Japanese market for instant film, compared to Fuji's 30 percent.

Kodak's efforts to draw attention to the case were, at times, comical. At one press conference, Fisher appeared with New York's controversial U.S. senator, Al D'Amato, prompting fears in the audience that the senator would say something embarrassing, even racist when he took on Japan. D'Amato was, after all, the senator who was widely chastised for his tasteless impersonation of O. J. Simpson judge Lance Ito during a radio interview. (He later apologized for his remarks.) D'Amato was a dangerous bedfellow for a company trying to win friends and customers in Japan.

To his credit, Fisher does seek feedback from everybody he meets. That's a change from his predecessors, who spent most of their time inside their offices in Rochester. Fisher prefers to talk to outsiders. While attending the Kentucky Derby in 1995 with board member and former Kentucky governor Martha Layne Collins, Fisher quizzed professional photographers about what Kodak could do for them. Bill Prezzano, vice chairman, recalled a trip to China with Fisher. The two arrived at the government offices for a meeting with a vice premier, then learned that they had arrived inappropriately early. In the twenty minutes before the meeting, Fisher wanted to "get down into some side streets and get a better sense" of the market, Prezzano said.

One of Fisher's greatest challenges was convincing the world that Kodak could do much besides make film. The company's past attempts to manufacture equipment, ranging from cameras to copiers, hadn't been successful. One problem was that Kodak always attempted to do things on its own. "We were very arrogant in dealing with other companies," Fisher conceded. Because of the company's strength in film, "we didn't need other companies; by and large, we did everything ourselves." For instance, Kodak had a lot of problems when it tried to get computer companies to incorporate Photo CD into their products. Fisher needed the help of the computer industry as he pushed ahead with digital imaging products; he and Gustin spent considerable time in their early days meeting with Microsoft's Bill Gates and other leaders of the computer industry to convince them that Kodak was changing. Fisher had also formed alliances with other companies that can help develop products.

The new CEO's efforts to work more closely with the outside world were one reason that Joerg Agin, once a senior executive in Kodak's motion-picture-film business, decided to return to the company after leaving in 1992 to work for Universal Studios in Hollywood. Fisher sought Agin's help in finding new ways for Kodak to sell its imaging strengths, especially in partnership with the movie business. He was working on developing programs with Disney and Universal Studios. One idea is to offer personalized videos of theme parks. Instead of lugging their camcorders and trying to record all of Disneyland by themselves, families could pick different sites where they would be videotaped. At the end of the visit, they would have a personalized video postcard, without hours of boring footage. Another idea was to offer "imaging centers" at the parks, where families could create their own posters. After seeing *Pocahontas,* for instance, they could make a poster of their children in a canoe with the movie characters.

To help convince the outside world, Fisher and Gustin put on an elaborate mini–trade show in San Francisco to publicize Kodak's new partnerships with Microsoft, Sprint, Wang, and Kinko's, among others. Microsoft and Kodak had developed software to allow consumers to use their home computers much like the digital image-enhancement equipment Kodak sold retailers.

Eventually, consumers would be able to view prints and place orders with photofinishers from their home computers. At Kinko's, Kodak was testing software that would make it easy to put photos and text together in documents.

The show cost $1.4 million, prompting some inside Kodak to snarl. But Gustin figured it was worth every penny, because it generated considerable press coverage and got industry insiders interested in seeing more of Kodak's digital products. "It just kind of ignited a flame in everybody."

Kodak has a decent shot at making at least some of its new initiatives work. The key is that the company has finally learned to hook up with established firms and leaders in the computer industry, while previous CEOs were too arrogant to admit that Kodak couldn't do everything itself. To be sure, it's hard to get too excited about some of the more esoteric ventures when many people in the world still can't program their VCRs, much less figure out how to use their home computers to view pictures. "We still have not made digital easy enough to use for the average consumer," admitted Swift, by this time a vice president in charge of the digital business. "There are a lot of wows and whiz-bangs, but for the average consumer, it's still too complex." Besides, Kodak has launched, then killed more products than many companies, sucking a lot of funds down the drain. It badly needs to make at least a couple of the digital ventures work, if it ever hopes to make money on anything besides film.

There were early encouraging signs. For instance, Kodak took some of its toys to the 1996 NBA All-Star game and used a digital camera to take pictures of the basketball players. Kodak's logo and with the words "NBA All-Star" were printed on each picture. Kodak sold them for $15 each, but people liked them so much that some offered to pay $400 or $500 if they could jump the long line of people eager to buy. "Digital imaging gives you instantaneous gratification," Swift said. "Consumers are willing to pay a lot for gratification."

Fisher was confident that Kodak could make money from its own manufacturing, despite the company's past failures. For instance, just six weeks after taking office, he told employees that the troubled copier business was not for sale. He called it an "important business" for Kodak, considering its digital efforts; besides, he wanted to expand Kodak's servicing operations, so the company could fix what it sold. Success in the copier business would depend on Kodak's ability to improve its market share and profitability. "Having sold off the health businesses, I'm not strapped for cash," Fisher said. "But it's gotta show that it's gonna be a good business on its own, in addition to having those synergistic benefits. Those synergistic benefits are the reason that we're willing to be more patient with it than some other people might like us to be." (He *was* patient, not resolving the copier issue until 1996.)

His patience was good news to the people who worked at Elmgrove. By the time Fisher arrived at Kodak, Elmgrove had been labeled a ghost town because so much production was gone. Fisher made that plant one of his first stops during his initial trip to meet employees.

Near the end of 1995, Elmgrove was about 98 percent full. This was partly because Fisher had consolidated other Kodak operations. (One financial indicator of his efforts to cut costs was real estate: by 1995 Kodak had reduced its annual real estate costs by $100 million.) But much of the plant's revitalization came from expanded production lines for hot-selling products like single-use cameras. Fisher wanted Kodak to make and sell more products like the cameras, rather than just relying on film to build sales growth.

To that end, he set ambitious goals for the manufacturing people as well as everyone else at Kodak: He wanted a 50 percent reduction in the cost of quality in two years. Each business would be required to calculate its customer satisfaction index and to show improvements. Every division had three years to reduce defects and improve reliability. Fisher wanted the rate of improvement to be rapid; and the company was to hit six sigma by the end of the decade. Cycle times on everything from routine paperwork to manufacturing goods were to be improved by a factor of ten over three years.

Couple those improvements with selling leading products, and you have the "formula for a very successful company in a very simple nutshell," Fisher said. "Life is fairly simple. The difference is some people do it, and some people talk about it."

The big question: How could Fisher force such dramatic change on an often reluctant workforce and bureaucracy? It would be difficult in a company that had a monopolistic and civil service mentality, and where everyone felt that lifetime employment was guaranteed. To hammer home his commitment to change, Fisher put the topics "quality" and "customers" first in each policy committee meeting with his senior staff, so there was no danger of their falling off the agenda. He also insisted on accountability and on constant improvement in cycle time.

Change was painful, especially when so many inside Kodak had come up through the ranks at a time of little competitive pressure. But Kodakers had seen what happened to thousands of their colleagues tapped for layoffs, so they were getting the message that they would all lose if Kodak didn't make some radical changes. Although they felt pressure to deliver, the rank and file liked what they heard and often cheered Fisher at meetings. Those in management liked him too. Some said he would've been a great evangelist if he hadn't become a businessman. "He's got that intangible quality to get the troops lined up behind him," said Van Graafeiland.

Fisher would need that quality as he applied his rigorous standards to overhauling the troops. He issued mandates about increased diversity inside Kodak and about training. Beginning in 1995, each employee had to take a minimum of twenty hours of training. By 1996, the requirement climbed to forty hours per year. That was met with much skepticism, because previous management teams had talked about the importance of training, only to cut it from the budget when money got tight. So Fisher had some campaigning to do to convince employees to view training as a sacred entitlement, even as he talked about changing a corporate culture that was choking on its massive entitlement mentality. Training, he believed, was one entitlement that worked, because it was an investment for both sides—the company and its employees.

A broader part of the training plan was to make sure every

employee had a written development plan, a roadmap of where each one was going, which clearly measured their progress each year. Part of a CEO's job is to plan for his own succession; Fisher did that in 1995, by creating the post of chief operating officer. To decide who should get the job, Fisher reviewed everyone in upper management. He asked all of them to look at their last five jobs, their accomplishments, their failures, and what they had learned. At the end of the process, he visited two managers, one in Europe, the other in Rochester, and invited them to join him in the senior circle as assistant chief operating officers. He delivered the news over sandwiches.

Fisher didn't go outside the company to fill the jobs, as he had in other cases. Instead, he chose two veteran Kodakers, but picked them from nontraditional businesses rather than following the historic practice of grooming film-manufacturing managers to become CEO. Dan Carp, who ran Kodak's European operations, and Carl Kohrt, who ran Kodak's health business, had shown they could produce results. Carp's overseas regions saw revenues climb at twice the rate of the European economy, and profits rose by 25 percent. Kohrt's health sciences division posted a 50 percent increase in earnings and sales in cardiology markets in four years.

Neither is comfortable with the notion that they've been dubbed the heirs apparent for when Fisher steps aside, something no one expects for several years. "This is not the Pillsbury Bake-off," as Kohrt put it. But both show they are intensely eager to cut through Kodak's maze of processes and procedures. "I hate bureaucracy, even though I'm part of it," Kohrt said. One of Kodak's biggest challenges was to grow profitably by speeding up the process of pushing new technology out the door. One project that Kohrt and Carp worked on was simplifying the business. For instance, Kodak's health sciences division had 1,200 different sets of terms and conditions for contracts in the United States.

Another part of the assistant chief operating officers' job was to tell the boss when he's wrong. Kodak was traditionally too polite—especially in formal meetings, where good manners prevented managers from speaking their minds. Fisher wanted to drop the pretense. He wanted some heated discussions, not just puffery. "I think sometimes at Motorola, we carried it to too much of an extreme. But it's because most of us grew up with each other. It was like brothers fighting it out. You're still brothers, and you're still friends." Dissension was also easier at Motorola because the tradition began when the firm was small. "Kodak has developed a much more nonconfrontational culture, and it's very comfortable. I must say it's definitely easier in a sense to work through issues here than it was at Motorola, 'cause there's not a war on every issue."

Fisher tried to instill Motorola-style ease with debate by not "killing the messenger" and by forgetting who's the boss. In meetings, both with his lieutenants and with outsiders, he did make it clear that you'd better not waste his time. On one particular morning, Fisher was meeting with Vaughn Morgan and Reid Callahan, who wanted Kodak to help sponsor a workshop, called the Santa Fe Digital Imaging Center, where people could go to learn how to use new digital technology in their businesses. Gustin, Sculley, Dick Pignataro (vice president of professional and printing imaging), and others were also seated around the table for the sales pitch. Morgan saw a need for seminars to educate corporate types about digital imaging. And he wanted Kodak to help foot the bill.

"You see top-level executives in the company as the target for this?" Fisher asked.

"Yeah, top and middle level," Morgan answered. "They're the people who have the vision to change the way you're going to do business."

"And how long is the program?" Fisher asked.

"I think all you need is a three-day survey for people."

Fisher shook his head. "Believe me. You're not gonna get me for more than a day. For me to give up three days for you to sell me is gonna be a cold day in hell."

The group discussed this point a bit. Morgan revised his plan; he'd offer CEOs a one-day class. "Maybe we'll have George Fisher be a guest speaker at that class, which is a nice draw."

Fisher retorted: "Then for sure you're not getting me."

Morgan tried again: "If we could convince you to bring your spouse, and come to Santa Fe for the weekend . . . and she can go shop. We have some marvelous shopping there."

"Won't work."

Indeed, Fisher didn't appear too impressed by the pitch. He sat back while the rest of the group mulled over the proposal. They concluded that it would be more useful as a training tool for customers who were newcomers in using Kodak's digital equipment, like Photo CD, and that it had to focus on the folks in the trenches, such as copywriters and designers at advertising agencies. Sculley reminded the group that Apple Computer launched its success from the bottom up, not from the corporate suite down, so it was more important to get "the doers converted to know how to use those tools." Corporate chiefs wouldn't make it a priority. "The model of corporate America just isn't the same as it was years ago," Sculley said.

Another way that Fisher tried to change Kodak's culture was to revamp performance appraisals, pay, and benefits throughout middle management. Managers were now evaluated by their employees and peers, not just their bosses, and they had more pay at stake because compensation would be tied to customer satisfaction and the other measures Fisher had laid out.

Every employee would feel the pinch of the stricter system, because Fisher also changed the long-time wage dividend to link it to RONA. While in the old days employees were virtually guaranteed a several-thousand-dollar bonus, now there would be no minimum or maximum payout. The problem was, under the former system, Kodak often had to borrow money to pay the bonus. Fisher calls that practice "stupid." "It doesn't make sense to give away five percent of salary, which is about a hundred million dollars, if the company is losing money." Under the new plan, "the company will have to do very well for people to get back up to the levels we were at, but they're achievable levels, and hopefully we can, over time, get back to those levels, and higher." The results for 1994 showed that Kodak had a long way to go: net earnings from continuing operations were down 11 percent, reflecting the need to get rid of more costs.

Fisher knew that the continued cost cutting had hurt people throughout the company, and that most employees were feeling beaten down by all the turmoil and changes. At the same time, people felt that the company had hit rock bottom and had to go up—and that they needed a leader. "I know we still have serious morale problems, but I think generally speaking, people feel better about the leadership directions of the company and are more optimistic about the future as a result. They're not so happy yet about their personal state, other than they have jobs. That's a big plus today."

The issue of trust was a difficult one. In the past, management had repeatedly promised that layoffs would end, then turned around and said more workers would have to go. Now along came Fisher with new ideas for rebuilding Kodak. He was a good messenger who knew the importance of mingling with the troops even when there was bad news. But even those who supported him were still waiting to see whether things would improve for them personally. "How can factory workers have great trust in senior management if it led them into the problems we got into?" Fisher said. "I think all of us in management are somewhat suspect—until proven otherwise."

7

Pawning Rolexes
in Smugtown

It was Friday morning on the corner of Rochester's North and Herald streets, and a crowd was gathering in front of the brown brick building. A woman comforted her baby as she paced the sidewalk. She stopped and smiled as Margaret Oberst stepped out of her van to unlock the building's front door, a sturdy steel guardian that protects St. Andrew's Area Food Cupboard. The metal door had to be added because an old wooden door was peeled off its hinges during six burglaries in eighteen days. The thieves stole $2,000 worth of food.

Margaret is a mother of five, but finds time to run the food cupboard, which feeds more than 300 households each month. She hurried to unload today's offerings—200 pounds of macaroni-and-cheese dinners, beans, and other goods she'd just bought at Wegman's grocery store. Four other volunteers quickly stashed the groceries on shelves in the back room as Margaret headed for the front counter to hear the stories of distress from the six men and four women who have shown up for free food.

The mother and child were first in line, with a hefty order: she had a family of nine, including twins. "Double up on the pasta and beans," Margaret told the others, who raided the freezer for some ground turkey, butter, and hot dogs. Another box was filled with eight loaves of bread, nonfat dry milk, and tuna. The volunteers worked quickly to send the woman on her way with enough to feed her family until she received next month's food stamps. It was the last week of the month, so most people were here because they'd already used up their monthly allotment.

The people who needed food all had the same desperate look on their faces. This was their last hope—they were jobless, and the unemployment checks had run out. The mother smiled with relief as she carried away her boxes of meager rations, knowing her family would eat today. The pantry was a sobering place for the volunteers, all ensconced in a middle class that had once been immune from hunger and poverty. They now saw at first hand the ripple effect of the daily headlines about layoffs in Rochester. They saw how short the trip was between the people in line and their own neighbors—even their own families.

"People used to think that those who go to a food bank are in another class," said Mary Ellen Heyman, a board member at St. Andrew's and one of this morning's volunteers. "I see that's not true. We are all part of this." She had noticed that people in her neighborhood now donated less: they were anxious about their own future. Even cans of peaches and beans became something to hoard. "People would buy an extra can and give it to the food cupboard. Now they buy an extra one and save it for themselves." Even those who still had comfortable, well-paid positions were being more cautious. "The Kodak people are really worried." Like her neighbors, Mary Ellen was trying to be more conservative in her spending because she realized her family could suffer the same trauma as the folks on line at the pantry. Both her husband and Margaret's taught at a local Catholic school, and Mary Ellen worried what other people's belt-tightening would mean for her family. "Enrollment gets cut back because people can't afford to send their children to the school anymore. What if they get fired?"

Some of her best contributors had given up food drives because they were too busy trying to find work. One woman, who organized food drives at Xerox, was laid off, so she no longer collected canned goods. Her food drive used to bring in about 10 percent of the cupboard's monthly total.

Margaret stepped through the doorway to ask: "Do we have any cake mixes? We have a birthday boy." Robert Antonelli, a student at Rochester Institute of Technology, searched the shelves, but the only dessert in sight was a package of Jell-O. It would have to do.

Antonelli volunteered as part of a class at RIT. Students had a choice: either write a term paper or help out at an agency like the food cupboard. He found himself in the minority: "Most kids would rather write a fifteen-page paper instead of stepping down here." After a month of handing out free food at the cupboard, he had become less optimistic about the economy and his own future. "I grew up well off, so this is my first eye-opening experience. Now I see how bad it is out there."

Food Link, an agency that distributed food to ten counties in the greater Rochester area, gave away 8 million pounds of food in 1995, ten times the amount it handled in 1980. "Some of the very people who were generous now need help themselves," said Tom Ferraro, founder of the agency. "In some suburban areas, we've seen quadruple increases in the past couple of years." Likewise, food stamp use was up. Almost one in nine Americans received food stamps in 1993. A research study by Second Harvest, the country's largest hunger relief organization, found that 55.4 percent of those who turned to food pantries did so because of unemployment. Underemployment, from low-paying jobs, was the reason 52 percent more showed up for help. One of the biggest problems was that it took many people a long time to find a new job, even one paying less than they used to make.

Throughout the Rochester area, there were signs like the food cupboard that showed how deeply layoffs shake a community, from the violinists who played Beethoven in the Rochester Philharmonic Orchestra to the single mothers standing in line at the St. Andrew's Food Cupboard. No one was immune. In a town where unemployment was typically below the state and national figures, there were scores of indicators that people were stepping down the economic ladder rather than moving up to the next rung. And there was a realization that big companies could no longer help cure social ills or guarantee jobs for all. "Rochester used to be fat city. There was a polite arrogance," said Mary-Frances Winters, a local consultant who headed United Way's 1994 campaign in the city. "That's not the case anymore. We don't perceive Kodak as our savior anymore."

That's a harsh realization in a town once dubbed "Kodak City" and "Smugtown." In 1980, Kodak accounted for 21 percent of local payroll. By 1993, it was 12 percent. At its peak, in 1982, Kodak employment locally was 60,200 workers. By 1993, employment was down to 36,800. Likewise, Xerox, Mobil, Bausch & Lomb, General Motors, and other local employers had trimmed their workforces. Of course, many of those laid off found work at smaller companies in Rochester or started their own businesses, but others simply moved on. Monroe County, where Rochester is located, lost 37,680 people between 1980 and 1990, according to U.S. census figures.

Rochester's unemployment rate tends to be lower than New York's and the nation's. In 1993, the unemployment rate was 5 percent in Rochester, below the nation's 6.8 percent. By 1995, the figure fell to 4.6 percent, compared to 5.6 percent nationally. But local economists warned that the unemployment rate is a "biased and restrictive measure of the economic well-being of a community." One reason is that the rate doesn't include discouraged workers, those who have stopped looking for work. Furthermore, there were questions about the numbers' accuracy. The 1990 census showed that unemployment numbers were actually higher than those reported by the state. In Rochester, for instance, the rate for 1990 was 3.9 percent, but the census found unemployment of 5.2 percent. The official U.S. figure was 5.3 percent, but the census concluded that it was actually 6.3 percent.

Rochester was a microcosm of New York State's problems and, to varying degrees, of the rest of the country. The same impact can be seen in IBM's neighborhoods, where dry-cleaners see business falling off because fewer suits are going to work. And in the poshest southern California neighborhoods, aerospace cutbacks have sent thousands to the unemployment lines. In Rochester, service jobs accounted for 27 percent of local employment in 1994, and manufacturing jobs were down to 25 percent of local employment. Such jobs were disappearing throughout New York. Between July 1990 and July 1994, the state lost 384,000 jobs, including many in manufacturing. New Yorkers were struggling to hang on to the jobs that remained. And they were angry that so little had been done by state leaders to keep companies in the state and preserve their jobs. In his 1994 re-election campaign, Governor Mario Cuomo told voters that he shouldn't get too much blame for the state's economy. But voters expressed their disgust at the polls, casting their votes for newcomer George Pataki instead. A bumper sticker seen during the election said: "Time's up, Mario." The same thing happened across the country, as voters ousted Democrats who failed to deliver on promises of help for the middle class.

The outrage about the loss of jobs poured out daily in the local newspaper. "I'm just tired as hell of picking up the paper and reading about a new batch of folks being put out of work," wrote Bob Lonsberry, a popular columnist at the *Democrat & Chronicle*. "I love how the great economic machine our parents and grandparents built has taken to chewing people up and sucking them dry and spitting them out."

Even those still employed were scared. A 1994 poll by the *Democrat & Chronicle* showed that nearly 54 percent of people who earned $35,000 or more were concerned about their own, a friend's, or a relative's job security. Even more respondents between the ages of forty and fifty-nine—56 percent—were worried.

The U.S. Census Bureau found that workers who left a full-time job or were laid off between 1990 and 1992 saw their wages drop an average of 23 percent when they found another full-time job. Wages for manufacturing jobs in the United States that were $8.97 an hour twenty years ago, were $8.10 an hour in 1995. Small wonder that people didn't feel optimistic about their ability to get ahead financially.

What was happening in Rochester reflected the entire country's struggle to deal with a new economy. Unemployment figures looked great, hitting seven-year lows in the fall of 1996. But the new jobs were lower-paying and lacked the career-advancement opportunities and security once offered by a paternalistic corporate America.

William Julius Wilson, the Malcolm Wiener professor of social policy at Harvard University, wrote in his book *When Work Disappears* that the shift has been especially stark in the nation's inner cities. In Washington Park on Chicago's south side, most adults had jobs in 1950. In 1990, just one in three did.

Throughout the Northeast, towns have lost jobs to overseas manufacturing and the migration to the southeastern United States. Textile mills and shoe factories in New England are almost gone because of cheaper foreign imports. Many of Detroit's auto plants are shuttered. When visitors to Pittsburgh want to see a steel mill, many locals reply: "Go to Japan."

Rochester and other towns like it have a tough time competing. New York State has the United States' highest taxes, highest utility rates, and highest premiums for workers' compensation insurance. Florida, on the other hand, is less expensive and even offers corporate tax credits for companies that move into the state. Basically, companies can get refunds of up to $5,000 per job created. Indeed, Florida governor Lawton Chiles personally courted Al Dunlap, known as Chainsaw Al for his massive hacking of jobs at Scott Paper Company, to move Scott's headquarters to Boca Raton from Philadelphia. Chiles flew to Boca Raton to meet with Dunlap and offered the company a variety of grants and credits from the state and county. A bidding war has developed among states, counties, and towns to see who gets jobs. Economic development groups compete to lure companies away from old locations. But, again, the jobs created are often low-paying, as with the boom of back-office jobs and telephone marketing centers in the Southeastern states. There are fewer opportunities for people who could once graduate from high school, walk down the street to factories like Kodak's, and expect to find a well-paid job for life. Now employees must cope with a lifetime of changing jobs and companies, as the new economy adds and subtracts people as needed.

These trends have created anxiety and problems in a town once spoiled by its Yellow Father. Through the years, Kodak had been benevolent, in both jobs and charity. Local author Curt Gerling wrote in his 1957 book, *Smugtown U.S.A.*, that success in Rochester was as "unburdensome as getting a job at Kodak and learning to pat the proper posteriors." Gerling called George

Eastman "the Kodak king" and likened a post at the company to being a prelate: Saying "Daddy is a Kodak man" was like saying "Uncle Dan is a Bishop of the Catholic church." The company's place earned it loyalty among the masses. And the mere suggestion that someone might sell his Kodak stock was "a blasphemy comparable to matricide." Indeed, the original investments in Eastman's enterprise helped fund a number of local fortunes. Gerling estimated that 90 percent of Rochester's "important" probated wills listed a nest egg of Kodak stock as a "sort of hedge against the failure of their own enterprise or the end of the world."

George Eastman himself also bankrolled considerable philanthropy, especially in education, the arts, and music. In a 1923 interview, he said he believed it was "more fun" to give his money away while he was still alive than just to will it to others. He established the Eastman School of Music and the Eastman Theater. He donated millions to the University of Rochester, the Massachusetts Institute of Technology, and other universities. He also cared for the less fortunate, paying for dental clinics where children could receive free care because, in Eastman's words, "money spent in the care of children's teeth is one of the wisest expenditures that can be made." In 1919, more than 48,000 patients visited his Rochester clinic. He even took pity on the federal government: he had company auditors total their profits from war contracts in World War I, and returned $335,389.76 to the Secretary of War.

One of his most important projects was to establish the Community Chest, the forerunner to United Way. Henry W. Clune, who worked as a newspaper reporter in Rochester for fifty years, recalled: "He was always interested in the city." He told a story about Eastman's fund-raising for the Community Chest: "A socialite sent him a generous check for five thousand dollars. But Eastman sent it back, which was pretty nervy. He told her that it wasn't enough."

Collecting for the United Way was made easier because companies like Kodak made supporting the agency an obligation for both the corporation and its employees. One former Kodak secretary recalled how she had to contribute, despite a low salary. "I

was given a card, and I said, 'I don't want to do this!' " Her supervisor told her to reconsider. "There was big pressure. I gave just to
get my name off the hit list."

Despite the company's continued efforts, United Way has
been losing ground in Rochester and across the nation. The 1993
national campaign raised $3.05 billion, up just slightly from the
previous year and down from the $3.27 billion received in 1991.
In Rochester, fund-raisers struggled to meet their $36 million
goal, largely because of corporate layoffs.

Local campaign results had started to slip in 1992, when the
total fell to $35.4 million from $37.4 million. For the first time
since the 1940s, the campaign took a step backward. And the
total rose just slightly, to $35.5 million, in 1993. One big factor
was Kodak's layoffs and early retirement buyout program: those
who left Kodak in 1991 had donated $1.2 million to United Way.
In 1992, the same groups gave $100,000.

Administering the United Way program has become more
complicated as big companies cut back. For starters, the agency
had to beef up its reserve to cover lost pledges because "we've
been told by Kodak and Xerox there will be more layoffs," says
Joseph G. Calabrese, president of the local United Way. That's
money that doesn't go into programs to help those in need. The
agency also incurs higher administration costs when it has to
campaign in more places to raise the same amount of money.
"It's less expensive for us to solicit a large number of people
in manufacturers than it is to solicit in three- to ten-employee
operations," Calabrese says. And the corporations are giving less.
Kodak is still the single biggest corporate giver to any United Way
campaign in the United States. But its donations have declined
20 percent.

In 1994, for the first time, United Way in Rochester ran
infomercials and mailed pledge cards to households in the
county. But it's difficult to get individuals to donate when many
are still wary of pink slips themselves. Sometimes people are
afraid to donate anything, even blood. The American Red Cross
has had trouble getting blood donations, hitting a low point
entering the July 4 holiday weekend in 1994. Blood banks try to
keep a three- or four-day supply of blood, but reserves fell to just

one day. "It's getting harder and harder to get people to come in and give blood," said a Red Cross spokesperson. Because of downsizing, "there are fewer employees to tap into"—and those who remain say they are reluctant to do anything but sit at their desks and work.

Those who have moved into lower-paying jobs are a challenge, too. They earn less, so naturally they give less. And they require more free services. "Many people who used to pay for support services now earn less, and the community has to pick up the tab," Calabrese says.

Food Link is a good example. The need continues to grow, but both funding and food donations are hurt by downsizings and restructurings. Ironically, corporate campaigns for "total quality" in production means food manufacturers also donate less food. "Ragú never puts too much oregano in the sauce anymore. And Mott's never puts too much cinnamon in theirs," says Ferraro, Food Link's founder. "We used to get mass quantities of food because there was no end to their glitches." Such packaged food was cheaper and easy to pass out to food cupboards. Now Food Link has to replace it with perishables, which spoil faster, making it tougher to feed the hungry.

Ferraro, a Rochester native, sees the ripple effects of corporate cutbacks and the changing profile of those in need. And the impact the damaged economy is having on children. "We are throwing dented cans of food at the symptoms. The problems are getting bigger and bigger, and we're not laying a glove on them. People are hungry because their money doesn't go far enough to buy food. And it's taking a toll on our ability as a society to be normal."

He is particularly troubled by government programs that allow manufacturers to buy cheap raw materials, yet won't do as much to feed the hungry. "Companies can take five cents' worth of grain and it hits the store shelves as a four-dollar cereal box." And some of the same companies then lay off their workers in search of fatter profits, creating more need for free food.

This spiral effect shows up at places like Rochester's Webster Avenue Family Resource Center, where families in need can get everything from advice to free diapers and milk. The center's

United Way funding fell to $50,000 in 1993 from $63,000 in 1991. Two staff positions were cut and the office space was halved to save money. "The layoffs have trickled down to us," says Carolyn Micklem, who was director of the center before becoming director of the Rochester Family Resource Network. Since 1980, "the rich have gotten richer and the poor have gotten poorer. The middle class is stuck. Those who have lost jobs—and some who retain them—are falling down dramatically," she says.

Micklem sees more cases of abuse and neglect after unemployment hits a family. "An increased number of people come in and ask for referrals on where to get food and clothing." The center revived an old program of giving away Christmas baskets because "parent after parent came in and asked for help." Others come in asking for help paying their gas and electric bills. Requests for diapers and milk are up.

A disturbing cut in the center's programs came when Xerox and other corporate donors pared their contributions. "Half our budget was for job-skills programs. Not anymore. That's been painful for us," she says. Likewise, the Genesee Settlement House, which provides tutoring and other after-school programs for youths, had to trim its employment counseling service because of funding cuts. Not only were there state cuts, but the group's United Way allocation went down $18,000. Robert W. Hunter, president of the agency, finds that way out of balance, considering that the state of New York spends $84,000 per year to jail one youth, but spends just $22 to provide young people "a safe place to go after school." Because of funding cuts at the settlement house, he can spend just $4.22 per person in need.

"Layoffs show up in our numbers, especially in the number of people who need emergency assistance," Hunter says. "Traditionally we saw the poor people who had been poor for years. They would come through over and over again. Now we're seeing more and more people who have never used our service before. Because of Kodak layoffs, people find themselves in the same line. They thought they were self-sufficient. But nothing is sacred anymore, not even Kodak."

The effect on young people? "Children are affected not only economically, but their self-esteem is hurt, too." Budget cuts cost

Hunter some of his summer jobs programs. In the past, the agency had summer jobs and a camp for 200 children. That required ten or twelve counselors, among other help. But he had to cut back. "That creates problems for the community. Instead of having them in camp, they're running around."

Likewise, cuts in Kodak giving ended a popular summer athletic program that had offered baseball, tennis, softball, and soccer to thousands of kids since 1942. The program was started when fathers had to go off to fight World War II, and mothers had to take their husbands' factory jobs to support their families and the war efforts. Kodak paid for counselors, T-shirts, and equipment for the sports camp, but all this was cut, along with other programs, to save money. Tom Castle, who was an instructor in the softball team back in the 1940s, recalls that it "was more than a sports program. It taught kids about leadership, working together." No more.

Parents and teachers also see the impact of layoffs in their neighborhoods and classrooms. Consider Jackie Gottfried, a teacher who lives with her husband, Henry, and two sons, David and Jason, in Pittsford, New York, a village built alongside the historic Erie Canal. This is where Kodak managers move after they've achieved a certain level of success. Residents shop at Pendleton and other boutiques on Main Street. Pittsford is charming and quaint, with its lampposts and red brick town hall, built in 1890. Wood-paneled Jeep Cherokees park on the quiet streets. A sign advertises an election-night pancake supper, hosted by the Rotary Club at the local high school.

Gottfried sees the change in her own neighborhood and in the nearby Henrietta school district, where she teaches. "We've seen a lot of David and Jason's friends have to leave. It's become more common in the affluent neighborhoods. There's been a steady exit of people. You drive through neighborhoods like this in Pittsford and it's wall-to-wall 'For Sale' signs. People are more concerned about expenses. Nothing is secure anymore." Only about five of the Gottfrieds' original neighbors remain. One nearby house has been on the market at $899,000.

Traditionally, Jackie was the exception because she had a job outside the home. That's changing, too. "When I moved to this neighborhood, the attitude was: This is Pittsford. Pittsford women do not work. They do tennis. They do lunch. They volunteer. Then, as things changed, a lot more went to work. That's an indication of insecurity."

As for the working-class and middle-class children who fill her classroom in nearby Henrietta, those from less privileged families have parents who work for smaller companies, or in construction or other service jobs. "One student's father was unemployed for over a year. [The student] was forced to get a job at McDonald's at the age of sixteen," Gottfried says.

She finds this disturbing, as a teacher and as a mother. "I don't like to see kids working during the school year. But the kids do feel that if parents are unemployed, this is something they can help with. A lot of kids don't want to talk about it. They are sort of ashamed of it and they'd rather keep it to themselves."

Even more disturbing, some students have permission to leave school early each day so they can go to their jobs. In some cases, school officials have had to send letters to employers warning them that they are giving teenagers too many hours. "A child's first obligation is to school," Gottfried says.

That pressure from real-world problems and a troubled home life limits what teachers can do to keep students interested in finishing high school, much less attending college. And there are fewer incentives from corporate America to help pay their tuition bills. Rochester mayor William Johnson was head of the Urban League before taking public office in January 1994. The Rochester Urban League's United Way allocations were trimmed 10 percent a year in his last two years at the agency. In addition, there was less direct giving from big companies. Kodak had agreed to fund a leadership development program that cost $25,000 a year. "It took almost a year for the company to honor its commitment. That delayed us starting the program." And when Johnson sought funds to start another youth program "I was told quite bluntly: 'Which one of these do you want? You can't have both.' "

Kodak also funded special scholarships for minority students, covering all tuition at any college for those pursuing degrees in certain fields, such as engineering. The Urban League had been assured that a minimum of two would be awarded each year, but then Kodak decided to lump the scholarships into its larger Kodak Scholars program. "They were essentially reducing that scholarship program," Johnson said. Some of the recipients would go to Harvard or Yale. Kodak guaranteed the scholars jobs if they wanted to come back after graduation. "But these opportunities have almost disappeared in all the companies." Johnson hears from a lot of college graduates whose degrees don't win them a higher-paying job. Instead, these graduates settle for jobs that require only a high school or community college degree.

As mayor, Johnson worries more about the lack of opportunity for the people who used to graduate from high school, then take a place on the factory floors of Kodak or Xerox. "We have not done a good job of creating or maintaining the low-skill jobs. They've been almost wiped out of existence. We are creating a new underclass." Another problem is that less-educated workers are competing with laid-off Kodakers even for low-paying service jobs. "They [the Kodakers] are taking jobs from somebody who's trying to raise a family and who may have to piece together two or three part-time jobs in order to make a living."

The latest cutbacks come at a time when Rochester is already vulnerable on many fronts. While the situation is not as bad as in Flint, Michigan, or other one-industry towns where Johnson has lived before, Rochester has severe social and economic problems. The mayor had to slash spending on the city services and schools. As of October 1993, projections indicated that fiscal year 1994–95 would find the city and its school district with a deficit of over $30 million. If nothing was done, the deficit would grow to more than $85 million by 1998–99.

The city's neighborhoods are in turmoil as people who can do so move to the suburbs to escape crime. Downtown Rochester can be a dangerous place. The evening newscasts are full of stories about drug busts and murders, some of which sound like what you might expect in bigger cities like New York. In one case, an elderly woman was stabbed fifty-four times and nearly decapitated in her kitchen. Tom Golisano, chief executive of Paychex, a local company, and candidate for New York governor in 1994, is quite blunt on the subject of Rochester's decline. He calls downtown "a dinosaur." His company's headquarters is now in suburban Penfield, next to the woods.

Mayor Johnson was well aware of people's fears about crime; during his campaign, he told the story of how his mother was assaulted in her own driveway. Yet during his first year as mayor, Johnson had to propose cuts at the police department. The city didn't have the money to meet the requirements of the 1994 federal crime bill. And despite growing crime, cutting personnel is one of the quickest ways to slash a budget.

Johnson wasn't optimistic about solving the problems, even if private money were available to help. Collaborations among government, business, and social service agencies had been a bust in the past. In 1988, a "New Futures" initiative promised resources for youth and families in need. The Kodak CEO sat on the board, along with city and school officials. The group failed. The mayor saw little hope that the once generous not-for-profit groups would be around long enough or have the means to address the city's problems: "Those halcyon days are becoming dim memories."

Finding jobs for more people was an urgent item on the mayor's agenda. "It doesn't take a wizard to predict what is likely to happen if we can't accommodate them. A lot of our violence is attributable to folks who feel they don't really have a stake. It's survival of the fittest. We have got to understand all the ramifications."

Johnson did not believe that the titans of corporate America understood the impact of their layoffs. He gave them low marks for remembering the community in decisions about cost-cutting. "Companies have been more concerned about their shareholders and their bottom line." At Kodak, "they made it clear that they weren't concerned about the impact they would have on the local community." Indeed, George Fisher told local leaders that he wasn't going to become a "Yellow Father" like his predecessors. Noting that his first priority was fixing Kodak, he didn't get involved in local activities. He figured that everyone prospers when Kodak makes money.

The mayor was right in saying that the company paid little

attention to the town when it announced its last 10,000 layoffs. Kodak's formula of adding up performance appraisal scores meant that the firm's best performers were often the ones laid off. They often relocated to Silicon Valley or to new high-tech centers in the Carolinas rather than stay in Rochester, where fewer jobs are available. Many former Kodakers did stay in Rochester, but most could not find comparable work and often went from one temporary assignment to another.

Fisher had the right idea about analyzing each department as part of its ongoing strategy, rather than executing massive cuts every few years to rein in costs. Under Fisher's system, people could be retrained and, it's hoped, moved into new jobs as old ones disappeared. At the same time, the leaders of Rochester now realized that no single CEO or company could be the town's savior. Job creation is central to rebuilding an economic base. But so are a good public education system, crime prevention, and better social programs that help people learn to be self-sufficient. Those are tasks beyond the capacity of any one company.

In Rochester, the ripple effects of unemployment increased the burden on county and city social services. At the Monroe County Social Services office, Richard Schauseil said that in his 20 years with the county, things had never been this bad.

To get to Schauseil's office, one had to be attended by security guards who chaperoned the visitors, from those who needed food stamps and welfare to those who helped provide safe homes to foster children. Schauseil's desk and table were stacked high with charts, graphs, and budgets, all showing how the system was ready to explode. "The loss of manufacturing jobs here over the last ten years has had an effect. The creation of a manufacturing job has a multiplier of about 2.7 or three to one." For example, suppliers to a company can expand and hire when new manufacturing jobs are created. Service jobs don't have that multiplier effect. "Many of our clients today, ten years ago might have been able to get a job as a factory helper in an unskilled labor job that would've paid him eight-fifty or nine bucks an hour. Today, that's not possible. Most of the jobs being created are in the health care industry, services, information systems.

The man who started it all: Kodak founder
George Eastman (*left*) talks with fellow inventor Thomas Edison
during a 1928 visit in Eastman's terrace garden.
Courtesy of the George Eastman House.

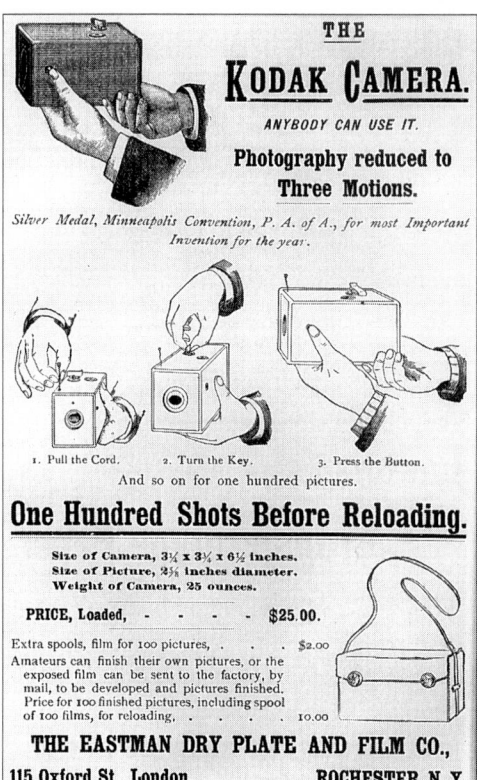

As these early ads attest, the ease and convenience of Kodak cameras were a huge selling point in Eastman's mission to popularize amateur photography. *Courtesy of the George Eastman House.*

Eastman Kodak's first factory. *Courtesy of the George Eastman House.*

Today, Kodak Park is the heart of Eastman Kodak. Each year the massive Rochester complex churns out enough film to stretch to the moon and back. © *Charles Bertram*

Kay Whitmore (*right*) with Colby Chandler. By the time Whitmore took over the CEO post from Chandler in 1990, the company-wide problems that would plague his tenure were already in place.

Kodak's board of directors asked Whitmore to resign in August 1993, the same month that the company announced it would cut an additional 10,000 jobs. An editorial cartoon in the local paper captured the feelings in Rochester. *Cartoon by Bill Mitchell courtesy of the* Democrat and Chronicle, *Rochester, NY.*

Meredith and Bob Couture, along with their Newfoundland Rosie, tried to relocate after he lost his job at Kodak.
© *Charles Bertram*

ABOVE: When Al Waugh looked for work after being laid off from Kodak, his wife, Mary, and son Rob found jobs of their own. © *Charles Bertram.*

RIGHT: Tom Walker, who lost his job at Kodak, volunteers at a local support group to help others find new employment.© *Charles Bertram.*

Michael Donnelly started his own consulting business after he lost his job at Kodak. © *Charles Bertram*

ABOVE: Rochester merchants have witnessed Kodak's good and bad times. Giacomo "Jack" DiPisa, owner of Rubino's Italian Subs, sees his noontime lunch trade as an economic indicator. © *Charles Bertram* BELOW: Niramon Toner checks a package of film inside the final production line at Kodak Park. Kodak has lost market share to Fuji and private label film, as consumers look for cheaper alternatives to the yellow box. © *Charles Bertram*

RIGHT: Current Kodak management has tried to break with the company's paternalistic past by involving employees in problem solving. In some parts of the company, a poster called Ground Rules serves as a reminder. © *Charles Bertram*
BELOW: A Kodak employee takes part in an outdoor exercise intended to foster teamwork.
© *Charles Bertram*

PERSONAL BEHAVIOR GROUND RULES

1. I will honor my commitments.

2. I will only make statements that add value and stick to the purpose at hand.

3. I will come to meetings prepared and determined to contribute.

4. I will offer alternative proposals to those things with which I disagree.

5. I will avoid working in isolation and will seek the thinking of others.

6. I will not be limited by current (perceived) boundaries and limitations.

7. I will look for "how we can" rather than "why we can't".

8. I will focus on helping others towards their purpose through listening and sharing of thoughts.

Earnie Deavenport saw the old Kodak stumble. Now he's chief executive of Eastman Chemical, which was spun off as part of Kodak's restructuring. He changed the rules to make sure the chemical company didn't repeat Kodak's mistakes. © *Charles Bertram*

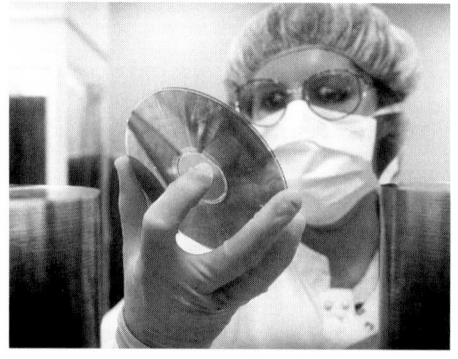

LEFT: Part of Kodak's digital future is producing CDs used to store information. MCI and other companies use the discs instead of sending paper printouts of phone bills or other documents. © *Charles Bertram*

The single-use camera is one of Kodak's fastest-growing product lines and is an important factor in the company's attempts to reverse its fortunes. The disposable camera harkens back to George Eastman's "you press the button, we do the rest" philosophy, reflecting the new Kodak's emphasis on its core business. © *Charles Bertram*

Kodak CEO George Fisher, holding one of the company's Oscars for contributions to filmmaking in Hollywood, sees Kodak's future as a combination of old and new—traditional filmmaking and new ventures in digital technology.© *Charles Bertram*

You have to work much longer to get that nine bucks. And many of our people are coming out of school not reading or writing and doing mathematics at the level they're supposed to be at."

A survey of the county's social services clients in 1993 showed that about 25 percent had been laid off; 14 percent had temporary jobs that ended; and 16 percent were on long-term health leave when they learned their job had disappeared. Schauseil was critical of the state's policy of maintaining two separate tracking systems in the labor department and social service agencies, with no cross-referencing of clients: "We need to put something in place so that when the last unemployment check comes, we've done some planning to help them."

Not that Schauseil's agency needed more work. Annually, the group helped about 86,000 people, so that each examiner handled about 225 cases a year. Those who administered the federally funded food stamp program handled 350 cases each. And the client base continued to grow, especially as need crept into once-comfortable suburbia. In the mid-1980s, about 92 percent of Schauseil's clients were from the city. A decade later, 88 percent live in the city, 12 percent in the suburbs.

Once people could also supplement public assistance with some charity from their churches. But Sunday collections were dwindling; churches couldn't provide the same outreach programs they once did. Rochester' Sacred Heart Cathedral saw its collections drop 15 to 20 percent. "We are a Kodak parish, so it's affected collections," said Pat DiFabio, director of religious education at the church.

The Church of the Transfiguration, home to the local unemployment network, suffered the same impact. "Churches don't just lose money. They lose the wife who's the religion teacher. They lose the children. We lose a lot who have to move. You lose the crux of your community," explained Mary Presutti, the head of religious education at the church. Since her family went through the trauma of her late husband's layoff, she had cut back. "I don't even know where the dry cleaner is anymore. If it doesn't wash, it doesn't go."

Like Rochester, the smaller towns nearby couldn't depend as much on county, state, or federal programs to help them through the tough times. The town of Greece, which is home to parts of Kodak Park, saw a slowdown in new home construction to about 300 a year, down from the boom of 700 to 800 a year in the 1980s. "The good news is we're still building," said Shaun Groden, finance director of Greece. Still, he was tightening up the town's budget. And he was pushing the town to issue less debt for big-ticket items like trucks: "You've got to work yourself to the point where you can pay cash for everything."

One reason he wanted to hold the line was a growing revolt among taxpayers. Business leaders refer to New York state as "Tax Hell" because state and local taxes per capita are 68 percent above the national average. "Taxes are another one of those mandatory expenses that everybody has. Maybe in the heyday you didn't worry so much about it because you knew you were gonna get a raise next month or next year. And you weren't worried about your job. I don't think that's there anymore. People are very conscious about stretching the paycheck."

So Greece's budget for 1995 included its own downsizing. "We've got to focus on public works and safety," Groden said. About 75 percent of the town budget covered clearing snow and providing a police department. And the town overspent on snow removal for three years in a row, 1992 through 1994. One of the cuts eliminated a $250,000 counseling program for teenagers on problems such as drug and alcohol abuse or teen pregnancies. And two of the five library branches were closed.

One reason Greece hadn't seen much growth is a deal it made with Kodak to reduce the company's tax bill on its plants. An appraisal of the land showed that Kodak was being overcharged. To avoid a long court battle, the town promised to reduce the company's taxes over a ten-year period. "If Kodak had taken us to court and won, the reduction would've been immediate. It would have been awarded back payments, and it would have been a devastating blow to this community. We would've had to raise taxes triple or quadruple what they are." Instead, in 1996, Kodak's property tax bill was cut from $13 million to $5.8 million. It will drop again when the town does the next reassessment in 2001.

Now residents throughout the area were questioning their

appraised values and property taxes. This was no wonder, considering Rochester's problems in maintaining an image as a good place to live. *Reader's Digest* ranked it as the most altruistic U.S. city, on the basis of a study of whether people were helpful to strangers. But on the real estate front, there was little reason to celebrate. *Money* magazine's April 1994 issue ranked the nation's largest fifty metropolitan areas according to projections about home values. Rochester was number 46 out of 50, with a 2.6 percent projected twelve-month gain in price on an $84,400 (median-priced) house. *Money* also listed the top 300 places to live, giving Rochester the depressing rank of 199, just ahead of Erie, Pennsylvania, one of the bleakest spots in the Northeast, and Johnstown, Pennsylvania, which has never rebounded from layoffs in the steel and coal industries. Rochester was even beaten out by El Paso, number 191. By contrast, Pittsburgh was ranked at 53, Los Angeles at 66. Rochester had been ranked 159 a year earlier.

Fewer new houses are being built throughout Monroe County. Many people who can afford to buy a house are opting for an existing home, rather than building a new one. The new housing total fell 20 percent in 1994 from 1993. And it's about 40 percent of the level reached during the building boom in the 1980s.

But for many, housing is not a matter of deciding between an old and a new house; it's a matter of keeping any house. The Housing Council, a not-for-profit agency that provides counseling to help people avoid foreclosures, has seen a rapid rise in people fighting to keep their homes. "For a number of years, we had a little under two hundred default cases a year," says Allison Columbus, deputy director of the council. By 1990, the number was 469. In 1993, it had climbed to 914. "Increasingly, it's people with higher mortgages in the suburbs." Some mortgages ending up in default were as high as $3,000 a month. Some strapped homeowners can't even sell their house and pay off what they owe because the house has lost value. And some have borrowed heavily against their house. The temptation of easy loans from finance companies has hurt many of them. Jim Palmer, the Hall of Fame ball player, pitches easy credit at the Money Store, which appeals to people who are hard up for cash. "We've seen a number of people with second and third mortgages with these companies," says Lindley Pryor, the director of the Housing Council. "They see him on television and think, 'He's my buddy.'"

The foreclosures impact everyone. "In the suburban areas, it could lower property values around adjoining properties," says Pryor. In Rochester itself, there's an even bigger problem: vandals break in and strip copper pipes and other valuable materials from vacant houses. Some even lose their aluminum siding to thieves.

Still, it's difficult for Pryor and Columbus to make their case for more public or charitable funds to help people avoid foreclosures. They are competing with other projects deemed more important to urban renewal. "You can't cut a ribbon on a house you saved," Pryor says. His United Way allocation has been flat at $41,800. "How many of those nine hundred and fourteen foreclosures could we have helped prevent if we had the resources?" His staff of four counselors spends about twenty hours on each case. "I've got people who are overworked. I don't know if they're gonna snap and jump off the top of the roof. But you can burn out."

Helping to depress the Rochester real estate market is the large number of properties for sale around Kodak Park, a collection of 200 manufacturing buildings in a four-mile stretch of land straddling the city of Rochester and the town of Greece. Kodak's chemical emissions have made it the state's biggest polluter. Many residents have moved from the neighborhood, which some have dubbed Rochester's Love Canal, because of their fears about environmental problems at the huge manufacturing site. To its credit, Kodak created a "value protection program," which, for instance, guarantees the value of homes from 1988 to May 1998 and provides grants and low-interest loans for home improvements. Kodak also pays the relocation expenses of homeowners who want to move from the neighborhood.

Besides paying a $2 million fine for violating environmental laws, in October 1994 Kodak reached a settlement with the U.S. Environmental Protection Agency and the U.S. Justice Department, including a $5 million fine for violations of federal haz-ardous waste regulations. The fine was reduced from $8 million because Kodak agreed to spend millions to fix its leaking sewers and take other steps to clean up the plant.

Some neighbors saw the EPA fines as a good start that did little to ease their worries about the impact on their property values and, more important, their health. "We're all living in a dump," concluded Audrey Parkman, who had lived on Ridgeway Avenue, which borders Kodak Park, since the late 1960s. "I actu-ally would feel guilty selling my home to somebody. I have a con-science. With that company sitting in your backyard, I wouldn't want it for anybody's kids."

Parkman walked to the edge of her backyard and pointed to the smokestacks that loom over the neighborhood. "That is ugly for a lot of reasons." She had been bothered by the smell from Kodak and other industrial neighbors ever since she moved to the area. "When it's strong enough, it comes through into your house."

Her artist husband, Paul, painted a scene depicting the smokestacks and clouds of gray smoke. He had shown his other paintings at local galleries, but this one was "way too controver-sial," he said. "The galleries wouldn't touch it." Audrey had con-sidered sending it to George Fisher so the new CEO "can look at it all the time like we do. . . . Companies can do a great job and make a lot of money, but [they] leave safety out of the equation." Kodak was improving its efforts to work with neighbors, but she worried that the company's restructurings would make environ-mental concerns less of a priority at Kodak and eventually cut the number of community-liaison people assigned to work on envi-ronmental issues. "The community is going to suffer." Indeed, one of Audrey's longtime contacts at the company "was holding his breath about losing his job because of the downsizing."

Some of Kodak's neighbors sued the company. Others moved away to escape the environmental worries. Dick Streeter, a former Kodak employee who lived near the park, called the people of Rochester "yellow canaries," a comparison to the birds that coal miners used to keep in the shafts with them because of their sensitivity to toxic gases in the air. Like others, he was concerned about the health impact of Kodak's pollution. His wife, Linda, died of brain cancer in March 1991. He moved to California after her death.

Health officials did conduct some studies to determine whether there were health risks associated with living near Kodak. One study, which evaluated health records from 1976 through 1986, found that women living near the park had a rate of cancer about 1.7 times greater than expected. Kodak conducted its own study of male workers exposed to methylene chloride and found a higher-than-expected number of deaths from pancreatic cancer. But, the company argued, the workers studied had other risk factors for the cancer.

Kodak officials maintained that the company had reduced various emissions dramatically since the late 1980s. For instance, methylene chloride emissions dropped by 63 percent from 1987 to 1993. Total atmospheric emissions were cut by 52 percent, and releases into water were down 70 percent. Jim Blamphin, a Kodak spokesman, said no conclusive evidence proves a link between the company's plants and health problems: "The only thing that came back was maybe they have more frequent headaches and runny noses." Blamphin said that employees who were asked the same health questions as residents produced results that didn't support the findings of surveys of residents. The study on pancreatic cancer was inconclusive, he argued; Kodak epidemiologists who had studied the situation didn't believe there is a problem with cancer.

Streeter was not convinced: "We seem no closer to the truth than the victims of Love Canal." He figured that in the process of cost-cutting, Kodak would eventually sell some of the contaminated properties. "They'll leave a terrible health legacy to the community."

Some who joined Kodak's citizen's advisory board, which gives the company feedback on its environmental programs, were criticized by others loyal to Kodak. "Some people in the community are so worried that if we put too much pressure on them, they'll close up," said Mary Sevilla, who was the Sierra Club's representative to the advisory board for a year. At times, people suggested that Kodak wouldn't have to downsize so much if "we didn't have these left-wing, pinko commie environmentalists after us," Sevilla said. "We become the scapegoat."

Kodak seemed to be dealing with its environmental problems more aggressively after Fisher took over. The company newsletter now devoted more space to the Kodak Park cleanup. And, unlike a lot of companies, Kodak was actually cleaning up its mess and paying its fines to the government. Fisher had linked part of his own compensation to the company's progress in cleaning up the environment. Rarely do such issues figure into a CEO's paycheck. Even though Fisher was not spending a lot of time on Rochester events, he was at least putting a piece of his compensation on the line for an issue that did matter to this town. That was much more effective than just chairing some board or making a bunch of speeches. Fisher said he didn't know of any other company that spent as much money on environmental matters. "We are all concerned about environmental issues."

On the other hand, some Rochester residents fear that the new Kodak will slowly shift some of its operations to new locations, as other companies have done in an effort to cut costs. Fear is already hurting some local businesses. "The community may be clinically depressed," said one Kodak supplier. She doesn't expect the Kodak cost-cutting to end anytime soon, so her accountant has advised her to consider her own downsizing. "In the eighties, [attracting business] was just a matter of answering the phone. Our problem was hiring enough people."

Retailers are watching established businesses, such as McCurdy's Department Stores, close their doors after decades. John Page, a partner in the family-run Page Appliance in suburban Spencerport, sees "a reluctance to spend money." The store offers more financing programs to help customers defer payments. "If a retailer runs an ad without stating 'interest free,' he might as well not run the ad," Page says. He hasn't made any major investments or changes at his store because he's nervous about the future.

Each March used to bring a bonanza to retailers and car dealers because of the Kodak wage dividend, the annual bonus, which often amounted to several thousand dollars per employee.

The dividend is generally paid around St. Patrick's Day, so it's called St. Kodak's Day when the checks arrive.

The dividend, established in 1919 by George Eastman as a reward for employees, had shrunk in recent years as Kodak slashed spending. And beginning in 1996 new formulas for computing the amount linked it more closely with the company's performance. "That's going to have a more roller-coaster effect on the economy," said Shaun Groden, the Greece finance director. "Everybody used to bank on it as an extra paycheck in March."

Groden grew up in a Kodak family, so he remembers bonus week because he got $10 from his father when the check arrived. "It was an exciting week." His ex-wife also worked at Kodak, and the couple used her bonus check to make big purchases or pay off their credit cards. "It's gonna be a real culture shock for people."

The new reality is that no company or CEO can guarantee employees a job for life. To think it can is to be naive about the changing marketplace and global competition. If Kodak was going to rein in its spending, its employees also had to take the hint, better controlling their own personal finances. But when consumers tighten their belts, there's less business for retailers, restaurants, and other local firms. For instance, Kodak's new emphasis on doing more with less meant less traffic at some area restaurants. Groden used to work at restaurants near Kodak Park. "People would come in at eleven and stay until two for lunch. It wasn't unusual. The mentality was, 'Hey, you're at Kodak.' " He helped pay for graduate school on the tips he made from those jobs: "I could always count on fifteen or sixteen people being in the restaurant at any given time."

Now Kodak employees ate fast, restaurant owners said. The desire for a quick and cheap lunch had its advantages for Giacomo "Jack" DiPisa, owner of Rubino's Italian Subs, across from Kodak's headquarters on State Street. For eighteen years, he has watched the lunch trade for economic indicators. "My sandwiches are so cheap that they don't have to pack a lunch. When you sit down in a restaurant, it will cost you eight bucks. Here, for five bucks, you get a sandwich, pop, chips, and dessert." Still, his business was slower because of layoffs, and those who remained were jumpy. "One lady came in every day for lunch. One day we were busy, and she left without ordering. Next time she came in, I asked her why she left." She was worried that "I wouldn't have a job when I got back to work." Some Kodakers now went to the company's cafeteria to get an even quicker meal, DiPisa said.

Edith Lagas had been tending the front counter at Silver Cleaners, on the same block of State Street, since 1987. She watched a soap opera because business is slow, and leafed through a notebook to tally how much business had been lost because of Kodak job cuts. Since the end of 1991, business had dropped by $300 to $400 a week. "When they're laid off, they don't need to come in here anymore."

Dennis Cerame, owner of Flower City Jewelers, was the most optimistic of the block's tenants, but he, too, saw more conservative spending: "The big items haven't been selling so rapidly. They're not going for the diamond necklaces or tennis bracelets." One unfortunate bright spot at the jewelry store was a new service, which Cerame began in 1992: pawning. He deemed it his "community service" for people in need, and calculated that was up 30 percent. Cerame pawned only jewelry, but more and more often got phone calls from people wanting to borrow money against a television or other items.

"I've had guys come in here with Rolexes," he said. "It's happening to everybody."

PART THREE

Snapshots of the Future

8

Changing the Picture

The full cup of coffee that Mike Hornak poured at five o'clock this morning sat untouched at 9:30. A supervisor in Kodak's single-use-camera production line, Hornak had parked the coffee mug on his desk before dawn, then headed to the shop floor to lead his team of several dozen camera assemblers and machine operators in a quick round of exercises to loosen up their wrists and backs. They had to be limber for their work snapping plastic pieces and film together at the demanding pace of 200,000 cameras a day.

The team members took their stations. The cameras began a steady *clickety-click, clickety-clack* down the conveyor belts to Packaging and Shipping. Summer 1995 was drawing to a close, so the team was busy making the flash cameras to stock retailers' shelves for the Christmas holiday. Consumers were buying in record numbers; they liked the convenience of using a camera that comes loaded with a roll of film and is then returned to a photofinisher for prints. With no film to load and no lens to focus, the camera represents a return to the basics espoused by George Eastman in his early advertising slogan: "You press the button, we do the rest."

Demand was so strong that no cameras were stacked in the warehouse. Some days, the air-fright team paced at the nearby Rochester airport, waiting for pallets of cameras to arrive from assembly for shipment to Japan and around the globe. Indeed, thanks to the annual growth of 35 percent in the single-use-camera market, Kodak had to do something it hadn't done in a decade: open up the Elmgrove plant's employment office to take applications for production jobs. During a two-day period in the summer of 1995, more than 5,000 people waited to apply for 200 openings. At $7.25 an hour, these were among the lowest-paid positions in the company, and among the most tedious. But applicants flocked to the plant because the jobs offered benefits in a town where many college-educated people were flipping burgers or stocking grocery store shelves. It was a reflection of the times: people were thrilled to see a company like Kodak hiring for a change. And they'd take any entry-level job, even if there was still fear of being laid off someday. They had faced up to a new reality: workers are disposable, too.

Strong mixed emotions are created inside companies like Kodak when the old paternalistic ways clash with the new reality of no guarantees. Little is seen as either purely good or bad news. A fast-growing product line shows that Kodak can be successful, but the folks working on the line aren't like the old Kodak employees, well-paid and showered with generous benefits. Yet those who lined up to apply were happy to have work, because they had seen what it was like in the service industries, where dead-end jobs offered even lower pay and few benefits. Some of the new employees worked alongside longtime Kodakers, who were often frustrated by the changing workplace. They wanted to believe that times were changing for the better, but it was difficult to stay optimistic when they were never quite sure if more layoffs would come. They wanted to endorse Kodak's new leadership, and often did. But they also hesitated to believe that the chaos at the top, which had brought them so much hardship, had really been replaced by a management team that could get the job done. It left them feeling ambivalent and focused solely on getting through each day, rather than dwelling on what might happen down the road.

Today, Hornak was focused on getting jobs filled on the assembly line. He met with a group of two dozen applicants who had made the first cut, an aptitude test that measures basic reading and other skills. If these applicants passed a drug test, they would become part of the single-use-camera team. Hornak carried a box of cameras and parts into a conference room at the edge of the production area.

"We need you," Hornak told the group. "Chances are very good that you'll be hired." Some of the applicants wore ties and starched shirts and sat up straight, paying close attention to the supervisor. Others were more casual, in T-shirts, slouching in their chairs. Hornak, who had worked at Kodak since 1974, showed them the various types of single-use cameras, from the older cardboard-boxed models to the newest version, a sleek, trim plastic camera that fits in your palm. He showed them how to assemble the camera around a roll of film. "You are building these at your own rate. Quality is job one," he explained. "Kodak used to have an incentive program that paid you a bonus for everything you built above a certain number. We made a lot of cameras. But the quality suffered." Now, he explained, everyone had daily targets and marked each camera with his or her personal symbol to help supervisors track down the source of defective assembly or parts. This was one way the group was carrying out CEO George Fisher's marching orders: hold people accountable. Those who didn't perform wouldn't last long; turnover in this area was about 25 percent. "I need you. I need your cameras," Hornak said. "It's fast-paced, noisy, and hectic. But it's the place to be at Eastman Kodak."

He took the group on a tour of the assembly area, where operators sat in chairs, busily snapping parts together. Some had taped fingertips because the repetitive motion of winding the film-advance knob tended to gnaw away the skin. Others wore headphones, so music would drown out the hum of forklifts and stamping machines around them. A chart on the wall showed why they were focused so intently on their tasks: their performance goal was to produce fewer than six rejected cameras per week per 1,050 cameras built daily by each operator. As each worker advanced, goals became steeper: fewer than two rejects per week per 1,250 cameras a day.

The pace didn't bother Roxann Fiser. She was eager to know when she could start her shift. A single mother raising five children, ages four to fourteen, she was desperate for a full-time job. In a world where jobs with benefits were hard to find, her best shot at improving her home economics was this. She had a college degree and yearned to eventually become a manager—an increasingly elusive piece of the American dream. Instead, she had held a string of part-time jobs. "I can't keep doing that."

Back in the conference room, she asked to look at one of the cameras in Hornak's box, and practiced snapping the pieces together. Others took pictures of each other. Hornak told the applicants that they would likely be asked to work afternoon and night shifts and weekend overtime when demand was high. Lately, that had been every week. "I've had two Saturdays off since Christmas," he told the group. Fiser chimed in: "I'll take all the overtime I can get." He assured her that she'd have plenty.

Back in his office after the meeting, Hornak saw his cold coffee and a fresh stack of memos and other work piling up on his desk. "Where did the day go?" he asked. It was almost noon; he had already logged about seven hours and would put in another five before thinking about going home. Some Saturdays, he swung by the doughnut shop to buy several dozen for the overtime crew. And he often stayed after they went home—to build a few more cameras himself. His philosophy: don't ask anybody to do anything that you haven't done yourself. It was clear that this guy really got a kick out of working on Kodak's hottest product line—"It is very satisfying," he said—but the long weeks were beginning to wear him down. "You wake up Sunday morning comatose. You're still so physically tired, but you want to take a weekend and condense it into one day." His wife worked part-time at Kodak, so their life was often a juggling act to make sure their two children didn't get lost in the shuffle. At work, his colleagues routinely called each other "No Life."

Such intense demand for a product should equal some type of job security for the 600 or so people building these cameras, one of the few fast-growing parts of the photography business. But the sad reality was that many of them worried about losing their jobs anyway. There were no more guarantees for anyone. After living through two restructurings and demotions, Hornak was conservative and a realist in all aspects of his life. Indeed, in 1995 he still drove a 1984 car with 140,000 miles and was struggling with the idea of replacing it with another used car.

No one understands such a worker's mixed feelings better than Lane Riland, a psychologist who had been taking Kodak's pulse for nearly four decades. After a decade of upheaval from downsizings and restructurings, he said, the typical employee of the 1990s was "moderately depressed" and displaying symptoms of stress, such as headaches and colitis. Kodakers, like other middle Americans, craved the basics of the American dream: a house, a job, college educations for their children. "This generation," said Riland, "won't do as well as its parents." And he worried about the ripple effect when the people left behind inside Kodak were expected to shoulder the workload once shared with those who took buyouts or were laid off. How long until somebody went ballistic? How many of the heart attacks among Kodakers were caused by the stress of the job? Beyond that, Riland worried about the impact on the next generation. Applicant Roxann Fiser, who wanted lots of overtime, had five children at home. In twenty years, those kids would be applying for Kodak jobs. "What's the effect on the five kids when she has to work all the overtime she can get?" Riland asked.

It is the key to any company's effective recovery from repeated downsizings: doing more work with fewer people, without burning out those who remain. Kodak's massive bureaucracy had to be dismantled, and work had to be changed to eliminate outdated tasks. That was a huge project. In some ways, it was easier than changing Kodak's culture to one based on performance and accountability rather than lifetime employment. There were deep feelings of entitlement among employees, who wanted to cling to the days when Kodak could spend freely on lavish benefits and buyouts. But now employees from CEO Fisher to the workers on the factory floor knew that they would have to deliver on promises to change Kodak. Like other U.S. companies, Kodak would have to follow through with reforms, not just a lot of hot air about change, and generate new sources of revenue growth. Otherwise, the company risked repeating the cycle of layoffs.

One thing was certain: Kodak people wanted someone to believe in. And most backed their new CEO. There were signs that Fisher's message was getting through. Machine operators, long relegated to menial labor, were signing up for college engineering courses. Supervisors were nixing bushels of frivolous paperwork. And factories like Elmgrove, once dubbed Elmgrave, were humming with new production lines of cameras and printers. Most of all, Fisher and his team were clearing out those who didn't perform. Employee surveys in the summer of 1995 showed that a record number of workers believed the company was well managed. And other measures showed improvements.

Kodak didn't have a major layoff in the months before the summer 1995 survey, which was one reason for the improved results. In fact, a fair amount of cynicism remained—and still remains—throughout the company. For starters, some are still bitter because their friends were laid off. And they fear they will be next, should Kodak sell off another piece of the business or see a downturn in profits. Even workers in areas that are growing fear that nothing will ever be stable. All the talk of changing the picture had yet to translate into reality in their own lives. The 1995 survey showed that only 25 percent of employees felt secure in their jobs. One reason Riland cited was cynicism about whether more layoffs are on the horizon. "I wouldn't work on commission trying to win them all over," he said.

Some of the efforts that Fisher endorses, especially in manufacturing, were already under way when he arrived in late 1993. But improvement had been sporadic. "You can create centers of excellence in any organization like this. The challenge is to permeate the place with it," said Frank Zaffino, head of the Elmgrove plant. Before Fisher joined Kodak, Zaffino sent a team of managers to Motorola to learn about its improvement programs, then come back and train others at Elmgrove. The initiative was met with considerable skepticism, said Zaffino. The reaction was: "Oh, my God. Zaffino read another book this month."

Likewise, some workers at the biggest Kodak facility, Kodak Park, went to Motorola to learn the fundamentals. One area in which Kodak's efforts took hold was photographic paper manufacturing, which supplied paper to both professional photographers and the photofinishers who develop amateur photographers' pictures. Inside Kodak Park's building 319, a paper mill was churning out almost all of Kodak's worldwide supply of paper.

This was one of the earliest sites for reforming the old wasteful ways, largely because Kodak felt a lot of pressure from foreign competitors. Since the early 1990s, production time had dropped to a fraction of the thirty days it used to take to produce a roll of paper. The ultimate goal was to cut the time to about two days. The efficiency of the operation was becoming increasingly important as archrival Fuji opened a new South Carolina plant to make photographic paper for the U.S. market. More important, with the traditional market for photographic paper dropping, the department came up with new products, such as special papers for ink-jet printers. With demand for such products growing, managers predicted the department would actually hire some new people in the years ahead.

One improvement was team efforts that included operators, not just engineers, in problem-solving. And all shifts shared information, in contrast to the days when each shift worked independently from the others. Each of the sixty different expense categories now had a designated watchdog among the thirty people in the department, so everyone kept tabs on even the tiniest expenses. One new manager was chided for keeping the office thermostat too high, raising the group's utility costs.

Part of the team-building resembled what Fisher and others had done at Motorola. (In fact, some of the managers in the area were among those to visit Motorola to learn about six sigma and other measures.) For instance, everyone in paper manufacturing got a pocket card listing "Personal Standards of Excellence," such as "I will honor my commitments" and "I will look for 'How we can' rather than 'Why can't we.' " Ralph Olney, an industrial engineer who was unit manager of the group, said meetings were often punctuated by operators pulling out their value cards to challenge a statement that "doesn't align with what we believe in the Park. They've used that on me several times." Sometimes, Olney, an Eagle Scout, recited the scouting pledge in his meetings, reminding his coworkers to be trustworthy, loyal, and helpful.

Another change concerned how people could advance. Employees could now write personal development plans outlining where they wanted to go in their career. Typical Kodak limits on performance appraisals, which closed doors when people tried to advance to the next wage grade, were removed. "It used to be that you'd come in and sweep floors for a while," Olney said. Only as someone moved on or retired could you advance to a better job. Now employees could advance more quickly by showing that they had mastered skills needed to take on tougher assignments. Performance appraisals were written by each worker rather than a manager.

The changing environment was apparent in a conversation with Rick LaDue, who started on the cleanup crew in 1975 before moving to the instant-camera production line. Eventually, he joined Building 319, making paper. Formerly the workers reported to a general foreman, whom he not so lovingly referred to as El Supremo. To hear LaDue describe it, Kodak was the bureaucracy from hell. At every shift change, for instance, foremen would tell operators to tinker with the machines, just to show they were trying to improve the product. But when customers complained about problems with the paper, some foremen would order the crew to do nothing, but would tell the customer that the problems were solved.

The foreman jobs were gone. Now team members trained to use statistics for controlling the paper-making process, leaving little room for the old tinkering and inspection at the end of the line. "If your process is in control, you don't need four people testing the product," LaDue said. Workers were trained to quiz suppliers of pulp about their quality to ensure that the raw materials were as good as they should be.

LaDue was ambitious about improving himself and those around him. For a time, he worked as a team coach, setting up what he dubbed LaDue University. During night shift, when there were fewer interruptions, he would train one operator in a new job in the department. Trained in broader areas, they understood more about the entire paper-making process, not just their task of pushing some buttons on one piece of machinery. "They didn't do any more because they weren't expected to do any more. I threw that by the wayside and said, 'You're whatever you can be.'" Now that Fisher was pushing for company-wide training, LaDue took a moment to crow. "I like to think I was ahead of George."

Despite his desire to upgrade his skills, though, LaDue worried about what the future might hold. "If something happened next year and paper becomes obsolete, what would I do?" He had never earned a college degree and had always said he would like to go to school. "That's been one of my failures in life." A father of three sons, he lectured them about education and living within their means.

LaDue was a cheerleader for Kodak's efforts to live within *its* means, shedding debt and parts of the company that didn't fit with its imaging core. But it was one thing to cheer that effort for the company, another to realize what those reforms meant to his own career. For instance, Kodak's old suggestion system was generous to those who found ways to save the company money. In 1985, LaDue and others received $50,000 each for a machine maintenance program that saved his department $1 million.

Now suggestions netted far less, maybe a couple of thousand dollars, so LaDue put all of his ideas on his performance appraisal, hoping for a better raise. Still, he was part of the Windows of Opportunity (WOO) team, which looks for ways to cut out downtime for the paper-making machinery. Indeed, he worked late into the night to train people when there were changes in the machinery. And he got his share of kudos—but he hadn't seen the payoff where it counted the most: his paycheck. He didn't get a raise in 1995. "That's where the system has failed me and where I want George to change it so these types of inequities are remedied."

Kevin Rogers, another operator in paper manufacturing, was equally disheartened about how difficult it had become to get ahead financially even when one worked hard. A college graduate, he started at Kodak's Elmgrove plant making Disc cameras, was laid off when the product went bust, and was called back to the Park on a contract job, only to be laid off again. His fiancée, Darlene, was also laid off, so the couple had to downscale their wedding plans. Kevin eventually returned to Kodak, while his wife joined the Rochester police department, working on drug abuse prevention programs in local schools. Despite having two incomes, they still found it tough to support a family of five. Like so many Americans, Rogers saw a widening gulf between the haves and the have-nots. Wages weren't keeping pace with the times, and he and Darlene were working more hours just to try and maintain their lifestyle. "I call it the working poor. That's what we are. There's no more middle class. It is the rich and it's the poor."

Rogers did understand that he and the rest of Kodak would have to improve constantly if they were to succeed. "It's a way of saying, 'Hey, guys, let's wake up. If we don't get ourselves straight, we're not gonna be here.'" His oldest son wanted to become an engineer and work for Kodak. "That gives me an incentive to really be motivated and try to work hard to make our company survive."

Olney, the unit manager, had his work cut out for him in trying to explain why individual rewards weren't always higher. When raises were given, he came in at 1:30 A.M. to talk to the night shift and stayed around the clock to either congratulate or console. He tried to offer occasional extras, when possible. For instance, the group went more than a year without an accident, so he gave out $50 gift certificates for Wegman's grocery stores, and a note of congratulations that was tucked in everyone's personnel file.

Making changes in the culture and rethinking work processes had proven equally challenging for other units at Kodak. The trick was to get change to really take hold in the biggest profit centers, where it could deliver the maximum results. One of the biggest challenges was to improve Kodak's core product, 35mm color film. Inside Kodak Park, machines churn out a quarter of the world's 35mm film. The process had been improving. Kodak claimed its manufacturing costs were now below Fuji's. Still, it would take much more to meet Fisher's ambitious goals for improvement in cycle time, measured from the point of making the Jell-O–like film emulsion to the time the yellow boxes land on K Mart's shelves. The Kodacolor improvement program was so big that Fisher personally sponsored the team. Tony Fedor, who managed Kodak Park, held quarterly meetings with Fisher to review the progress, and saw how Fisher accelerated the pace of improvement on all projects: "He actually has convinced a lot of people that we're gonna make it. That's the biggest impact."

One of the company's role models for improvement was the 35mm finishing team, which had made progress in both self-management and cutting costs. Output per employee doubled from 1990 to 1995, and costs dropped by 27 percent. The process began with a redesign of the work area, guided by the operators who staff it. "We built an operation so you can see all the supplies coming in and then the finished product leaving," explained Ken Bowers, team adviser in finishing. "So it gave you a sense of some accomplishment."

The team was learning about issues such as cycle times, and also taking classes on conflict resolution and dealing with stress. Bowers was one of the first Kodak employees in a new program, set up with the help of the Rochester Institute of Technology, under which RIT professors visit Kodak Park and teach a class of about thirty students who want to earn their college degrees. Bowers, hoping to get a bachelor's in production and quality management, went to school a couple of hours during the workday, with Kodak paying for the classes. Others studied issues like time management, which they discovered helps at home as well as at work. "I don't watch much TV anymore," said Bill Granger, a fork-truck driver, who delivers goods to the area.

The classes were an adjustment for many, who had been out of high school for decades. Early classes included a review of basic skills, such as listening and test-taking. Eventually, the program might be expanded to other parts of Kodak as the company searched for ways to invest in people.

The 35mm finishing team also made strides in self-management, hiring their own colleagues when they needed to replace someone or expand the group. When supervisors did the hiring, "people didn't have a lot of ownership for getting somebody up to speed because they didn't hire them," Bowers said. "Now they help them make it." Team members decided who would work overtime and how to cover jobs during vacations or sick days. They also did their own performance reviews. Each person selected four coworkers to review his or her performance, and three others were picked at random.

The finishing team was ahead of the curve on learning about Fisher's mantra: return on net assets. They knew how their inventory and the amount of space they used in the building affected their bottom line. When people on the shop floor decided they needed a lift to move cartons, the team went to a company purchasing agent to look over a supply catalogue. Then they went through Kodak's various plants and found a lift that wasn't being used; they moved it to the finishing area and installed it, at no cost to the company. It was easier to win over employees to the notion of return on net assets when quarterly earnings reports offered some positive reinforcement.

One reason Kodak was seeing some improvement was a shift away from insular thinking. More people throughout the company were doing something that seems pretty simple: listening to the consumer. In film packaging, that meant workers on the packing line went to class to learn how to talk to consumers who called Kodak's 800 line. The operators took personal responsibility for resolving complaints. Sometimes that involved tracking down a problem that was beyond Kodak's control, such as damage that occurred after the film hit a retailer's shelves. The operators rehearsed their telephone manners in front of a mirror, because "people on the other side can tell what kind of mood you are in," said Niramon Toner, a member of the group.

In its push to improve, Kodak found that the lesson of listening and responding quickly applied in other areas. In the past, Kodak would study issues to death and often drag its feet on getting a product to market. In the era of Fisher, there was evidence that the company is getting better at moving faster. The reinvention of the single-use-camera project serves as a case study of how a variety of processes, from manufacturing to marketing, had to be put on a fast track in order to succeed, and how Kodak could return to the basics of camera and film making to create jobs and a return for shareholders.

Kodak was helped by worldwide growth from the Funsaver

cameras, which were gaining in popularity even in mature markets, such as the United States and Japan, where households already own several cameras. The business was similar to film sales. Kodak had the dominant share in the U.S., while Fuji had captured the bulk of single-use sales in Japan.

The product got off to a rocky start at Kodak: The company was too slow to patent its inventions, so it had to pay Fuji for the use of some inventions. And the disposable camera faced critics inside the old Kodak film clique, who thought it was almost sacrilegious. They believed it was easier and cheaper to just sell film, not film inside a disposable camera. "They thought it was the worst thing they ever heard of," recalled Jack Thomas, executive vice president.

The early model, called Fling, was quickly labeled an environmental nightmare, because, after a consumer used it once, photofinishers disposed of it. It went through several changes before Kodak's management decided, in late 1993, that it had to do something drastic to take advantage of a market that was growing out of consumer demand, not Kodak's innovations. Thomas, second in command to CEO Kay Whitmore, put Bob LaPerle in charge of designing a business plan. That plan called for investing in a new, more-automated production line at the Elmgrove plant, which many had figured would eventually close because of Kodak's cost-cutting. Even Elmgrove's head described the outlook at that time as bleak. Getting assigned to Elmgrove, Zaffino said, was like "being exiled to Stalag 17." The new production line was made even riskier by the fact that the project started just as Whitmore was getting the ax and the board was searching for a new CEO. If the new guy didn't endorse the project, they'd all be looking for work.

But the Funsaver team found that job security came with a solid business case for spending money to expand the product. Research showed that the bulk of buyers wanted convenience like that offered by Kodak's earlier 110 and Disc cameras, which were easy to load and use. To really see what consumers wanted, LaPerle and his team decided to do market research first in Japan. When young women were asked why they buy the single-use cameras rather than use one of several cameras their family already owns, they replied that the others were old-fashioned. "It has become a trendy thing to do," LaPerle said.

Kodak was at a disadvantage with trendy consumers because of the camera's style. Amateur photographers said the camera was too square and boxy. They wanted something sleeker, with rounder edges, easier to hold. "We wanted to make the product even easier to use. One-button simple. Our vision is the same as George Eastman's original vision," LaPerle said. And with improved recycling efforts, about 86 percent of each camera is now used again. Sometimes, the same parts can be reused six or eight times. Others are recycled elsewhere inside Kodak. For instance, the batteries inside a single-use camera are repackaged by a rehabilitation center that employs people with disabilities. The group makes money by repacking the batteries for Kodak, which saves about $25,000 a year by reusing them.

Other problems with older camera models became apparent once the team started to listen more closely to the marketplace. The underwater model, though encased in plastic, sometimes leaked. And the defect didn't always show up until consumers used the product, despite an expensive and time-consuming inspection process at the plant, in which a conveyor belt carried each underwater camera into a twenty-foot tank of water and then on to an inspection table. Consumers also complained that they couldn't tell whether they had taken a picture, because they couldn't feel or hear the camera click under water. Finally, when photofinishers tried to pry open the plastic casing they often incurred injuries.

Kodak heard all this feedback through a team of operators, engineers, and finance and marketing people who worked the 800 line fielding consumer calls. Some worked the night shift at photofinishing plants and interviewed snorkelers and skin divers about the underwater models. "We're getting technical people out of the labs and the manufacturing people off the factory floor and they're actually visiting customers."

When LaPerle first presented the business plan to redesign the single-use camera to an audience of 1,000 employees inside Elmgrove's auditorium, the response was skepticism: "People basically said it's a dream." So he and his colleagues dubbed it the Dream Project. The group showed Whitmore their plans just two days before he left the company, and kept moving forward although they didn't know if the new boss would support the plan. They figured it was solid enough to survive even the toughest cost-cutter.

The new camera became known as Falcon, because the team wanted it to resemble a bird of prey, picking off rival products. "You gotta have a little bit of the killer instinct," said Steve Rumsey, manufacturing manager on the single-use-camera line.

The Falcon was first launched in the Japanese market in November 1994, under the Snapkids label. It was introduced in France and the United States in 1995. Fuji's immediate response in Japan was to lower its prices by about $2 a camera. But Kodak's sales were so strong in the first months that the region's managers raised sales estimates three times in two months. Advertising for the product was unconventional by Japanese standards: the TV commercial featured a typical school setting, in which a stoic principal is lecturing students about the importance of conforming. His speech is interrupted when a popular actress marches into the auditorium with the new Kodak camera. The principal takes the camera and shoots a picture, prompting all the students to rush to the stage with their own cameras. "It's a counterculture, in-your-face type of ad," LaPerle said. The public responded. Japanese press reports on the Falcon were favorable, and it was named one of the best photographic products of the year.

In the United States, Kodak's marketing strategy was to persuade retailers to drop prices on older single-use cameras and sell the newer models at a premium. Wal-Mart, Kodak's single biggest customer, gave the product a boost when CEO David Glass picked the single-use-camera category as his choice in the company's annual contest to see which product line did the best business for the year.

On the manufacturing side of the business, the strategy to deliver the new cameras quickly relied on reengineering production in three stages, simultaneously. The oldest camera production line used a lot of manual assembly and outsourced some basic work to local companies. The second line was a bit more advanced. And the final line was highly automated, with robots doing many of the tedious jobs and no manual inspection at the end. Some of the automation had its roots in the old Disc camera project, which was considered state-of-the-art at the time. Indeed, LaPerle, who was a product manager for the Disc camera, played tour guide on the factory floor for curious manufacturing executives from Japan. "The reason why we've been able to restoke this is some embers were kind of still burning out here," he said. A big change is the volume—five times more than Kodak ever made on the Disc, 126, or 110 camera lines, he said.

At the Elmgrove plant in the summer of 1995, the Falcon team was eager to show off its progress to CEO Fisher, who had visited them when Falcon was still on the drawing board. Back then, he framed one of the first plastic pieces from a Falcon and hung it in his office. Even his wife, Ann, brought guests through for occasional tours. Now he returned himself to see how much progress they had made. The place was being expanded to keep up with demand. Indeed, the weekend before his visit, the team was reorganizing the plant layout to increase from four to six lines.

LaPerle and Rumsey greeted Fisher at the factory door and immediately started telling him about their plans. "The factory isn't the way it used to be," LaPerle said, "and that is one of our major accomplishments. We've run out of production space." Now the team was taking over offices to make room for production.

"Fantastic," Fisher replied. "Fantastic."

"We'll be bringing you an SER [special equipment request] in about three weeks. We need more money to build more lines here," LaPerle continued. The company would double its capacity by 1997, including expansion at its plant in France.

"Can you get the French government to give you anything for putting that in there?" Fisher asked.

"We should look hard at that," answered LaPerle.

"Yeah, you should," Fisher said. "I'm trying to teach everybody that everybody wants us, and why give it away?"

He was enthusiastic about the expansion and about news that the team is eyeing the Pacific Rim for the next wave of growth. "I'll sign the SER within twenty-four hours of when I see it," he promised.

He asked about cycle time on various processes. "Get them to count minutes, because then minutes begin to mean something. You talk hours, then hours mean something. You talk weeks, you'll get weeks."

Fisher learned about one glitch in the works: the flash model production was slowed because of a faulty part from an outside supplier. Fisher studied the part. "Is it from Motorola?"

"I didn't want to say that," replied Rob Fischmann, product team manager for single-use cameras. "They were breaking their butts to get it fixed. They were almost apologetic."

"They better be," Fisher said.

They discussed plans for a new product, an outgrowth of the market research on the underwater camera. That model was redesigned with a new push button and other features to correct problems. It was also tougher. But market research revealed that some consumers were still skittish about using a plastic-encased camera. Although the redesign was pretty tough, the clear plastic looked almost glasslike, creating the impression that sharp pieces might break off. That prompted the team to develop a more rugged model. (To make the point, LaPerle gave the camera a toss. "You could literally throw this against a cement wall. It takes a whippin' and keeps on clickin'.")

During his tour, Mike Hornak told Fisher about the process of operators marking cameras they make. "They take ownership of it. They control their own destiny and they control their own product." He explained how he tracked defects. Fisher walked past the reject tray on the automated line. It was empty.

"Did you just clean that off?" he asked.

"No," Hornak replied. In fact, the team later joked that the plant floor was a bit of a mess. This visit was a radical change from Kodak's old days, when a CEO's visit was orchestrated to provide for where he would walk, stop, and talk, and hallways and stairwells along his route were spruced up with paint.

Fisher made it clear to the Falcon team that he wanted worldwide designs for manufacturing equipment, so machines could be installed and serviced anywhere. That would also send a strong message that manufacturing doesn't necessarily have to be in the headquarters hometown. "I want this thing to fit on a 747 so you can move it into Korea or Singapore overnight and have it up and running the next week," Fisher said.

The CEO was clearly pleased with the Rochester team, which was breaking all kinds of records on production. "They exceed the number of cellular phones we used to make," he remarked.

As he walked along, Karen Koksal slipped out of her chair at the flash camera line and dashed over to tap Fisher on the shoulder. She asked him to please take time to say hello to her teammates on the line. "We're working our butts off," she said. Fisher was already behind schedule, but he told his handlers to hang on for a minute.

"How are you doing? Good to see you," he said, shaking the line workers' hands and thanking them for their work. Some took his picture. Some gasped when they saw who was walking by. Some cheered. "Come again," Koksal said. "I will," he promised. She was frustrated by Fisher's rapid changes, but his few moments of handshaking scored big points on the factory floor.

Fisher was obviously pleased by the response. "It gives you hope. I see a phenomenal difference. You see people who are smiling, who have energy to them again."

LaPerle and others also saw the new energy. But they worried about the toll the project was taking on people. "I had to grab people and physically throw them out of the building. They were canceling family trips. We had people close to burnout. I think sometimes the price gets too high. The number one reason we're all doing this is so we can have a nice family life, support our families. Sometimes it gets out of control. I worry about that."

Sadly, the single-use-camera group—and all of Kodak—soon experienced a loss that made them think about the balance in their own lives. In the fall of 1995, LaPerle was promoted and Jane Lanphear was named as his replacement in the single-use-camera business. The team was preparing for the transition in management when, at the age of forty-one, Lanphear had a heart attack and died. A Ph.D. in chemistry, she had been considered a rising star inside Kodak. "She could have been CEO of this company," says Carl Kohrt, who worked with her in the health sciences business. He had seen her a few days before her death and recalled how excited she was about taking her new job. "We lost a spark."

At Lanphear's funeral service, the eulogy included a message that hit home with many in the audience: don't let work take over your life. "I think it was a good message for that whole room, because those people have been burning the candle at both ends and working harder than ever," says Ann Fisher, who attended the service. It's difficult to keep a balance, because the job pressures remain. "But for a moment, we all went, 'Oh yeah, there *is* something more important in the long run.'"

CEO Fisher saw the strain in his employees. And he knew that morale was still a serious problem. People seemed hopeful, but they were exhausted from the pressure of doing more with a smaller staff. One big problem was the lack of personal rewards. The employees all feared that Kodak would once again cut jobs, so they worked hard to keep theirs. But they were waiting for some signs that their efforts were worth it. Or would they just work and work, only to be laid off, too?

"We are not at the point where our employees generally see the rewards for them, other than the fact that many people have jobs today that wouldn't have on the track we were on," Fisher admitted. While the prevailing sentiment among management in late 1993 was that Elmgrove should be shuttered, "the more likely issue today is can we hire some more people rather than work so much overtime." Indeed, one woman on the line asked Fisher to hire more people to help.

Others, like Karen Koksal, showed that many still yearned for a bit of the old paternalism to calm their nerves. An unrealistic wish, it demonstrated the difficulty of the transition from the old Kodak to the new. "If Fisher could guarantee a job for good, hardworking people, you'll see a big improvement here. People won't be afraid." Yet Koksal was quick to criticize past managers—exactly those who were known for their paternalism and failure to make tough business decisions that might have helped Kodak sooner. "How come the last CEO didn't do the job?" she demanded.

Those left inside Kodak needed occasionally to rehash the past as a salve for their hurt feelings and their uncertainty about their futures. One of their concerns was how to advance beyond entry-level jobs like single-use-camera assembly and into something more challenging. It wasn't easy to motivate everybody. Some could move into a more challenging line, such as the thermal-printer production team. The printers, which were more advanced, provided more opportunities to learn new skills.

At the time of Fisher's tour, the printer team was celebrating some milestones, such as clearing out back orders. Frank Zaffino, head of the plant, wanted the CEO to reinforce the team's good work with a quick visit.

On the way, Fisher recalled his last visit to the printer team. "This is Mary Burkhart's group. She used to be a schoolteacher." He asked Zaffino whether the group knew he was coming even though it was a last-minute addition to his schedule.

"I didn't tell," Zaffino said.

"Bullshit," Fisher said quietly, laughing.

"As God is my judge . . ." Zaffino countered.

At the printer area, a crowd was gathered around an overhead projector and Burkhart. Applause erupted as Fisher and Zaffino interrupted the presentation.

"Is this a birthday party?" Fisher asked.

Burkhart explained that she tried to keep Fisher's visit a secret, telling only one of her associates. Apparently, though, news got around fast. As she joined the group, she now told Fisher, she overhead someone say: "I came to see George."

She resumed her praise of the crew. They had doubled their original plan of production. "This team has just been pushing and doing everything that they could do to build above the schedule." Productivity was improving. "It took us twenty-one and a half hours in January per printer. We'll go down to thirteen at the end of May and we're headed for eleven and a half at end of June. That's due to drastic quality improvements that people are making. We're gonna smoke!"

Fisher offered to say a few words to the group. "You should hear the enthusiasm of customers who use our digital print stations, which use your printers. There is excitement in their eyes and in their voices that just makes you happy. And also it makes for one of the highest growth opportunities that Kodak has seen in years. So I hope you all feel the importance of what you're doing here for our customers and certainly for the profitability of the company and for the well-being of the company. I said when I came into this company that Kodak, in order to succeed, was going to have to be successful in the equipment business. . . . You are demonstrating that you are winners." He gave Burkhart a lot of credit. "Let's give Mary a round of applause, too," he said. She had tears in her eyes.

Burkhart reminded the group that it was unusual to have her manager and her manager's manager on hand for a celebration. "What she's trying to tell you is we've got too much management," Fisher joked.

He was peppered with questions as he tried to leave the building. Some simply wanted to know why his ID badge was different from everybody else's. He was wearing one of the newest ones, with a hologram. Another employee asked whether Fisher had received his letter with suggestions on marketing. "I didn't get it. Send me another copy." Another woman said she wouldn't wash her hand now that she had shaken the CEO's. Once again, he saw how employees can have split personalities: they got mad as hell about his big paycheck, but they wanted to believe he was a white knight who could save them. If he did that, they would forget that they ever grumbled about the money.

It was a refreshing change to hear some good news, especially for Zaffino, who had orchestrated more than his share of layoffs at Elmgrove and saw the daily toll they had taken. "Those that are left are looking over their shoulder, saying, 'Frank, every year you come and tell us we've done what you've asked us to do. And every year you have another layoff. What the hell are you doing up there?' So anybody's credibility pretty soon starts to get a little ragged," he said. "But everybody senses now this is our best shot ever."

One reason the Elmgrove lines were humming was new efforts to build on Kodak's traditional photography business. For instance, the thermal-printer business was growing, partly thanks to Kodak's efforts to increase consumers' use of existing photographs. Driving that growth were copy print stations, digital enhancement stations, and creation stations, which provided many ways to alter, enlarge, or duplicate photos. Only 2 percent or 3 percent of photos ever get enlarged, so there were about 150 billion pictures stashed away in U.S. drawers and closets. A test in Australia showed a 30 percent increase in enlargements and reprint sales at Kodak's stores equipped with the copy print machines. Frame sales soared 25 percent.

Some of that growth came from sales to the over–fifty-five crowd, a slice of the population that doesn't tend to use as much film as younger folks. The results of the Australian test were so strong that copy print machines were now rolling out in other markets. "This will grow our core business by fifty percent in the next five years," predicted Ziggy Switkowski, head of Kodak's Australian operations. "This has the potential to be a home run."

The copy print machine was also a bridge product that showed how to take traditional photography into new arenas—something that Fisher and others wanted to do with digital photography. Kodak faced many skeptics because it had stumbled badly whenever it tried to make money on expensive electronic gadgets, like the Photo CD. Shortly after taking office, Fisher injected some new blood into the company to bolster the digital business.

One of the first outsiders to join was Carl Gustin, a veteran of both Apple Computer and Digital Equipment who started his professional life in jobs as diverse as composting garbage into fertilizer and hawking snowmobiles for an advertising agency. He wasn't a real fan of Kodak; his first exposure to the Rochester company was during his time at Apple, where he worked as chief executive John Sculley's assistant. At the time, Sculley was riding a wave of popularity—as Gustin puts it, "He had become the number one icon of American business." Eventually, Sculley's star faded, and he left the company. Gustin decided to move to Digital because he wanted to work in line management, not just advertising and marketing. Shortly after he took the Digital job, Kodak started recruiting him.

Gustin remembered his days of trying to convince Kodak to launch the Photo CD as a business product rather than a consumer toy. "I spent a hundred thousand dollars on original research to convince Kodak not to make this a consumer product. John and I spent meeting after meeting here. We could get nowhere." The problem was at the top. Kay Whitmore "just didn't get it. He didn't want to get it," Gustin said.

So Gustin was reluctant to take Kodak seriously. "My vision of Kodak was, 'This is a film and paper company. Period. I just don't expect them to make it in technology.' " He knew Fisher from his dealings with Motorola while at Apple. And Sculley, who'd been hired as a consultant to Kodak, called Gustin to get him to talk to Fisher. "It's different now," Sculley told Gustin.

Gustin did spend a day with Kodak's senior management. "The two hours I spent with Fisher completely changed my mind. I came in apathetic, wondering what the hell I was doing in Rochester. I left saying, 'This place has really got a future.' " The key was Fisher's statement that digital imaging wasn't "the dirty little secret to be kept in the closet."

But Gustin faced a problem: his family was sick of moving. Rochester would be their third new city in less than a year. But his bosses at Kodak agreed to let him commute from Atlanta, so the family could return to an old neighborhood with familiar schools and friends.

Like Fisher, Gustin wasted no time making his mark. For starters, the sales force on the digital side of Kodak was put on commission, a first for the company. "That did not make everybody real happy," he said. But he emphasized: "Accountability for performance is not just to be talked about, but to be implemented."

He also tackled one of the stickiest problems inside Kodak: performance appraisals. At Kodak, there seemed to be a dozen different ways to evaluate performance. In some pockets, employees were doing their own, with a manager signing off. In other corners, appraisals were a group effort. Yet other departments used the old-fashioned manager-writes-it method. Gustin found that his division still suffered from the Lake Wobegon effect: everyone was considered above average. About 85 percent of the people were rated a 7 on a scale of 1 to 7. "If they were, then digital and applied imaging would be the biggest, most successful, most profitable company in the world," Gustin quipped. "And we're not."

So in his first round of performance reviews, he returned all the appraisals to managers and told them to redo them with the following measures: a 4 meant the staffer was meeting expectations. A 5 meant the staffer exceeded some. A 6 meant he or she generally exceeded all expectations. And a 7 meant you were incredible.

"It set off a firestorm," Gustin allowed. But he defended the move: "How are you gonna develop your people if you don't give them intellectually honest appraisals?"

So what did Gustin get on his own performance appraisal? A 4.

"That's what I thought I deserved."

The group had missed sales targets by 45 percent in 1994, so he told them that, beginning in January 1995, they would have to meet their plan. Two months into the year, the group was still off target, so Gustin made some personnel changes. He hired a channel development vice president to reach new markets, a new vice president of sales and marketing, and others.

He also went on a campaign to make sure the message of reform was being heard, loud and clear. He sent a video crew out into the plants and offices to stop people at random and ask them to explain the mission of digital and applied imaging. What was the vision? What was the strategy? "Nobody knew," he said. "All these managers were feeling really good that they were communicating." He held an employee communications meeting and opened it with the Video of Blank Looks. "Sixteen different people in nine different languages all saying 'I don't know.' "

Two months later, he sent the video crew out again and got the same response. So he told his managers: "If I find any more people that don't understand what we're doing, I'm gonna tie it in to your performance. And I'm tying it in to your pay." Suddenly, signs about the group's vision began to appear, taped to the hallway walls. Still, adopting a mission takes time. At another employee meeting, Gustin picked six people from the audience with the promise of extra days off to the winners of his version of *Jeopardy!* Everyone got a pad and a pencil and was given sixty seconds to answer the question "What is our mission statement?" As the theme song to *Jeopardy!* played, the group sat and pondered the question. "The six of them didn't have the answer," Gustin said.

As for the sales force, he said they were making their numbers as of the summer of 1995. "They may not like me very much, but I think a year from now, when they're doing a billion dollars in revenue, they'll feel good about themselves." He thought the thermal-printer business had set too low a goal, despite big improvements. "The projection was to sell five thousand in 1995. That's nonsense. I could sell five thousand out of the back of my trunk." He moved the target to 20,000, which he considers reasonable, despite some glitches with supplies and some quality problems that have slowed progress. "If I have demand for a hundred thousand printers in 1996 and I can only make thirty thousand, I won't get those seventy thousand [sales] back. They'll buy something else."

One of the biggest new-product projects was the relaunch of Photo CD in 1995. Gustin and Fisher met with computer-company leaders to persuade them to work with Kodak. They dropped the royalty payment to Kodak and lowered the price tag to encourage more customers to incorporate Photo CD into their systems. They also found new markets for writable CDs, which resemble music CDs but can be used like floppy discs, to store documents instead of music. The advantage of the CD is that it holds a lot more information. Major companies fueled the growth of the market because the discs were replacing outdated methods of record-keeping. For instance, some phone companies now shipped major corporate phone bills on a CD rather than printing the massive documents on paper. Kodak predicted that it would sell 7 million to 9 million discs in 1995, quadruple its earlier projections. Both the Rochester CD manufacturing plant and one in Mexico were expanding to keep up with demand.

It used to take fifty-six days to move a digital product, from the date of order to delivery to the customer. Dave Swift, vice president of operations and general manager of the group, was working on speeding up the process of producing special orders of discs. He hoped to reduce those fifty-six days to three. "I think we can even do better than that," he said. One big problem was the paper shuffle. "There were sixty to seventy handoffs on a given order." The new cycle would reduce that to one. "That's where Kodak is gonna get some of the significant changes in the future," Swift said.

He was constantly trying to cut out layers and waste. He realigned the division into five groups to provide more customer focus. And he moved his office from the Kodak office tower to a manufacturing site to be closer to his team.

Swift admitted that all the change was sometimes over-whelming—as was apparent on a walk through the CD manufacturing facility, an old baby-food plant that Kodak bought. Kodakers still call it the Gerber plant. Lynn Streber, a Kodak employee since 1985, had been a training coordinator in the CD area for the past few years. Lately, she saw morale improving because "you're so busy." At the same time, workers were "still afraid." And with good reason. A couple of years ago, the factory was busy making discs for the Photo CD project, only to find the discs warehoused when the market never materialized. "We had to downsize," Streber said. Now the task was to convince people that the results of *this* boom in production were really moving off the loading docks to customers, not collecting dust.

Those who saw the discs moving off the manufacturing lines into boxes and onto pallets were symbolic of all those in the Kodak trenches. They were happy to see the products moving out the door—it meant they had a job—but they were still struggling to see how Kodak's improved picture would give them something else they lacked: a sense of security. Some found it impossible to forget the past. Lynn Cooman, a lead operator in the CD finishing area, had worked at Kodak for fourteen years in each of its Rochester plant sites. Her father worked at Kodak for about four decades, but she had been laid off twice, including one stretch that lasted almost a year. Even during the downsizings that spared her, she had been bumped to various jobs. As a single parent of four children, Cooman had learned to survive. Like others, she was fairly cynical: "Nobody has much faith," she said as she folded cardboard boxes for the CD packing area. It was undeniable, though, that in her search for more security she had learned new skills that in the long run would make her more independent of the rise and fall of any corporate employer. For instance, she was now more conservative in her spending and she prepaid many of her bills, just in case she was laid off: "I don't ever want to be in that situation again." And she told her children to look outside Kodak for jobs.

The nature of the job contributed to employees' mixed elation and cynicism. Some tasks, such as folding boxes or inspecting a disc for flaws, were boring. Turnover in the department was high, so there was a prevailing sense that nothing was permanent, even the presence of the person in the next chair. There were other problems as well, evidenced by a sign on the door reminding employees that illegal drugs were forbidden in the workplace. A cartoon of Clint Eastwood saying "Go Ahead. Make One More Change" hung on the wall. All this upheaval made for a difficult adjustment, especially for the longtime employees who remembered when a job at Kodak meant steady raises and little turmoil.

Cos Palermo, the son of a barber, got his job at Kodak right after high school. He recited the day—July 12, 1965—just as he would a wedding anniversary or birthday. "We would bowl Thursday nights at the Kodak alleys and go to the Maplewood Diner for breakfast." On the weekends, the theater presented family shows hosted by Kodak. It was family, inside and outside the plant.

Now Palermo worried about the high turnover. Contract workers came and went. "We've had people come in for two hours and go on break and walk out." Some were former Kodak employees who had been laid off; they were paid about a third of what regular employees made for doing the same job, and they received no benefits. "How do you think they feel?"

Even more important than money, Palermo believed, was restoring some of the old ways of treating people like family members. He still resented the fact that Kodak closed the bowling alley, even though it had been gone for years. "I think a lot of people were really mad. That was a big deal."

During his fourth twelve-hour night shift, he took a break in the lunchroom to reflect on why, at the age of fifty, he was now ready to leave Kodak. He resented missing the last big retirement buyout, in 1991: he fell short of the necessary age and service by just a few months. "I would've gone. I've got thirty years in, and I'm tired." He was also steamed because raises were now few and far between. Unlike some others, he did get one this year, his first in four years. "It amounts to eleven dollars every two weeks." The March wage dividend, which was once virtually guaranteed, regardless of the company's financial health, was now at risk. Palermo considered the dividend more than a bonus: "It was the number one reason that a union has not stepped into Kodak," he said. "If Kodak workers didn't get a good bonus, he predicted, a union could try to organize them."

Despite their frustrations, Palermo and others showed some signs of trying to change their views on how Kodak should be. Palermo volunteered to join the "winning team," a group that met regularly to discuss improvements in teamwork. The people in CD manufacturing modeled it after CEO Fisher's winning team; the idea was to "stop looking at yourselves as losers," according to Rick Tette, an education consultant at Kodak.

The team learned to work together through a program called Headed for the Future and other group seminars and outdoor exercises on rope courses designed to build teams. They began their sessions at Camp Eastman, a rustic lodge nestled in the trees along a lake.

One afternoon, Palermo, Lynn Streber, and others formed a circle outside the lodge. Engineers, administrative assistants, and operators stand around a rope and numbered discs. As a group, they had to figure out how to step in and out of the circle formed by the rope, touching all the discs, in the least amount of time. They tried it again and again, perfecting who should shout

out the location of the next number and who is agile enough to do the running.

Tette, who began his Kodak career as a messenger in 1968, led the group's discussion of their teamwork. They consumed the bulk of the allotted period planning, and only a tiny amount of time actually doing the task. The discussion moved indoors and focused on rebuilding the team, which was now over a year old. Several members wanted to quit, some because of other pressures on their time at work, some because of how difficult it was to implement real change after seminars. "I have a degree in physics and that's easy compared to this stuff," said Scott Chase, a technical consultant at the "Gerber" plant.

They read Fisher's statements about individual worth and trust and respect, all the things these workshops discussed. Groups like this occasionally hit walls because some in management were skeptical, seeing the program as a social gathering, until they tried it themselves. Participating in the program changed their minds. Everyone realized that changing a company's culture with programs like Camp Eastman took a lot of effort. But employees like Streber were determined. "It's sacred territory. It's not like changing the budget or changing the schedule. It's something scary," she said.

The effort to teach teamwork was valued by senior management, although it almost got lost in the shuffle of restructuring. Tette began the program in 1989 for a limited number of Kodak Park manufacturing teams—for example, the paper manufacturing group. He eventually hooked up with Project Adventure, a nonprofit group based in Hamilton, Massachusetts, that works with companies on building relationships. Some initially dubbed the project playing games in the woods. But productivity rose and defects fell after more of their crews attended Tette's seminars. One by one, managers became believers when they saw the payoff.

Tette's success didn't insulate him from Kodak's restructurings. In the summer of 1994, he was reassigned as a tuition-aid consultant, which made little sense to anyone. His boss came out to the woods one day to deliver the news. "I can't say that I was happy," Tette admitted. But he tried to be positive about change, just as he preached in his seminars.

News began to spread that Tette was now at a desk job and Camp Eastman was history. One by one, his clients throughout Kodak began sending E-mail and voicemail messages to George Fisher. Tette met with the current tuition-aid consultant, who was being bumped to another job, and began the process of making the switch. "While that's going on, these people just kept hammering away," he recounted. Manufacturing people asked Fisher and others to visit their workplace so they could demonstrate what Tette's programs meant in terms of improved results. One employee told Fisher that the program was "the most beneficial thing I've ever done."

Within a month, Tette's manager asked for a Saturday meeting, where he delivered the good news: Tette would be reassigned as an education consultant to restore his old programs.

Tette hired Project Adventure as his consultants; they began training Kodakers to lead the groups so that the company could eventually do the job itself.

One of his first projects in the Fisher era was to design a pilot workshop, "Personal Pride, Power and Performance," a primer on living the corporate values. The idea was to make sure the values didn't just sound like more fluff, to make them part of everyday life at Kodak, and to show clearly that Fisher's words weren't a lot of hot air. "Part of the corporate values is continuous improvement in personal renewal. I can't make an improvement in this company until I make an improvement in me." And true to Fisher's mission to reduce cycle time, Tette collapsed his original four-day program into three.

For his test group, he invited various people from throughout Kodak to the new Starfish Lodge. The name came from a story that Tette likes to tell in his seminars: A man goes to the beach at dawn each day, picks up a starfish from the beach, and flings it back into the water. Another man asks him why. The rescuer explains that starfish will die if left in the sun. There are millions of beached starfish, so why bother? "How can your effort make any difference?" The man tosses another starfish back into the ocean and replies: "It makes a difference *to this one.*"

Eventually, the now-bare wall under the Starfish Lodge plaque would be covered with photos of Kodak people trying to make a difference. For now, there were posters to remind the group of some basics: "Trust: Knowing with confidence that others have your best interests at heart." A dinosaur cartoon read: "If I always do what I've always done, then I'll always get what I've always gotten. You can change without growing, but you can't grow without changing."

The group gathered at 7:30 A.M. for their final day: a trip to the woods and the rope exercises in the trees. As they drank coffee and munched on muffins, Tette turned up some Yanni tunes on the CD player and read from *Gold Nuggets,* a collection of readings for experiential education. The passage today was from Shel Silverstein's *A Light in the Attic:* a little boy and an elderly man commiserate about how grown-ups sometimes don't pay attention to them. "We don't pay attention to a lot of people," Tette said. "We should."

A test of the group's efforts to build trust and commitment to others came when they headed for the woods. They learned to tie themselves with security ropes of teal, pink, and yellow that would keep them safe when they climbed the trees. Mark Murray of Project Adventure coached them on their Studebaker wraps, so named because, like the car, they look the same in front and in back. "It will take an act of God for you to fall out of this," he assured the team. They tied square knots and wound the ropes around and around themselves, squirming a bit: wearing ropes isn't comfy or natural.

The first exercise was the flying squirrel. Each team member was hooked to an overhead rope, hoisted off the ground, and swung through a clearing. "This takes a strong commitment by the group," Murray said. "If you let go of the rope, the squirrel becomes roadkill."

One by one, they took turns swinging from the rope. Some were nervous; others seemed to relish the idea of swinging fifteen feet off the ground. "It's awesome!" said Dan Long, a supervisor at Kodak Park, as he returned to earth. Bob Streber, a supervisor in analytical services at Elmgrove, the husband of Lynn from the CD-manufacturing group, paused before taking his turn. "Should we do a test first to see how I hang?"

"By the neck till death," jabbed Jim Rogers, a supervisor in motion-picture finishing.

The team ran to pull Streber off the ground. It looked as if he might career into a nearby oak or beech tree. But he cleared both. "A guy could get used to this."

Monica Rigney, an instructional designer, had waited until the end to take her turn. She was nervous, but said: "Squirrel ready for a slow and gentle ascent." As she was being raised off the ground, she relaxed and offered her best Mary Martin impression. "I'm flying!" She was voted best flying squirrel for showing courage. It is an emotional scene as the others congratulate her for overcoming her fear.

The next task was far more challenging: the team members climbed spikes set in a tree, to reach a telephone-pole bridge, which leads to another tree. Once across the pole, they leaned forward and dropped to the ground. For some, climbing the tree was enough. Rigney got to the top, farther than she had expected to go. Proud of her efforts, she leaned over and kissed the tree.

Tette coached her to apply the feeling of accomplishment to her life inside Kodak. "You took a risk here. What are the types of risks you're willing to take at work in order to allow personal pride to be seen by more people?" She stayed aloft for a few minutes, then returned to the ground.

Streber walked slowly across the pole. "I'm definitely out of my element," he said quietly, focusing on the pole. "You're doing great," called Rigney, anchoring the rope below. The hardest part of the exercise was letting go so the group could lower him to the ground. "I was focused and then I started thinking: 'How am I gonna get off this log?' " says Streber.

Rogers related the climb to work. "It was a rush. I got out of my comfort zone." He figured that was what he needed: "This gives me more discipline to do uncomfortable things at work."

They had all seen more than enough uncomfortable tasks in round after round of downsizings and reshufflings. Some, like

Rigney, were relative newcomers to Kodak. An instructional designer, Rigney joined the company in 1991 after leaving Anderson Consulting. "Since I've been at Kodak, we've had five reorganizations and three downsizings"; the most recent one to shake up the human resources department, she said, was "a bloodbath." Many resented her because she kept her job while others were let go. "I had a skill that was needed by the company. But it caused a lot of resentment from people who were friends." The experience was traumatic; Rigney likened the aftermath of layoffs to that of the Holocaust, when survivors pondered why they made it while others perished. "It's a horrible sense of shame. Why am I still here when people with twenty-five years of experience are affected?"

One of the people in her division was Bill Lembach, a second-generation Kodaker who became director of the company's food service, the largest industrial food-service operation in the world. At its peak, the team fed 46,000 people every day in sixty-four dining facilities. Lembach ran a $40 million business with 340 employees and turned it into a profitable part of the company. He was featured in food-service publications as one of the country's leading experts in the field.

But in one of Kodak's various reorganizations, senior management decided to farm out the service to an outside vendor. Lembach tried to buy the business, but Kodak sold it to Marriott instead. When human resources downsized, losing 28 percent of its jobs, he was demoted to director of administration and operations at Kodak Education and Development Center. He took a $24,000 pay cut and lost some vacation, stock options, and performance bonuses. "That was not an easy thing to do," he admitted.

But his response to those material losses was tempered by the perspective he had gained from earlier events. In 1992, Lembach suffered a heart attack. Today, he spoke of his life, his career, and his future with a clarity that others lack. Recovering from the heart attack gave him a second chance at life. He had plenty of reason to resent the upheaval at Kodak, but his brush with death had left him determined not to let resentment suck the life out of him. "It gave me a different perspective on life. It tells you what's really important. Material things no longer have that same priority for me." He looked forward to retirement; he plans to visit Australia for an extended vacation with his wife. He was eligible for the big retirement buyout in 1991, but passed up the chance. "I can't change the past."

Lembach was a believer in the outdoor exercises. After completing the course, he reflected on how the various tasks helped him let go of the past. "We need to focus on the good things." He was so impressed with the program that he planned to go through the course again, this time with those in his department.

Letting go of the past was difficult, especially for those who believed that Kodak had made promises it was now breaking. Employees and retired workers were especially vocal when Fisher tinkered with the benefits that had made Kodak one of the most generous companies in America and helped get it into financial trouble in earlier years. A 1993 survey of benefits showed that Kodak ranked third overall in the United States—a rank it had maintained for more than twenty years. The wage dividend was 172 percent above average for companies with profit-sharing plans. Kodak's retirement plan was 33 percent more generous than average, and its life insurance was 53 percent above average.

So the retirement plan was changed to, in effect, require workers to stay longer to get the same benefits. Life insurance for future retirees was reduced. Health care for retirees was also changed, prompting an angry response by some. Of all those affected by Kodak's changes, retirees were often the most bitter. The paternalistic employer they once knew is now changing the rules, and in their opinion, breaking promises that came with a job at Kodak. Hugh Race, a retired structural mechanic, called the changes callous and accused Fisher of "going back on Kodak's promises to us and attempting to steal our hard-earned benefits. In the meantime, Mr. Fisher's nest continues well-feathered by his overly indulgent board of directors. . . . This is the first time I've ever been ashamed to be a Kodak retiree." Race and his wife, Laura, picketed Kodak's headquarters in the summer of 1995, carrying signs that said, "Kodak Unfair to Their Retirees."

Explaining the changes, Fisher wrote to employees that Kodak had to make radical cuts because "we cannot survive based on our reputation alone . . . we must fundamentally change the way we run the business." The employee newsletter published a chart showing how Fisher's performance would be measured. Half of his performance score was based on financial measures that reflect improved operations, such as how much return Kodak made on its assets. Another 30 percent of his pay was linked to customer satisfaction, and 20 percent to employee satisfaction and public responsibility. Fisher said the balance would change after Kodak had assured shareholders of "our financial viability."

Indeed, shareholders were being rewarded for his efforts, as was clear from the steady climb in Kodak's stock price. But the company was delivering the results through focusing first on what employees were doing to make better products and get them to customers faster. Fisher believed everything could be measured and tracked, making it easier to see problems and gauge progress. In the end, how well the products sold would show whether the company was really making progress. But by using such formulas on everything from cycle times for product development to the CEO's pay, Kodak was making strides in emphasizing real improvements, not just short-term fixes to boost its stock.

Fisher got plenty of feedback on his efforts from all corners, especially employees. The company had formed a corporate "ombuds" office to act as a neutral party to whom employees can take complaints or concerns without fear of being tagged troublemakers. The corporate ombudswoman, Deborah Cardillo, takes careful measures to ensure her visitors' privacy. Her office waiting area has high walls, and telephone records for her line are mailed directly to her rather than being part of Kodak's general phone bill. She shreds her notes and keeps no files on an issue once it is resolved. Cardillo reports to the ethics committee, which included Fisher, and to the public policy committee of Kodak's board of directors. She is represented by outside counsel not linked to Kodak's other law firms.

Messages to her office range from complaints about performance appraisals and job changes to calls from whistle-blower types who want to report wrongdoing. One such call led to what she considered a "serious" investigation related to hiring practices at a Kodak office outside of Rochester. She declined to elaborate.

The idea of using an ombuds office started on a small scale at Elmgrove in 1987, when Frank Zaffino went through rounds of layoffs and saw that people needed an outlet and he needed a neutral source of feedback. Since then he had heard a wide range of problems: increased family tensions, financial trouble, and drug abuse. "Part of it has to do with society in general," Zaffino said. "Part of it has to do, however, with the working environment that we're creating here." Absenteeism at Elmgrove was low, a fact that he attributed partly to fear. "I wish I could say they all come because they just can't wait to get to work. There might be some of that." But there were also some who said: "This son of a bitch is gonna let me go."

Many Kodakers mentioned their fears that someone would eventually reach a breaking point and react violently to pressures. Some left messages on factory walls, spewing obscenities at management. The company's security department had dogs trained to sniff out bombs. "We get a fair number of threats," said one manager. One Kodaker recalled how everyone feared that a particular colleague would react violently when he got the news that he had been laid off. His coworkers dubbed him "Defense," the name of the character portrayed by Michael Douglas in the movie *Falling Down*. The movie character goes berserk after losing his job, shooting up a fast-food restaurant, among other acts. Thankfully, the Kodak version of Defense left without incident. But to help avoid such problems, in 1994, the ombuds office began a program called "Preventing Violence in the Workplace."

Lane Riland worried that the increasing tensions and violence in society would eventually infiltrate Kodak. In a different era, mad-as-hell workers produced the trade union movement. But Riland figured that younger workers didn't see unions as a solution. So what was the alternative? "It's pretty easy to buy a gun if you want," he said. "I'm starting to worry 'cause I see this" just as the post office has. "Life has gotten pretty cheap. But that to me is normal human behavior if people are pushed too far. And in our culture, I wouldn't expect us to be the first, I'd expect that maybe in fast-food restaurants. Sooner or later, it will probably creep into different businesses."

Riland was working on keeping even closer tabs on how the workforce felt, expanding the company survey to reach 25 percent of all worldwide employees each quarter. More important, the results are being more widely distributed to employees, not just to some in management. "We used to only share the good news," Riland said. But that was "an insult to people's intelligence. They know what reality is." He sometimes found as much as six pages of single-spaced commentary attached to his survey sheets. Responses ranged from "Will there be a company to retire from?" to "Hallelujah! George has come!" Most writers were happy that the company finally had a focus, rather than a "direction *du jour,*" as Riland put it.

One of the best ways for senior management to understand what's going on is to mingle with the troops. At "town meetings," held at least twice a year, Fisher hammered away at the basics and delivered news about improvements. He reminded employees that improvements, such as progress on his lofty goals for improved cycle times, would take time. "I'm sure a few of you throw up your hands and say they must be smoking pot. Well, we weren't. And I'm not." He paused. "I don't even have to talk about inhaling." Without progress, he declared, "we're gonna fall behind."

Fisher reviewed the progress to date. Sales rose by 14 percent, and earnings climbed 20 percent, in the first quarter of 1995. Return on net assets stood at about 19 percent, meaning that everybody's wage dividend would be 5 percent in 1996 if the RONA figure didn't climb or fall. "We would hope to be able to do better than that." The company's stock price had gone up, too, adding about $5 billion in market value to where it stood when Fisher took over in late 1993.

Fisher faced a tougher job of persuading people inside the company that Kodak is changing. The majority of employees still craved the security blanket that used to come with a Kodak job.

When asked if they felt secure, about 25 percent of employees said yes; the national figure was closer to 40 percent. Kodakers got nervous whenever there was a report of the company selling off another chunk of its business.

Fisher read more grim figures. Only 30 percent of the company's employees thought Kodak had a "sincere interest" in their future. Feedback on benefit changes was negative, reflecting changes in the wage dividend and retirement plans. But in overall job satisfaction, the score had moved up for the first time in a long while. Fisher asked Kodakers to keep believing. "This company is no better than the sum of its parts. You are the people that really make the difference. It's you who are changing the picture."

9

The Class of '93

Each Sunday morning, Al Waugh and his family drive down Wegman Road to Gates Presbyterian Church, a brown-and-red-brick sanctuary with a tall steeple that opens on one side to reveal a giant bell. A large white cross looms on top of the steeple, a stark contrast to the gray clouds overhead this morning.

The Reverend Bob Kaiser, pastor of the church, delivered a message of hope to those who were trying to overcome problems. He was familiar with the strife in the community, troubled by economic woes and the social despair they generate. "People are desperate for hope," he told his congregation this Sunday morning. "God's presence enables us to be people of hope who put their faith into action." He encouraged the parishioners to do more to heal their troubled society—for example, by supporting the church's program to help eliminate violence by selling locks for guns and sponsoring programs to feed hungry families in Rochester. "Let us find those corners where people are lighting candles of hope and peace. God is at work in our world, and this God will never let us be totally crushed or diminished."

Al Waugh found he could escape the chaos of everyday life when he came to the church. Here he could think and pray. He could put his life into perspective and count his blessings as he sat with his wife, Mary. Waugh tried to share his hope with others at the "Class of '93" support group, which still met every other Tuesday night at the church. He shared stories of his own life to remind the others to live each moment. At one meeting, he broke the news that another friend had recently been diagnosed with cancer. "It takes these kinds of things," he told those gathered for the evening meeting. "When it strikes close to home, it's one of those reminders to hug the wife and pet the dog a couple more times."

The group, formed after the 1993 layoffs, was a place of comfort for Waugh and other regulars, among them Bob Couture and Paul Langlois. They looked forward to their twice-a-month sessions as an outlet for discussing everything from the day's news to their ongoing job searches. At times, the meeting was a spiritual time-out, when they reflected on their lives.

They met in the church's new annex, furnished with meeting tables, a kitchenette, and comfortable sofas, a switch from the early days in the basement nursery, with its cribs, rockers, and stuffed animals. Some nights, the church annex was a crowded sanctuary for a lot of troubled people. Down the hall were Alcoholics Anonymous and a bereavement support group. Walls were decorated with a poster of sandals and footprints in the sand, along with a verse from Psalm 25:

Show me your ways, O Lord.
Teach Me Your Path.
Guide Me in Your Truth.

Friendships in this life-after-Kodak group had helped the members cope with changes in their lives. Even after they found jobs, they came back to the group. It was their corner of hope and peace.

As they munched on chocolate chip cookies, Al passed around a cartoon he had clipped from the paper: Two men talking about the economy.

"For every job lost, two are created," says one.

"I know," the other replies. "I'm working both of them now."

It was too true to be funny for Al. He had found a job at another local manufacturing company, but he supplemented his income with a night-shift janitor's job here at the church. And Mary Waugh now worked full-time as a teacher's aide. With three jobs between them, they were barely matching Al's old Kodak salary.

At least he'd found a job. Bob Couture was still looking. After a couple of very quiet years, he was getting phone calls, mostly from out-of-town companies, ranging from Eureka, the vacuum cleaner company, to Hewlett-Packard. "When it rains, it pours," he told the group. A recent trip to Bloomington for the Eureka interview had gone well. "It's kind of a nice job. I'd be project manager responsible for a particular product." He was still waiting for a call-back. Meanwhile, another job interview had landed him a consulting job, helping a company design a paper machine. Cincinnati Microwave's headhunter called to see if he was interested in a chief engineer's job.

The Hewlett-Packard opening was for a reliability engineer. He had been invited out for a two-day interview, plus an extra day to look around Boise—which sounded great to Couture, who would have liked to live out west, close to the Rockies. "Once I'd get to Boise, I'd want to stay."

The most puzzling job lead had come from his local search: a Rochester headhunter submitted his name for an opening at Kodak's government systems division, which had landed some new contracts. "I have all the qualifications, and they were desperate to fill the job," he said. But the headhunter called back to say that he wasn't eligible for the opening. The reason? "They can't take you because you retired," he said. Obviously, this was news to Bob. "If Kodak would like to retroactively provide me with a retirement allowance, I'd be happy to retire. But I'm not retired." He told the headhunter to go back and remind Kodak that he had been laid off. He predicted one of two outcomes: either Kodak would invite him in for an interview, or they'd say, No, thanks. "Kodak doesn't want us back, for the most part."

The Class of '93 was part of the new lexicon of downsizing: you weren't laid off; you were impacted, rightsized, reengineered. Then there was the term "RED," an abbreviation for a bit of double-speak: "Reverse-employed." The group's favorite euphemism seemed to be "RIFed," from "reduction in force," a term Kodak once used for its layoffs.

Paul Langlois, who was on a contract job in Syracuse, had

driven back this evening for the meeting. He pulled out a copy of *USA Today* with a story that proved some people were finding work at shrinking companies. He passed around a clip about IBM's decision to hire an executive chef for $120,000.

"That does sound like a good career," Couture said.

"I'll start as a short-order cook," Langlois replied. "I guess you can't compete in the global marketplace on an empty stomach."

"Instead of feeding some CEO a line of shit, just feed him shit," Couture fired back, prompting a hearty laugh around the room.

Al pulled out further proof that even Kodak was looking for help. "Did anyone else get a chuckle from the Kodak ad? They're looking for copier technicians to repair Xerox machines. It would be a hoot to see if I qualify."

Couture wasn't optimistic about his chances, especially after the headhunter's call. "It will really piss me off if Gordon Urlacher gets a job before I do," he said. Urlacher, a former Rochester police chief, had recently been released from prison after his conviction for embezzling more than $300,000 in police department funds.

"You just have to get yourself put away for a while, Bob," Langlois joked.

Reviewing his place on the food chain, Couture offered: "There are real workers, ex-felons, and ex-Kodakers." He studied a second Kodak ad being passed around the room. He was qualified for several of the openings listed, and that made him rather sullen. He pitched the ad across the table and shook his head. "I'm sorry. This doesn't make fundamental sense."

Little had made sense for Couture and others in the two years since they were laid off from Kodak. Ever since Bob lost his job, the Coutures had had an ongoing debate about whether they should stockpile supplies for when money got even tighter, or whether they should start selling off possessions so they would have less to move if they needed to pay their own moving expenses to take a new job in a different city. They hadn't made progress in either direction. Stacks of magazines and books sat in the living room.

If Bob did get an out-of-town offer, they weren't optimistic about the prospects for selling their house. Neighboring houses were up for sale but were drawing little traffic, despite price cuts and frequent open houses. The weak real estate market was a big factor for the Coutures. They didn't want to slide backward, moving to an area where they'd get a tiny little house for the same amount they had already invested in five acres and a spacious home. Indeed, that was one of the biggest reasons Bob turned down the only job offered him in his first two years of unemployment. A medical equipment maker in Cleveland talked to him just before Christmas 1994. The prospect of work should've been reason to feel good at Christmas, their third unhappy holiday since the December 1992 rumblings that Kodak was planning a New Year's layoff. Every year, Bob was preoccupied with the job search. They had limited their purchases to practical gifts. In 1994, Bob's son, Chris, didn't make the trip back from Colorado. "I couldn't afford to bring him back," Bob says. The good news was that Chris had decided to return to school after taking a hiatus from college.

After the holiday, Bob and Meredith visited Cleveland. He was offered the job, and they began to search for a house. They also had their Rochester home appraised, a depressing exercise. Realtors said that prices in the Cleveland market should be comparable to those in Rochester. "We figured we could get something reasonably close to this," Bob said. "But the depression of the Rochester market hasn't caught up with the stats yet." They found that for the money they could expect for their Rochester home, they could get only a tiny ranch house on a small lot in the suburbs an hour outside Cleveland. The Coutures dashed around the city, looking at thirteen houses in two days. They even ventured an hour outside downtown to look at an Amish house that didn't have electricity. They found they would have to spend a great deal more money to get as much space. "You can always say we'll take less house, but that affects your whole perception," Bob said. The experience was a grim reminder of yet another piece of the American dream that's slipping away: buy a house and it will appreciate by the time you're ready to move on to a bigger place. Nowadays, many families are faced with losing money on a house in a sale rather than being able to trade up.

The Coutures agonized all weekend about what to do. Finally Bob turned down the job offer. With the high cost of housing and no guarantee that Meredith could find a comparable job, the move would have been very risky. Bob realized that was the smart decision in terms in their overall security, but found it hard to walk away from a job after so many months of being at home. "Here was somebody who wanted me. Having to turn it down was tougher than I expected."

The New Year brought other disappointments. Leads on other jobs didn't turn into offers. Bob did land a consulting job using the new computer equipment he had bought with his Kodak severance package. Spending winter days at the computer in their spare bedroom at least kept him in touch with his work. And he had become quite proficient at searching for all sorts of things on the Internet. Those days, their dog, Rosie, stretched out on the bed, watching him work.

Meredith was frustrated that Bob hadn't allowed himself to do much besides look for work during his two years of unemployment. They did take one vacation about eight months after the layoff: they met Meredith's parents at Rocky Mountain National Park, where he could watch elk and other wildlife. For the first time in his life, Bob kept a brief journal to chronicle his vacation. It offers a telling look at his frustration.

> Sunday: "Beastie patrol" at 6:00 A.M. Meredith is actually up. Deer and elk by the side of the road. Frame-filling shots with the 300mm. I need to live here! If I live here, I'll have to develop the same disdainful attitude toward the tourists that some of the locals seem to have.
>
> The sound of an elk bugling is like the sound of a loon, it stays with you and you want to hear it again soon.

By Monday, it had snowed two inches, which he described as "white velvet on ancient rock." They scouted around Boulder and Estes. By Friday, he was depressed.

> Friday: Our last full day here. I don't want to leave.
> The best morning yet for elk viewing. Try and take scenics and you find yourself elbow to antler with them. . . . Met Chris at the

appointed time. Took an old-time picture. Had a good time. There was not enough time to say what needed to be said.

This is the last night here. There was certainly not enough time here to do all we wanted to do.

I still don't want to leave, but I can't see any way to stay, not in the short term, not in the long term. This was vacation, life is life.

Trying to understand what's going on in his life, Bob studied the journal. "When I go back and read it, it kind of reflects the whole upward swing very early in the week and the gradual decline. The thing that isn't in the journal is the month-long crash afterward. It was a month when I was pretty much paralyzed." A box of his fifteen rolls of slides was sitting untouched in the living room. "They've never been looked at," Bob admitted. "I can't bring myself to do that."

Meredith regretted that they hadn't taken the trip long before the layoff, when they both gave far too many hours to work. "I had five weeks of vacation saved up in addition to the five weeks I had every year," Bob said. "It was saved up because I wasn't taking it, because I was doing the job, by God."

He confided that they did a bit of dreaming in the Rockies and that he'd like to start his own business. He and Meredith looked at an art gallery for sale near the entrance of the park; could have expanded it into a photography shop, "and we could live here," he figured. The daydream was perfect, except for the reality of running a small business. There is a bit of escape in the fantasy of never working for anybody but yourself. "There are times when I wish that we had more guts and less common sense. . . . I'm not sure that taking a gamble and losing would be any worse than what I've been through for the last two years." But soon, Bob came back to the reality of a job search and waiting for the phone to ring. There was little talk of other vacations.

Day trips were growing scarce, too. On the weekends, the Coutures ran errands, which used to keep them out of the house until five P.M. Eventually, even those trips were ending earlier. "Now we're back by two." One of their least favorite errands was going to the newsstand to buy a national employment guide, which lists job ads from around the country. "It's kind of a real downer," Meredith said. During the workweek, they sometimes fought about what time she was coming home. He'd call to find out, because he was making dinner and wanted to time its completion to her arrival. "You look at the housewives of the sixties. I'm making a lot of the same complaints." Bob's unemployment had put a strain on their marriage. "If somebody had posed the scenario three or four years ago and said: 'You're gonna go through this and are you gonna make it? Are you still gonna be married or not? Will you still be sane? Will you commit suicide? Will you just go ahead and dig the trail deeper into the woods? I would have probably said that I'd have crumbled . . . we would probably have crumbled also." But they had endured.

When Kodak raises were announced in the summer of 1995, Meredith didn't immediately tell Bob the news that she got one, and that it was above average. He figured it was an unintentional oversight, but she admitted that she didn't like to discuss work with him. "There's a piece of her life that I'm not sharing. Not good. Not good at all," Bob said.

And he worried that he'd never be able to make an impact again. At Kodak, he had felt he was making a difference. "Everybody wants to leave something behind them. I spent twenty-two years working at a job. Now there is nothing that's gonna be pulled out and identified as, 'You know, that good old boy Bob Couture took care of this problem.' As soon as you disappear, these things disappear. It bothers me. I've gotta go off now and try and leave something behind me in the second half of my adult life. That's gonna be tough."

Al Waugh also questioned what the future held: "I find myself back at the bottom of the heap starting over again." The jobs out there didn't come close to paying Kodak salaries. The Waughs and their two children had done a lot of belt-tightening in the months after his layoff, and money grew really tight after Al's severance pay ran out in the beginning of 1994. "We went into hunker-down, survival kind of mode." They cut back even on the basics. There were fewer trips to the grocery store, something unheard-of in earlier days. And when they did shop, they learned to buy cheaper food. "We introduced ourselves to brands of food that we never would have really thought of using before. It's the cheapest and that's why you buy it," Al said.

The money crunch was the factor that finally made Al realize his world had changed. Like many others who followed all the rules, Al and Mary Waugh were now learning to adapt to big changes. They no longer took things for granted. They knew they had enjoyed a taste of the American dream that many others never get. "I started thinking of myself as a poorer person. I once thought of myself as middle-class or upper-middle-class. It never really dawned on me why all these people were out there with two-income families and nobody at home taking care of the kids while I was making a good buck at Kodak and being able to do what I've always done. I had my wife at home, my kids going to school, and I was providing the income. All of a sudden, it was a lot more obvious to me why people were out there doing that. It's not because women's lib made every woman want to be part of the income-earning part of the family. It was that people were making a lot less, and they *had* to work." This really troubled him: "I've always been a believer that if there was any way possible, the best place for a mother if she could handle kids was to be there as a homemaker. You have the best long-term results in raising some decent kids."

But that changed at the Waughs', after Mary had spent more than a decade as a stay-at-home mom. After working as a department store clerk, she was hired as a teachers' aide, working with children with disabilities. "I'd still rather stay home with the kids," she said. Fortunately, their children were nineteen and fourteen when Al lost his job. Obviously, they were old enough to be less dependent on their mother than when they were small. But Mary's full-time job meant they had fewer meals together and less time for family activities.

After Al's severance pay ran out, he began to worry about finding a job, any job, just to keep some money coming in. He was rejected for a janitorial job at a nearby high school. "I was told that I was overqualified to sweep floors." Instead, he took on a part-time job as church janitor at Gates Presbyterian, where he had always been an active member of the congregation. He did it for the money, but also to spend time inside the sanctuary.

Sometimes, he was there thirty hours a week, mostly at night or during the weekend. Some of his friends wondered why he would bother with such a low-paying job, but Al didn't like the idea of having no job. And he hoped that he could turn the janitor's post over to his son Rob, as soon as he got another full-time engineering job. But there was a deeper reason to take this instead of some other minimum-wage job. "It's a spiritual kind of thing. I feel like I want to be there." He couldn't explain it: "I really am waiting to find out."

As the months pass, Al began to see some answers to the chaos in his life. The time away from work gave him the opportunity to help a Sudanese refugee family who moved to Rochester. Church volunteers helped them with everything from shopping to doctor's visits. Al spent a lot of time trying to ease the family's adjustment to life in a new country. He helped them find an apartment and even led mini–food drives to fill their kitchen cupboards. He showed them how to ride the bus rather than walk down the center of the freeways. No detail was too small for Al: he taught the family how to use Q-Tips instead of seagull feathers to clean their ears. When the expectant mother went into labor with their second child, the family called Al. "They wanted me to help push," he said with a laugh.

Seeing the refugees and hearing Mary's stories of working with disabled schoolchildren helped Al gain some perspective on his life and made him feel less sorry for himself. "I'm less driven by money now. There are a lot of things that mean more." Al and Mary spent more time with church friends and volunteered for all sorts of church fund-raisers.

By the summer of 1994, things were starting to look up. All of a sudden, the phone started to ring. Al had seven interviews in three weeks. And he got an offer—an engineering job at Alliance Automation, a company where he'd been applying for jobs for the past eighteen months. It was close to home, a plus, but meant a big pay cut. "Two thirds is better than no thirds," Al said. He kept his church janitor's job, because the Waughs had bills leftover from all those months when he was unemployed. His days began to stretch from dawn until midnight, because he often left

Alliance to go to the church. With the couple's three jobs, they were just about making what he did at Kodak.

After Al had spent nearly a year at the new job, the Waughs decided to treat themselves to a much-deserved family vacation at a relative's lake cottage. But Al decided that he had to stay behind. His new job offered just three days of vacation time. Besides, he could use those days to clean the church.

Al was busy and making money again, but that had its price. "We really don't do as much together. Life is just sort of turning into more of a survival state." One of his birthday gifts to Mary was a new pad of brightly colored Post-It notes "so we could communicate with each other."

Other long-term effects of his job loss remained to be seen. Their daughter, Katie, had finished a degree at a local business college, but she was having trouble finding a job other than a retail position, and at job interviews, she learned that she was qualified only for low-paying work. She was considering going back to college for another degree. Al wasn't sure he and Mary could afford another round of tuition bills; he was already wondering how they'd send their second child, Rob, to college. Thankfully, Rob was quite resourceful. A high school junior, he had a thriving business of pet sitting, lawn mowing, and other odd jobs, and had already saved enough to buy a used Jeep. Both at home and at school, he got a lot of lessons on the plight of the unemployed. In one class, he saw the movie *Roger & Me,* a satiric look at the impact of General Motors' layoffs on the town of Flint, Michigan. His own career plans had changed; from the age of five, he told his parents that he wanted to be just like his father and work as an engineer. But after Al lost his job, Rob started to talk about becoming a photographer. "I always sort of liked the idea that he wanted to do the same thing I did," Al said. "There's no more talk of doing like Dad did."

"Do you blame him?" Mary replied.

Other households had adjusted their long-term plans following layoffs at Kodak. Paul and Ruth Langlois found that his lost job forced them to adjust to a lot of time apart. After Paul's first year of unemployment, he finally got a temporary position at

Penn Traffic, a retailing company in Syracuse. Each Monday morning, he drove to Syracuse; there, he spent three nights at a Howard Johnson's motel. He drove home at least one night during the week, and for weekends. "It's a way of life for people who don't have attachments," he said. The commute was wearying, but both Paul and Ruth were happy he got the job after an entire year of looking for work. "There was a separation, but the alternative was horrible," Ruth said.

Paul, like other contractors, was paid 70 percent of the wages, with the contract house getting the rest as a commission for placing him in the job. Some houses offer contractors a chance to buy health insurance. It can be difficult working alongside the full-time employees, who often fear the contractors will end up replacing them. In Paul's case, a six-month contract turned into fourteen months. At that point, he decided that it was wise to return to school for more computer training, and enrolled in a ten-week program at Boston University. The contract house said it would help him land a job back in Rochester.

The Boston University class of twenty resembled his Kodak support group: people in their forties who were caught in cutbacks. Hearing their stories, Paul realized he was very lucky to have a wife who was still working. Even more important, they were both healthy: "Some of the stories are almost tragic. One man was laid off from Digital in his fifties. Now he has pancreatic cancer. It changed my attitude about a lot of things like health care. There are just too many people that fall through the cracks in the system the way we have it now."

Though he'd been out of college for years, Paul proved to be a good student, earning five A's and three A-pluses in the course. Now he faced a job market in which applicants needed to show they had experience, even though the computer program he studied was relatively new. So the Langlois family still didn't know whether they'd have to leave Rochester for a new job, or whether they could stay put. Ruth was now willing to go either way. "I found that difficult at first. Now it doesn't bother me." Paul was a little more tense about starting another job search. "You start feeling the stress again, just like two years ago." They got a chance to celebrate some good times during the summer of

1995, when two of their three sons graduated from college. Ruth called the ceremonies "the proudest moments of our lives." And both sons had jobs.

In the fall, Paul got a phone call about a contracting job—back at Kodak, in the same building where Ruth worked. He went for the interview and accepted the job. "It was kind of strange," he said. "It was the first time I was on Kodak property in two and a half years." Both he and Ruth saw some improvements at Kodak, but they knew that the company had a long way to go. Nor did Paul predict that he'd be at Kodak for the rest of his career. "I'm not sure I'll ever feel comfortable again with both of us working for the same company," he said. "You're putting all your eggs in one basket." He and Ruth had a healthier attitude now about working in the new economy, where jobs come and go. Paul wanted to have portable skills so he would be ready to make the next move if Kodak once again tapped him for a layoff. In some ways, he was better off than others, because he had realized the importance of polishing skills to keep a job or to help find a new one.

Another member of the Class of '93 also found that companies like Kodak still needed her skills. In late 1994, Patty Minisce, the systems analyst, found a contract job near where Ruth and Paul Langlois work at Kodak Park. The pay was similar to her old Kodak salary, except she didn't get the annual wage dividend. It was a huge relief after working as a waitress. "I fell right back into it. It's nice to be back at work." Her five-month contract was extended a couple of times, but she never knew how long she'd be employed. She was reminded of her temporary status at a staff meeting, when a manager asked for volunteers to take over her assignments when she was gone. "I darn near died," she said. Contract workers are often told that contracts at Kodak last only a year. But there are exceptions throughout the company.

The contract house assured Patty that systems analysts were in demand and she'd get a new job after her Kodak contract expired. "I get very nervous," she said. "I still remember when I was not getting any money." The family was still catching up on bills. "We have not totally gotten ourselves out of a hole we dug when I was not working. You end up turning to your charge cards." She wanted to save money, but found it nearly impossible. "You hear that rule of thumb: save up six months of salary. I don't know how anybody could do it. We can't even break even." The Minisces' twenty-five-year-old house needed a new roof, and the furnace quit shortly after their son, Zachary, was born. A planned trip to Disney World with their children was postponed indefinitely. "It's been very disappointing to them. They just don't understand."

Despite her initial anger about getting laid off, Patty's attitude toward Kodak had mellowed a bit. For instance, she didn't get as mad as she used to about George Fisher's multimillion-dollar pay. "If he gets some results for the company, I guess he is worth that much." Like others in the company, she saw the changes he was making, and was willing to give him time to prove he was worth his big paycheck.

A crisis can make families rethink their lives; for their part, the Minisces concluded that money can't be the primary fuel that keeps a family going. "You can't lose sight of what's most important," said Patty's husband, Skip. "You can get wrapped up in lack of money. But it doesn't cost money to focus on your family." Two-year-old Zachary, dressed in denim bib overalls, darted around the room, giggling and clapping. "You can draw from love you get from them." Naturally, Skip wished he was able to do more. "My pride got hurt. But that will always mend."

Some contracting jobs at Kodak led to more permanent jobs, if there was such a thing as a permanent job at the company. John Wise, another member of the Class of '93, got a contract position as a quality assurance engineer in the health sciences division in August 1994. The contract was extended, and he had a chance to attend an internal job fair for openings in the government systems division. He interviewed for three different jobs and was hired as a test engineer at Elmgrove. In his new job, he was seeing the difference in Kodak, as George Fisher pushed everyone to be more accountable.

"They're not happening overnight, but I'm seeing some culture changes." John had attended discussions about improvements and the push for six-sigma quality, as well as a half-day seminar on return on net assets. He sees less finger-pointing when there's a problem, and more emphasis on teamwork. "You don't see the kaffeeklatsch groups hanging around the vending machines or sitting in the break areas for long periods of time like they used to. There's more of an attitude of 'I need to get the job done.'" More information was shared by upper management via E-mail and company newsletters. "That was never the case before," John said.

Indeed, he got to meet the CEO, a rare occurrence in the old Kodak. Shortly after he was hired, he attended a town meeting at which Fisher fielded questions from employees. Later, they lined up to shake his hand. Wise waited patiently to introduce himself and shake the new CEO's hand.

"I was affected by the layoffs back in '93," he told Fisher. "And I was recently hired back in government systems. They had authorization to go outside. I was excited about that."

"Neat," Fisher said. "Glad to have you back."

Wise explained that he had worked in government systems, then been transferred to office imaging, where he was laid off a few months later.

"Oh, boy. That was poor timing," Fisher said. "How do you feel about coming back?"

"Great. Great. I think it's a lot of your efforts that are beginning to turn this company around."

"I think it's beginning, yeah," Fisher agreed.

Wise described his time as a contractor in health sciences, where he worked on the improvement projects.

"That takes a while, to really get going where people really believe it's real and can see that it's possible," Fisher replied. "It's energizing once it gets rolling."

"But it's a culture change," Wise said. "A lot of people were extremely resistant to that kind of a change, to that kind of ownership of quality in their work, and they're still resistant. But a lot of people are starting to come on board."

"It snowballs after a while," Fisher answered. "If we can reinforce the examples where good things get done, and where as a result, business performance is better, then all of a sudden, people start saying 'I'd better get on that bandwagon.' " A line of employees was waiting to meet the boss, so Wise stepped aside. "Good to see you," Fisher said.

Wise was remarkably optimistic about the new boss and Kodak's future. He had every right to be cynical, considering the roller-coaster path of his Kodak career. But getting over the past and focusing on rebuilding his piece of Kodak was a matter of survival. With his wife Janet suffering from MS, Wise was solely responsible for supporting his family. Getting his benefits and pay restored was a huge relief to the Wise family. Unlike some who credited their new jobs to luck, John and Janet considered it a blessing. "We have a very strong faith in God, and we really believe that He got us through this. I turned it over to Him and He gave me the strength to get through it."

The Wises gave each other credit for endurance, too. They put together a budget and used a stack of envelopes to divide up available money among various bills. "We continue to do that," he said. Janet cut up every credit card in the house. "I refuse to get another one. They're gone." Just as they learned that Kodak wouldn't take care of them forever, they were becoming more self-sufficient in their daily lives.

They still stuck to their grocery budget, even though John was back at work. They avoided store-bought snack foods and bought very little red meat. They did allow for an occasional indulgence: "Ice cream is a big problem," Janet said with a smile. "That's a staple as far as I'm concerned," John replied.

The Wises had become firm believers in being prepared should John ever be hit with another layoff. He took nothing for granted, especially after he saw how many people stood in line for entry-level jobs at Kodak. Competition means that more companies have to use the cheapest labor they can find, not the traditionally well-paid workers who expect raises and promotions every year. Wise counted himself very lucky, but "I still consider myself a temporary employee."

For others in the Class of '93, the time since their layoffs opened up new careers away from corporate America. Just as Kodak had to reinvent itself, so did they. Rethinking their careers meant stepping outside the traditional nine-to-five business world. For some, that meant working two jobs, both part-time. For others, it meant taking a detour on their career path. For still others, it meant making a living from the very fact of downsizing. There was a booming business in helping people like ex-Kodakers cope and find new jobs. Tom Walker spent his years at Kodak in human resources, helping others plot their careers inside the company. When his job was eliminated, he found another as a career counselor at an outplacement firm, Goodrich & Sherwood, just across the street from Kodak's headquarters. Now people seek his advice on what to do when they lose their jobs. Some of Walker's first clients came from Kodak, but the company stopped referring people to his office as it cut back on the number of outside vendors it used to provide outplacement services.

Walker found that life across the street had its benefits. His hours were more flexible than at Kodak. Now that his children were all grown and out of the house, the couple could live on less; he supplemented his salary by dipping into the money he saved from his Kodak severance.

Some days, he came home early—a shock to his wife, Gerry. "Last night I walked in at four-thirty and scared the hell out of her," Tom said. Seeing that he was scaling back his hours, she figured she should try it, too. She quit her full-time teaching job and now worked part-time. "There's more to life than your job," she said. "I don't have any of the hassles now." She spent some weekdays cleaning out closets and "cooking a decent meal." More important, she had had the pleasure of helping her daughter, Marcia, plan her wedding. And she reserved one day a week for her grandson, Shawn. "All of this made me assess my priorities," Gerry said. "I wasn't available for Shawn before. Or when I was, I was so darn tired that I didn't enjoy it."

Tom wondered what the ongoing upheaval in corporate America would mean for the next generation, especially Marcia and her fiancé, an engineer at Kodak. "They all work not knowing when the pink slip's gonna come," Tom said. "They all have to be prepared. There's no longer any loyalty or security."

Helping people prepare for a job loss was how Tom spent his days, and sometimes his nights. During one assignment, he worked the night shift at an Advil plant that was scheduled to close. Beginning at 10:30 P.M., he presented a résumé workshop and taught workers how to be interviewed and how to negotiate salary.

He also conducted a seven-week free course for laid-off workers at the Church of the Transfiguration in Pittsford. One Thursday night, he arrived early to plug in the coffeepot. It hissed as it brewed. This was week two, when Tom talks about marketing yourself to employers. One woman in the room held a Ph.D. in psychology and had six different résumés so she could apply for jobs ranging from dental hygienist to college professor. Tom preached the importance of selling. "Think of yourself as a business," he said, holding up a model résumé, which told the reader more than what jobs the applicant had held. It highlighted accomplishments, showing what past jobs delivered in terms of higher sales or cost savings. The "rule of thumbs" is important: "If you can get me to read past my thumbs, you've hooked me."

Though he had given up the idea of returning to a human resources job in a big company, Tom hadn't given up his job search. In early 1996, he responded to a newspaper ad for an opening at Drake Beam Morin, a big outplacement firm. He got the job. He would do the same kind of career counseling for the firm's Rochester, Buffalo, and Syracuse offices. The salary edged him closer to his old Kodak pay. And there was evidence that business would be booming; more restructuring at AT&T, Xerox, and Bausch & Lomb. Tom said he was happy with his new role helping others who have been laid off. More importantly, he had survived his own ordeal. "It makes you realize there's life after Kodak."

Michael Donnelly couldn't imagine how he would manage life without Kodak in the weeks following his layoff in 1993. At age fifty-five, he found it very difficult to land a job. That changed one day when he was attending Tom Walker's Transfiguration workshop. He noticed a story in the local business journal about Tom Golisano, an independent candidate in the New York gubernatorial race in 1994. The candidate had hired a local advertising agency that Donnelly used to work with on Kodak business, so he called one of his contacts and asked if Golisano needed a press secretary. Within days, he had the job. Golisano was a late entry into the campaign, so Donnelly spent a hectic six weeks trying to get him out among the state's voters. He arranged twenty-six news conferences in thirty-one days and logged 8,000 miles in thirty-two days. In the end, Golisano lost to George Pataki, but he won some support for his platform of less government and more self-sufficiency.

Helping with the political campaign was an uplifting experience for Donnelly, who had been frustrated by his job search. "I was on the job and within five minutes, I was right back in my element. That's the greatest thing that ever happened to me."

After the election, Donnelly found other consulting jobs, such as helping on capital campaigns for various churches around the country. That work was more productive than continuing to search for corporate jobs. "I gave up on the job search," he said. "I would find it hard to go back into the corporate world." He expected to match his Kodak salary with his consulting work in 1995, but he had scaled back his lifestyle, spending very little money except on essentials. His outlook was better than it had been when he first lost his job, though he occasionally slipped backward. "I keep saying to myself: What did I do wrong? I could've made a contribution if I was still there. Why am I on the outside looking in?" To keep a positive outlook, he recited the Serenity Prayer.

Donnelly gave the help of friends a lot of credit for his improved outlook. In particular, he leaned on a longtime friend, Helen Adams, a kindergarten teacher in Rochester. The two grew closer in the past year, and he proposed in early 1995. "I couldn't have gotten through this situation without her," he said.

The ultimate test of Donnelly's improved outlook was a return visit to Kodak. He was hired to help plan a touring exhibit of Smithsonian artifacts, starting with a float in the Tournament of Roses parade. Donnelly was visiting Kodak to see if the company wanted to become an official sponsor of the tour. The price tag: $10 million. "Everybody I ran into told me I looked great," he reported. Unfortunately, he couldn't say the same about them. "You can still see the tension. I don't think that will ever change." He was hopeful that Kodak's new marketing guru, Carl Gustin, would see the benefit in his proposal. If not, he knew where he'd go next: Fuji. "It doesn't bother me a bit. I'm an independent contractor now."

In time, even Bob Couture learned that he would make it without a job at Kodak. Of his colleagues, he endured one of the longest job searches, because he didn't take contracting jobs, relying instead on the occasional consulting work he did from home. In the summer of 1995, about two and a half years after being cut from Kodak, he finally got an offer that suited Meredith and him. The pay was substantially less than he'd earned at Kodak, but the employer is a Rochester company, M. D. Knowlton, so the Coutures could keep their home and Meredith could keep working at Kodak.

Bob found the prospect of a new job exhilarating. He and Meredith spent hours on the phone calling relatives and friends with the good news. But soon after he accepted the job, Bob realized he was in for another wrenching change. He had been at home for so long that he was accustomed to the routine. Now there wouldn't be many more nights when he could make a homemade quiche or potpie dinner for Meredith, a task he clearly enjoyed. "I'm gonna have to cook again," Meredith said. "And he's gonna have to eat whatever I make."

On Bob's first day on the job, Meredith took a box of doughnuts to her office at Kodak and announced that he had found work in Rochester. It was a huge relief to her. Knowing that she and Bob were staying put, she could now volunteer for longer-term projects.

The weeks flew by, and once again they were both working long days. Two months into his new job as manager of engineering, Bob was rising before the sun and going to work by 6:30 A.M. The job was consuming him. Meredith was worried: he was waking up often at night. "He can't sleep, because he's too busy turning things over in his mind about work."

They were both exhausted at the end of the day. Rosie seemed depressed, because she now spent her days in her dog pen rather than romping through the house or snoozing on a bed. Cooking had become a chore, not a pleasure. "We've had a lot of spaghetti," Bob said, "and some grilled-cheese sandwiches and tuna fish." They had canceled their weekday newspaper delivery: there was no time to read it. They were back in the rat race, running full speed ahead.

Slowly, they began to spend money again. They decided to replace their BMW with a used Saab. They borrowed the minimum amount, planning to repay it within two years rather than take on a four-year debt. "This purchase is at the upper limit of what we feel we can afford if I quit my job tomorrow and we have to pay for it entirely out of Meredith's salary."

Their biggest indulgence was a return trip to the Rocky Mountains in the fall of 1995. Bob packed up his cameras and lenses for another round of elk photos. "I probably felt the best that I'd felt in a long time," he said when he returned. The art gallery near the park was still for sale. "I spent the whole week avoiding that place."

But he daydreamed about it a lot. The new job didn't stop him from thinking about what came next—perhaps self-employment somewhere in the Rockies. He believed he was ready to handle almost anything. "At some point, you lose your fear of things that can happen to you."

Likewise, the people still inside Kodak were learning to overcome their fears about the future. The company showed many signs of improvement by early 1996; the wage dividend rose 20 percent, meaning an extra few thousand dollars in each worker's paycheck. "There are lots of unknowns where my job is concerned," said one employee. "So I'm just going to save the money." Another said she would use it to pay her bills and hoped to have enough "left over for a banana split."

That reaction to the wage dividend reflected the new reality of Kodak. Bonuses would be linked to performance, and little would be taken for granted. The company today had become a snapshot of American business bracing for even more foreign competition. Companies that didn't dismantle old bureaucracies would be left behind, and companies that strayed too far from their core businesses in the massive mergers of the 1980s would be dismantled and forced to return to their historic roots. That created a lot of mixed feelings for employees who had tried to hang on as corporate leaders changed course. But employee satisfaction at Kodak had improved as time passed. Overall satisfaction with the company rose to 52 percent by the end of 1995, up from 38 percent in earlier surveys.

In some ways, Kodak was ahead of the game in putting aside some of its traditional ways to get products out faster. Feedback from customers showed improvement. A survey of brand quality in the United States by Equitrend ranked Kodak as the top brand in the country, ahead of Disney, Mercedes, and Coca-Cola. And Wal-Mart has recognized Kodak as its outstanding supplier. Fisher was pleased with the progress, but knew there was a lot of work remaining. "I'm never satisfied. I run scared in life always. I think that's a healthy attitude, if kept under control."

Fisher found that it was even more difficult to fix the company's problems in Japan. Despite support from key congressional leaders, Kodak ran into all sorts of problems trying to get the Japanese government to investigate Kodak's complaints about that country's film market. Fisher was stunned when he heard Japan's senior trade officials say in early 1996 that the country wouldn't negotiate over the issue. "If I were in Congress, I would rally everybody and march over to the Japanese embassy and say: 'What did you say?' Then I'd march to Japan," Fisher said.

Still, Fisher embraced the concept of forming partnerships with his Japanese rivals if it meant that the company could move faster to roll out new products. This aspect of the new Kodak, and the future of other U.S. companies, was evident in February 1996, when the company unveiled its newest film and camera technology—the Advanced Photo System, a line of products sold under the brand name Advantix. The idea was to once again simplify picture-taking. For instance, the film cartridge doesn't have to be threaded on sprockets; it just drops into the camera. This is important for some consumers, because improper film loading is often to blame when pictures turn out badly. Besides, making copies of the photos is easier with the new Advantix film. It allows consumers to choose what size prints they want, regular or panoramic. In the past, a special camera was needed for panoramic photos. Most of all, Advantix is a further advance in the ongoing effort to simplify photography.

The biggest change was in how Advantix was developed. Kodak joined forces with its rivals Canon, Minolta, Nikon, and Fuji to design a new industry-wide standard for cameras and film.

Each company came up with its own products, using the new standards. But Kodak moved quickly to beat the others in unveiling Advantix. The product was shown off to groups around the world. In Rochester, the celebration took place about midnight at George Eastman's mansion on Rochester's East Avenue. Kodak employees in tuxedos and sparkling cocktail dresses mingled with Rochester's political and business leaders. A band played "In the Mood" as a waiter wove through the crowd with a platter of salmon and shrimp hors d'oeuvres.

In the auditorium, the crowd found noisemakers and Kodak hats in each seat. CEO Fisher greeted them via satellite from Hollywood, announcing Advantix just after midnight to ensure that the news would hit during Japanese business hours. His top lieutenants were in Tokyo and London to spread the news. "Kodak's message is one that will be heard around the world," Fisher told employees. Indeed, Rochester's mayor called the event "the snapshot heard 'round the world."

Everyone felt confident as they raised champagne glasses to toast the new products, unveiled ninety-six years after George Eastman's popular Brownie camera created home photography and a hobby that enabled generations of Americans to chronicle the "moments of their lives."

The morning newspaper carried headlines about the new product line and the promise it held for Rochester. Al and Mary Waugh saw them, but didn't dwell on how this or other developments at Kodak would affect them, until the phone rang one day in the spring of 1996. It was a manager at Kodak asking if Al wanted to come back to work at the Elmgrove plant. The company had been searching for someone with expertise in specialty motors that are used in everything from digital cameras to printers. His old friends inside the company remembered that Al had worked on such motors back in the 1980s. The offer was for less money than his old Kodak pay, but more than he was making at Alliance. His benefits and five weeks of vacation time were restored.

The job offer met mixed reactions at the Waugh household. Al had never dreamed that he'd have a chance to go back. And he'd often sworn he never *would* go back after the way he and others had been treated in the layoffs. In yet another irony of the bitter struggle at Kodak, some of those laid off in cost-cutting measures were now needed to help rebuild the new Kodak. If anyone doubted how poorly planned the layoffs had been, they needed only to look at how engineers like Al Waugh were ultimately asked to return.

In the end, a job at Kodak is still the best offer in town, so Al took the job. The old Kodak paycheck would come in handy: Katie Waugh had announced that she would be getting married in September, so Al was eager to stash away every extra dollar he could find.

His last day at Alliance was a Friday, and Al started back at Elmgrove on the following Monday, allowing himself only a weekend off between jobs. And he spent that Friday night where he had spent every Friday for the past few years—cleaning the church.

10

Beyond the
Yellow Box

For a snapshot of life after Eastman Kodak, just take a look at Earnie Deavenport in Kingsport, Tennessee. As chief executive of Eastman Chemical, he's not what you'd expect to find at the helm of a $5 billion company. For starters, he looks more like an Opie than an Iacocca: big ears, ruddy complexion, and an aw-shucks manner. Friends call him Red. He believes most CEOs are overpaid. And his tastes run far south of haute cuisine, as seen when he digs into a lunch of kidney bean salad and peach cobbler.

But to the locals here in the Smoky Mountain foothills, Deavenport is a hero. He led the campaign to cut his company loose from the Yellow Father and its corporate headquarters in Rochester in 1993. As a director and longtime manager at Eastman Kodak, he had an insider's perspective on what Kodak did right and wrong. And he's determined that Eastman Chemical won't repeat the Father's mistakes now that it's a separate company. Eastman Chemical, which makes ingredients found in everything from pound cakes to casket liners, offers some lessons to companies around the world about how to run a business that provides both a return to shareholders and steady work in a tumultuous industry. A look at its progress is also a primer on how other companies can fare after they split off from a corporate parent. Most of all, the story of Eastman Chemical shows what Kodak might have done, perhaps years before it fired its CEO and laid off thousands of workers, if such initiatives had taken hold beyond Tennessee.

The core of Eastman Chemical's efforts is accountability at all levels of the company. Deavenport has everyone from the plant clean-up crew to his new board of directors focused on how they can work on their part of the business in order to succeed. Everyone, including the directors, must buy a chunk of Eastman's stock, investing up to four times their annual pay. Every employee also has a substantial amount of pay at risk, linked to the firm's financial performance, so their paychecks reflect the company's ups and downs. Even entry-level workers are schooled in Wall Street concepts so they can monitor their company's progress. They all watch spending, even on simple things like whether to plant a shrub or to pave a parking lot. Maintenance workers have testified at congressional hearings about their cost-saving plans. Some workers who never attended college themselves are now on the lecture circuit, teaching MBA candidates at the country's top business schools. CEOs and quality gurus flock to the tiny town of Kingsport to hear Deavenport and others talk about their basic values. Indeed, the company has more than 10,000 requests for information or speakers a year.

It's easy to see why this company has become a management mecca. Eastman Chemical's stock price has risen more than $25 a share since it went public in early 1994. Earnings soared, so everyone got bonuses of at least 17 percent of their annual pay in 1995, and expected to receive 30 percent extra in 1996. And employees at all levels seem to like what's going on. Surveys show that 77 percent of workers are satisfied with their jobs, compared with the national average of 54 percent.

Deavenport doesn't hesitate to criticize the old Kodak ways of doing business. He likes to borrow one of Yogi Berra's lines: " 'The future isn't what it used to be.' Things here at Eastman aren't what they used to be, either. And that's good." Deavenport's emphasis on the basics has deep roots; he's a product of one of the poorest parts of Mississippi. His father owned an auto supply store, fixed cars, and raised cotton, corn, and cattle. His mother kept the books. The elder Deavenport never finished high school, but satisfied his craving for education by keeping a set of

Compton's Encyclopedia by his easy chair, so he could read each volume again and again. The parents pushed their three children to attend college. The youngest, Earnie earned his bachelor's in chemical engineering from Mississippi State University in 1960. Later that year, he drove to Kingsport in a new Chevrolet with $50 in his pocket to take his first engineering job at Kodak's chemical plant.

Toy Reid, who was general manager at the chemical company until retiring in 1989, remembered how managers identified Deavenport early in his career as "an achiever." It was equally important for newcomers to fit into the company's family atmosphere. "He came here already part of that culture that we have in this company," Reid said. "He's a southern redneck."

Deavenport worked his way up the ranks and succeeded Reid as president of Eastman Chemical in 1989. It was a time of change in Rochester as well. Colby Chandler was about to retire as Kodak's chief executive officer. Like his predecessors, Chandler didn't pay much attention to the everyday workings of Kodak's chemical unit. It just churned out cash and sent it back to Rochester. That money machine helped Kodak mask some of its problems in other divisions, so there was little meddling from headquarters as long as the money kept coming. "We were 'that part of the company down there in the hills,'" said Bill Adams, vice president of human resources.

Kay Whitmore succeeded Chandler as CEO shortly after Deavenport took over the chemical business. He showed more interest in chemicals than any CEO who preceded him, Deavenport said. But Whitmore's focus had to be on "the big gorilla," the imaging business in Rochester.

The chemical business had been founded by George Eastman in 1920, after World War I reduced the availability of the chemicals he needed to make film. He located the company in Tennessee because of its vast forests, a source of wood that was converted to make methanol and other chemicals.

By the 1980s, Eastman Chemical had grown well beyond its role as a captive supplier to Kodak; it faced different challenges and dealt in different worldwide markets than the parent company's other businesses. When Deavenport took over, only 7 percent of the chemical division's revenues actually came from sales to the parent company. The rest came from selling plastics and chemicals to toothbrush makers, soft-drink bottlers, and auto plants, among other industries. But few of Kodak's senior managers recognized Eastman Chemical. At each annual meeting, Deavenport would sit with the other top management of Kodak, but he "never got a question," recalled Virgil Stephens, chief financial officer.

Deavenport was frustrated by the restraints on his division's growth. The company generated all sorts of ideas to tap into burgeoning worldwide markets, such as the explosive growth of demand for polyethylene terephthalate (PET), used to make soft-drink bottles. But the message from corporate headquarters was always the same: Kodak had to pay down the debt incurred by its own problems and acquisitions, so the chemical division had to basically stand still—and send even more money to Rochester.

In 1989, Deavenport began to work on the idea of splitting off the chemical company, but nothing materialized. If he had to stay with Kodak, he felt, he at least wanted to make some changes. A major one was the March wage dividend. Deavenport wanted all employees to have some pay at risk, so they would see the connection between a good corporate performance and their paychecks. The plan was to reduce chemical employees' paychecks by 5 percent over three years. Depending on the annual results, employees would then get up to three times that amount back as a bonus under the "success-sharing" formula.

The Tennessee company also separated itself from the various buyouts and retirement plans that were decimating the workforce in Rochester. Eastman Chemical hadn't participated in the Triple R plan, the generous buyout that proved so costly to Kodak both in the money paid out and in the number of employees who left. Part of the reason the chemical division didn't need to use buyouts was their earlier efforts to use good management practices—in essence, doing things right the first time rather than doing them again and again. The issue of quality had been forced on Eastman Chemical in the late 1970s when a major customer said its cellulose acetate filter tow product, used to make cigarette filters, was inferior to competitors. Since Eastman Chemical had invented the product, the quality alarm served as a wake-up call to the entire company. Ironically, this was about the same time that the parent company was seeing advances by rival Fuji and not taking them seriously. But the chemical division did get serious, especially about good management practices, and it focused more on basics, such as building teamwork on the factory floor and eliminating wasteful spending.

Some of the changes were easier for Eastman Chemical than for Kodak because of its natural advantages when compared to its larger parent company. For starters, it has about 17,500 employees versus Kodak's 90,000. It's easier to tackle problems when there are fewer layers of people and less bureaucracy. The environment also helped. Kingsport is a small southern town with a strong work ethic. Eastman Chemical is concentrated in a handful of plant sites, and the corporate headquarters is right at the plant, rather than in a downtown office tower like the one at Rochester. Managers are physically closer to the workforce.

Earnie Deavenport is also different from George Fisher. Deavenport enjoys an advantage that Fisher lacks: he grew up in the plant, working alongside many of the plant workers. So they treat him like one of the guys. As hard as Fisher tries to fit in and mingle with the troops, he will always be the millionaire suit hired from Motorola. Besides, Deavenport really is, as described by many, a good old boy from the South. Fisher has a great sense of humor, but he's rather professorial in his demeanor. Even Ann Fisher occasionally tells him to lose the tie and loosen up. (She once planned a country-western barbecue for their backyard in Rochester, hoping it wouldn't be as formal as past company parties.)

Some of the initiatives taken by the chemical company were rather basic, but they sent a message to the troops that life was changing. For instance, the executive lunchroom in the headquarters building became a business dining room open to everyone in the company. Now anyone who needs a meeting place can go there for the buffet lunch, where the cook ladles out the soup of the day and quizzes those who don't want to sample it. Employees sign up as waiters, serving coffee and clearing plates. One day, Drendall Hurd, who designs pipelines for Eastman, was shuttling between the dining rooms and kitchen with glasses of tea and dirty dishes. Waiter duty nets him some extra cash, but he said he does it because he enjoys meeting the people who come through the lunch line. "I would do this even if they didn't pay me. I enjoy it. It's southern hospitality." Indeed, he believes it fits in with what he's learning in his classes based on Stephen Covey's best-seller *The Seven Habits of Highly Effective People,* which are open to anyone in the company.

Another change was turning the company plane from a private jet for the CEO into a shuttle for all employees going to other plant sites. The dress code was loosened up, so it's not unusual to see senior management in casual clothes. Deavenport wore khakis and a parka for his photo in a recent annual report.

Beyond the symbolic moves, the company began having employees dissect what was wrong in relationships with customers. To keep in closer touch, the company assigned a steward to watch over each issue, such as quality of products, delivery times, and other matters that affect customers. Employees at all levels began to see they could make a difference.

Management also took the heretical step of eliminating the traditional suggestion system, which paid a hefty bonus to employees who offered money-saving ideas. Under Kodak's old plan, employees could get thousands for an idea. But the chemical division decided that this system had to go if people were ever going to work as teams to solve problems, because "we aren't going to pay them separately when they use their brains," said Robert Joines, vice president of quality. Likewise, employees shouldn't have to live in fear that their improvement efforts might make the place more efficient and thereby eliminate some of their jobs. So the company is constantly studying which markets it should exit or enter, giving it plenty of time to shut down some processes or expand others. Usually that means employees have plenty of time to be retrained and then transferred to other parts of the company.

Eastman Chemical's progress was rapid, prompting the management to apply for the Malcolm Baldrige Quality Award in 1988. The award is one of the few measures of achievement for companies in all industries, and separate from Wall Street indicators that track only economic results. Applying for the Baldrige is an exhaustive process that includes reams of filings and interviews with hundreds of employees. Eastman's application led to a site visit that year—an honor in itself—but the company learned that it still had a long way to go to be a winner.

Deavenport ratcheted up the pace of change when he became CEO in 1989, instituting the pay-at-risk plans and building the foundation for an ownership break from Kodak. Cost-cutting measures were equally important to free up more money for growth, despite the constraints produced by Kodak's increasing financial problems. As employees saw their bonuses rise and fall with the company's annual performance, they began to pay closer attention to the details of budgets. Virgil Stephens, the chief financial officer, recalled when the company decided to do some landscaping around its marketing and sales building: "We got so much static from the employees." They questioned why the company was buying shrubs, because "you're spending this money that is going to reduce our returns." Others complained when they saw a crew repaving an old parking lot, although it had been full of bumps and holes.

It was especially frustrating for the Tennessee employees to watch as Kodak's senior management racked up more debt through acquisitions and fruitless ventures. They were doing their part to improve, but their efforts seemed to have little impact on the parent company's financial performance. In a way, the mistakes in Rochester helped seal the chemical division's future as an independent company.

By 1992, the pressure on Kodak was building. McKinsey consultants did a portfolio study to see what businesses Kodak should keep and what should be sold to pay down its billions in debt. Shareholders were growing restless over Kodak's poor performance. And former board member and retired Procter & Gamble chairman John Smale was leading a coup to oust the management of General Motors. That drew a lot of attention in Rochester and Kingsport. "The corporate boardrooms were undergoing a lot of change and pressure that they'd not seen previously," said Jimmy Tackett, Eastman's vice president of strategic planning.

In early 1993, Goldman, Sachs was hired to perform another study on what to do with Eastman Chemical. Possibilities included outright sale to another company, a leveraged buyout by management, or an initial public offering, making Eastman an independent, publicly held company. Kay Whitmore's hints that Kodak was considering selling pieces of the company sent shock waves through eastern Tennessee. The company draws employees from a fifty-mile area and has employed several generations of many families. Workers often stayed on for forty or fifty years. The 1,050-acre manufacturing site is the hub of Kingsport, which has a population of about 40,000. The town, designed by New York planners as a model city, is anchored at one end by a church circle and by the train station at the other. It is Mayberry-like with its free downtown parking and tough anti-noise ordinance.

The region enjoys low crime rates and affordable housing—the average house price in 1993 was $84,257—and is cheaper for manufacturing because of lower taxes, wages, and utility costs. For instance, the average manufacturing wage in Tennessee is $9.70 an hour, compared to $12.72 in Massachusetts. Those were factors Raytheon and other companies considered when moving manufacturing jobs to the region instead of to more expensive northeastern sites.

Kingsport is a company town in many ways. The mayor is an Eastman Chemical employee. And the company sold some of its land to the city for its new convention center and hotel. Merchants plan sales around when Kodak pays its annual wage dividend. Hills Department Store calls the company to confirm the actual pay date so it can stock its shelves with extra merchandise.

So it was traumatic when word spread that Eastman Chemical's future was uncertain. The region had already felt the impact of downsizing in earlier years when Unisys, the computer maker, laid off workers at its nearby Bristol plant. And other employers were undergoing changes that could affect local employment. For instance, there was worry that Arcata Graphics, a printing company, and Mead Corporation's local unit would be sold. "Don't be surprised if there's a run on worry beads in Kingston," lamented a local newspaper's editorial page. The newspaper estimated Eastman's economic impact at more than $1 billion annually, including salaries and taxes. Rumors spread about foreign shoppers coming to town to bid on the chemical company. Potential buyers included Mitsubishi, Shell, even Fuji, according to the grapevine. Every time a plane flew over the plant, employees panicked that another buyer was in town. "It was up front of everyone's minds," said Gary Mayes, a Sullivan county commissioner.

All of the speculation caused a major slowdown in the local economy. Lynn Shipley, president of First American National Bank in Kingsport, saw a change in the bank's usual lending as people put off big-ticket purchases like autos and houses. Indeed, Deavenport was among the few who bought a car that summer— his son wanted a new car as his college graduation gift. Deavenport got an earful from the car dealership manager about the lack of traffic in the showroom. "Everybody thinks Eastman's gonna be sold or shut down," he told Deavenport. "The economy, particularly in Kingsport and to a great extent, in this area, really began to kind of shut down."

But Deavenport couldn't reassure people, because the Kodak board hadn't decided what to do with the chemical business. That caused tension between Kay Whitmore and Deavenport. The Tennessee CEO pushed Whitmore—"We really need to go ahead and be definitive about what we're gonna do"—because it was getting more difficult to run the place with all the rumors. As a director of Kodak and also chief of the chemical business, Deavenport had to wear two hats: one as a director responsible for getting the most return for shareholders, and another as the leader of the Tennessee workers, who wanted to preserve their company and jobs. He believed that the best idea for all was to spin Eastman off as an independent company rather than sell out to another big company. "I looked out for Eastman Chemical, the people in it, and the communities that we have and also what's best for the shareholders," he said.

The board finally decided to spin off the chemical business as a separate company, giving shareholders of Eastman Kodak one share of Eastman Chemical for every four shares of Kodak they held. The spinoff was met with cheers. The same newspaper that forecast a run on worry beads proclaimed: "Economic outlook in Kingsport has gone from the outhouse to the penthouse."

The initial hoopla was dampened a bit when everyone realized that the price of freedom included a chunk of Kodak's debt— about $1.8 billion of debt was transferred to Eastman Chemical, giving it a debt-to-capital ratio of 63 percent. That's a hefty burden; the debt-to-capital ratio for the rest of the chemical industry is typically 40 percent to 45 percent. "We were all very nervous," said Tackett, the strategic planner. One reason was that at the time Eastman Chemical was leaving Kodak, the chemical industry was still in the trough of its usual cycles of ups and downs. "Things were not looking real, real bright in the chemical industry," Deavenport said. He knew the industry cycle would eventually turn, but the question was how soon. Though Eastman Chemical had fed Kodak a lot of cash over the years, it was still somewhat sheltered as part of a bigger company. Now it was on its own. That made some uneasy about leaving the nest. "People were so loyal that they said when they died, they thought they'd go to Kodak," said one manager. "Now we have to find a new place to go. Maybe heaven."

Deavenport and his management team began to work on big issues, like selecting a board of directors. Usually, when a company is spun off, some of the parent company's board members sit on the new company's board, too. Deavenport was determined to break with Kodak's traditional approach of loading the board with insiders and others from the old-boy network. He started the process by hiring an outside search firm that collected names of possible candidates. A list of about 1,500 was trimmed down to a handful, who met with Deavenport. He also wanted only two insiders, because he thought company managers were ineffective board members. In the end, the board comprised eight outsiders and two insiders, Deavenport and executive vice president Wiley Bourne. "You go on a board and there are always people there who tend to know each other. You get this board member saying, 'Well, I'm on another board, wouldn't you like to serve on that?'

At least starting out, I thought it would be helpful if I didn't get my friends. I wanted a diverse board."

Even more important, Deavenport wanted an attentive board. One of the biggest criticisms shareholders made of Kodak's board was its apparent lack of attention to the business problems of the 1980s. Only when shareholders nearly revolted did the board force some management changes, including the ouster of Kay Whitmore in 1993. So Deavenport instituted a policy requiring board members to hold company stock equal to three times their annual compensation—about $100,000 worth of stock. "My basic philosophy is that the board ought to have a stake in the company," he said. Because a board has such clout, he wanted a group that wouldn't just sit there "once every two months voicing an opinion based on reading something the night before. The more money I have in this company, the more concerned about the welfare of this company. I think that's true with the board members."

Board members tended to agree. Calvin "Tink" Campbell, Jr., president of Goodman Equipment Corporation, a maker of mining equipment and molding machines, went even further: "I think that directors should be paid in stock"—in fact, all stock and no cash. "Some people say that some directors due to financial circumstances would need some cash . . . but I think that should be the exception and not the rule." Indeed, Campbell refused to join the board of another company after learning that the other directors and senior management held little of its stock. That "told me that I should not spend my time pursuing that."

Eastman directors were trained from the start to be careful in their spending when on Eastman business. When in Kingsport, they usually stayed at the Ramada Inn, and they were encouraged to place long-distance phone calls through the Eastman switchboard because "it's cheaper than putting it through the Ramada Inn," Campbell said.

The directors were also active when Deavenport wanted them to meet with customers or otherwise keep in touch with the company. For instance, Campbell played golf with Eastman customers, and met others at trade shows and other events. To gauge the board's attitudes toward its role, the committee on directors put together a survey after their first year of working together. The questions covered a wide range, from basic matters like travel arrangements for meetings to a self-analysis of the directors' skills. It is unusual for boards to take such an introspective look at themselves, but Campbell believed it was the next frontier in corporate governance. "American business has arrived at the point that we can evaluate everything"—customers, products, suppliers. "But we have not evaluated boards." Eastman planned to repeat the survey in a year or eighteen months.

Back in Rochester, Kodak's board hadn't implemented changes like those seen at Eastman Chemical. In fact, very few boards have gone as far to review their own performance. Companies like Kodak are still run by clublike boards, where little changes. Few are willing to question their own judgment, pay, and performance. Many of the Kodak directors who allowed Kay Whitmore and his management team to drift off course are still seated in the boardroom. When asked if he would consider changing how the board is compensated, Fisher said the group had discussed the possibility, but nothing has yet changed. In his opinion, the board was doing just fine, considering the upheaval of recent years. True, the board did finally wake up in 1993 and change the management. But the practices that Fisher used to change how workers were compensated should start at the top. Kodak now asked all its staffers to measure everything they did and make progress on all tasks. Why not do the same in the boardroom?

Deavenport applied the same principle of accountability to his company's management. Eastman's top 500 managers were required to buy stock equal to one, two, or three times their annual pay. For him, the figure was four times his compensation. In addition, the pay-at-risk plan was expanded: instead of 5 percent at risk, an additional 5 percent to 35 percent of the top 500 managers' pay was at risk. They could earn up to two times their at-risk pay if they met annual goals. As for Deavenport, about 40 percent of his annual compensation was linked to the company's performance. Finally, the first 5 percent of every bonus went into an employee stock ownership plan, further boosting the amount of stock held by insiders.

With all these plans in place, Eastman Chemical got off to a solid start, despite the turmoil back at Kodak headquarters. Whitmore was fired and Fisher hired just as the chemical division was moving forward with its plan to go public. Deavenport met with Fisher, who agreed that the spin-off was a good plan. It also changed the companies' relationship: Now Kodak was an Eastman Chemical customer like any other. And as a supplier, Eastman Chemical could, for example, raise prices on certain product lines—a practice that hadn't really affected Kodak before.

Eastman Chemical got a substantial boost as a new company in late 1993, when it won that year's Malcolm Baldrige Award. After failing to win in earlier attempts, Eastman had kept applying and making improvements. In December, just before the company went public in the new year, Deavenport accepted the award from President Bill Clinton. He took the opportunity to remind all American companies that it's time to wake up. "This nation wants—and desperately needs—corporations willing to change, willing to transform themselves into national and world competitors," he said. "There is no room in America's future for couch potato corporations"—or, as Deavenport liked to say, SPUD: soft, petrified, undirected, and doomed.

The stock's debut on Wall Street was met with enthusiasm. Eastman Chemical's price began a steady climb from its January 1994 price of $45.25. The offering brought close scrutiny by Wall Street analysts, who had previously paid little attention to this part of Kodak's business. One of the first questions Deavenport got from stock watchers was "When are you going to downsize?" It was a natural question, considering that the parent company had just announced plans to lay off about 10,000 workers. Deavenport had strong opinions on the subject, as he did on most topics. "It's my philosophy that if management is really doing their job, and there's not something that comes out of the blue . . . if they wake up one morning and say, 'Oh, boy, the numbers look so bad I think I'll have to lay off two thousand people,' I just

think management has somehow failed to do their job correctly."
But he hedged a bit, because every company has to cut jobs when
a business goes bad. For instance, Eastman exited the Kodel poly-
ester fiber business in 1993 and transferred those workers to
other growing operations, such as PET production. Deavenport
once bragged in an interview that Eastman Chemical had had to
cut roughly 200 jobs in more than forty years. But just a couple of
months later, the company announced that market conditions
had forced it to stop production of Vitamin E products at its
facility in Rochester, resulting in the loss of about fifty jobs.

Deavenport realized that there were no guarantees against
downsizing. "There are businesses that are good today and next
year, they're terrible." And the company did use some contract
workers as a buffer workforce to fill in gaps. (Deavenport was
often corrected by colleagues when he used the term "permanent
employees": "Even you, Earnie, are not a permanent employee.")

Indeed, Eastman Chemical faced problems that make its
future difficult to predict. For starters, the company is subject to
swings in price and demand for all sorts of products around the
globe. But Eastman made substantial progress in its first year as a
public company. Deavenport set a goal of 10 percent annual
growth, double what it had ever done as part of Kodak. He also
pledged to quickly pay down a chunk of the debt, and, indeed,
about $600 million was repaid within the first year. By 1996, the
debt-to-capital ratio was down to 47 percent, very close to the
industry average. Investors are regularly updated; Deavenport
and his management team often meet two or three times a
month with various groups. The most important part of the plan
was for expansion around the globe, something that had previously been out of the question. By late 1996, Eastman Chemical
had plants under construction in Malaysia, Spain, and the
Netherlands, to name a few places. It had also acquired companies in Hong Kong and Brussels and was looking for partners
with which to enter China. Asia is expected to account for about
40 percent of the worldwide demand for chemicals and plastics
by the year 2000, according to industry estimates.

Innovation was seen as another way to build the company.
About 20 percent of Eastman's sales came from new products.

Constant feedback from customers makes it clear what works and what doesn't. Response time on complaints had improved. Customers can now get immediate information on inventories, prices, and delivery dates anywhere in the world. And the company's return policy for its commodity plastics is basic: If you don't like it, Eastman will come and get it.

It surveys customers, looking for feedback even from internal customers. For instance, at Eastman's warehouse in Singapore, product labels kept falling off, so the material handlers couldn't tell what was supposed to be shipped. An operator back in Kingsport figured out that the adhesive couldn't hold up in the country's humid climate. The label was redesigned with a different adhesive. The people in Singapore sent the operator in Tennessee a small Singapore flag and a thank-you note. The operator was so proud that he mounted the flag on his forklift and drove around the plant to show it off. Others sent telexes to Singapore to ask for their own flags. The reply was: "If you want a flag, you have to earn it." So the operators sent another note: "What can we do for you?" Pretty soon, the entire Kingsport warehouse operation was trying to collect flags from our customers throughout the world by asking them: 'What can we do for you?' " Deavenport recounted. "That's customer satisfaction on a global scale. . . . That's how we can stay ahead of the competition: by providing a work environment that thrives on reinforcing the right behaviors."

The effort by Eastman Chemical employees was already being judged favorably around the world. Eastman got about 10,000 requests for speakers or information each year. The Baldrige Award created such interest that Eastman developed its own lecture series, the "Chemistry of Excellence Seminars," holding twenty-three in 1994 and drawing managers from Germany, India, the Netherlands, and other countries.

Employees were encouraged to give senior management feedback during roundtables with the boss or by sending him E-mail messages. Deavenport always asked the question: What would you do if you were in my shoes? Invariably, employees asked about the company's financial outlook. They understood the quarterly reports about how much money they were making above the cost of capital invested, and they kept an eye on how their own departments could shave costs further to improve returns. "It's amazing the knowledge all of our people have about business issues. That's refreshing, because one of the reasons we have stock ownership plans . . . is that opportunity to educate large numbers of people about what makes a business tick." There is little difference, after all, between what a senior manager like Deavenport wants in life and what an entry-level person wants. "If we want all the good things of life, like stability of employment, a great community to live in, wages equal to or above the average, and good benefits, a precursor to having all of that is to have returns over and above the cost of capital."

The company newsletter offers steady reminders about how to get the most return. Every quarter, employees get updates on the financial results and the CEO's thoughts under the heading: "What Did Earnie Say?" One story reminded employees that absenteeism is a cost that all of them can help control. Hours lost to illness averaged 2.2 percent in 1994, up from 1.97 percent in each of the previous two years. According to the newsletter, this small increase cost $1.5 million, excluding overtime needed to cover for sick employees. The message seemed to be getting through. Productivity at the company continued to climb; it was up 15 percent in 1994 and another 10 percent for the first half of 1995.

The company was full of disciples who spread the word about how to improve a major corporation, one job at a time. Consider Gaines Fields, the son of a coal miner, who started at Eastman in 1966 as a laborer and worked his way up the ranks to become a team manager in the maintenance and services department. Since Fields put a chunk of his pay at risk, he had become an expert on how to improve his bonus. For instance, his team had saved the company $16 million by rethinking how to do simple chores. One project saved about $9 million by changing the timing of pipeline cleanings. Formerly, maintenance workers shut down different parts of the plant every two weeks and never had a chance to clean the entire system at the same time. Now the team shuts the entire operation down twice a year. Fields's group also compared their cleaning operation with outside vendors to see if they were competitive. They were cheaper. Employees are also in charge of the budget. "They will trace down a $10 discrepancy," Fields said.

Everyone at Eastman is connected via E-mail, and they keep a watchful eye on the company's stock price and news of the industry. Lunchtime conversation is often about Fidelity mutual funds and where everyone is investing their money—a change from the old days, when workers talked about fishing and race cars, Fields said. He encourages younger workers to plow more money into the company's 401K plan. His own money is in the Fidelity Magellan funds, among others. He also tells the lunchtime crew to "put so much into fixed income where they can have something to fall back on." Most of all, Fields urges newcomers and high school students to invest in their education and their "emotional bank account" with their families. "I don't want to sound like a politician, but I think an investment in family values is something they can really build on."

Fields's enthusiasm for empowering the workforce was noticed by senior management, and he was asked to fly to Pittsburgh and address graduate students at Carnegie Mellon's business school. "I never thought I'd be doing this," he said. "I started off sweeping floors."

Lori Garrett testified before a congressional hearing about her efforts to save money. Garrett is now a control systems mechanic apprentice, but when she was hired, she was assigned to general labor clean-up around the plant. She was dusting the electrical room when she found a yellowed piece of paper—an electrical inspection checklist. One of the items on the list was to make sure that the directories to the circuits were up-to-date. The directories show which circuits feed which equipment. Garrett realized that the directory was out-of-date, so she called the department head and asked for a meeting about the problem. He suggested that she try to fix it. So she put together a team, ranging from operations people to engineers. The result was a computerized system to update the directories and so improve the reliability of the equipment. The team saved the company more than $1.1 million the first year and another $500,000 annually. "It's a nice impact to have," she said.

Employees are encouraged to think about the company at every turn. The company newsletter featured a story about an "Eastman family" shopping trip: an employee walked through Wal-Mart to identify all the products that contained Eastman goods because it "pays to be Eastman smart." Every employee is encouraged to build skills, whether by taking classes to learn more computer systems or simply by standing to lead a group discussion. Some employees have monthly sessions with their team leaders to evaluate their development plans. Employees found this a path to advanced jobs. Patricia Jones, for example, started in the secretarial pool at Eastman and moved into the sales team as a sales force associate. She kept a list of her accomplishments ready for her performance appraisal. "I usually find that my supervisor's list is far longer than mine. I think the culture of East Tennesseans is we have a real hard time bragging."

The company continued to make progress, giving everyone something to brag about. Sales in 1995 were a record $5.04 billion, up 16 percent from a year earlier. Earnings were $559 million, up 67 percent from 1994. However, Deavenport warned that 1996 would be a tougher year because of higher raw material costs and predicted that earnings for the year wouldn't match the record 1995 results.

In the spring of 1995, everyone got a 17 percent return, out of a possible 30 percent. A divorced mother with one son, Patricia Jones stashed her bonus for his education. "There is much more pride of ownership in this company than there was before," she said. For Deavenport, the 65 percent increase from 1993 to 1994 meant a hefty return: his base salary climbed to $545,000 from $500,000 in 1993, and under the pay-at-risk plan he took home a $767,849 bonus, up from $276,028 a year earlier. He also received a stock award of 25,000 shares to reflect his role in taking the company public and winning the Baldrige award. The board said it had raised his pay to reflect his increased responsibilities as CEO of an independent company. And he was likely to see more raises, because the board's compensation committee reported that his base pay was below the median for his peers.

For his part, Deavenport struggled with finding a balance between paying executives a fair amount to keep them at the company and going overboard. "I do think there are some executives in this world that are grossly overpaid," he said. "But on the other hand, most of that pay for most of those people comes from the value creation that they make for the shareholders. And it's uncanny what some CEOs have been able to do for their shareholders." He cited Roberto Goizueta, CEO of Coca-Cola and a director of Kodak. Deavenport, too, had created value for shareholders. The company's stock price ended 1995 at about $62 a share, up from about $50 a share a year earlier. In 1996, shares rose to about $76.

Deavenport and the rest of his team were tested a bit in early 1997, when global competition increased and product prices dropped. The company's stock price tumbled, and many wondered if the CEO could resist cutting jobs to save money. He pledged that the company would be able to cut its expenses without significant layoffs.

Like others, he watched Kodak, now from a distance, and hoped that its worst times were in the past. And that Fisher would be worth every penny of his paycheck.

Deavenport believed the best indication would be Kodak's report card in three to five years. "We'll look back and judge that."

Epilogue

Kodak's annual meeting in the spring of 1996 was a reminder of how far the company has come—and how far it still had to go.

Kodak's stock price was hitting record highs, at times edging above $80 a share, nearly double what it had been when George Fisher joined the company. And the company was outperforming the Standard & Poor's 500 by 20 percent, after trailing it by 50 percent in 1993.

Besides producing numbers that impressed Wall Street, Kodak had started to chip away at some of its underlying problems. In 1995 the company cut $50 million from the costs of film and paper production. Cycle times on key processes, such as making film emulsions, had been sliced to a fraction of what they had been. What once took months could now be done in less than a day. Kodak no longer used 177 advertising agencies, having consolidated their accounts with only four and thus saving money that could be used to run more ads to promote products, not just feed a bureaucracy. And products such as the single-use Funsaver cameras were selling as fast as Kodak could make them. Indeed, 90,000 of the Funsaver cameras were used by visitors and atheletes during the closing ceremonies for the 1996 Summer Olympic Games in Atlanta. "In the short three years, you and your management have done a terrific job," gushed Anthony Yankloski, a shareholder from North Greece, New York, at the annual meeting in Rochester. "Let's give George

Fisher and his management team a big hand." The crowd applauded his remarks, and applauded Fisher twenty-eight more times during the meeting.

Quite a change from the meeting three years earlier, when Kay Whitmore was chastised by angry shareholders. But not everything at Kodak had changed. The company continued to struggle with some core issues in its efforts to grow. Competition from Fuji got tougher every month. For instance, the Japanese film maker outbid Kodak to buy the film-processing business of Wal-Mart, Kodak's biggest retail film customer. The move was expected to give Fuji more shelf space for its film in a popular retail store that sells a lot of film to consumers eager to save a few bucks.

For all of Fisher's finesse, even he couldn't find a quick fix for Kodak's battle with Fuji in Japan. He conceded in mid-1996 that resolution of the trade case was "a long way off." By the fall, the U.S. trade representative's office said the investigation would be expanded because it had implications for other industries. Some viewed the move as a delaying tactic and a signal that the U.S. government had doubts about Kodak's case; indeed, some at the White House acknowledged that the case was "just not there." The United States turned the case over to the World Trade Organization in Geneva, a move deemed a victory for Fuji because the WTO is considered more neutral territory.

Nor could the CEO's Midas touch fix other problems at the company. When he joined Kodak, Fisher pledged to be patient and not rush to judgment on the company's troubled copier business. But three years later, he finally sold off the sales and service side of the business for $684 million to Danka Business Systems, a St. Petersburg, Florida–based copier company. As part of the sale, about 10,000 of Kodak's employees were offered jobs at Danka. The move unsettled veteran Kodakers, who were used to the paternalistic ways of old Kodak and were uncertain what the deal would mean for their futures. But Danka pledged to build the copier business, something that Kodak had failed to do in numerous tries; and, lacking Kodak's bureaucracy, Danka is far more nimble. CEO Dan Doyle, a former salesman, built Danka from just one service center to a $3.5 billion company by focusing on one business rather than straying into unrelated turf, something that got Kodak into a lot of trouble. Analysts figured Danka got a good deal. Kodak, though, was still stuck with the more troubled side of the copier business, the actual manufacturing of the products.

Even the much ballyhooed rollout of the new Advantix photo system had its share of glitches. Production problems and other snafus meant a slow launch for the new cameras and film. Competitors were quick to call it a mess. "This has to be the worst product launch in the history of the photographic industry," said Paul Gordon, director of U.S. marketing for the Konica Corporation. By summer 1996, months after Kodak pledged to have the cameras and film in stores, many retailers still didn't have them. Some likened the Advantix line to one of Kodak's famous earlier flops, the Disc camera, or to Ford's notorious Edsel. Kodak called the problems temporary setbacks and said it expected to make 2 million Advantix cameras in 1996. By September of that year Kodak officials said they would make 50 percent more than expected to keep up with demand.

Kodak was enjoying similar demand for some of its digital cameras, but the company still wasn't making any money on them. Fisher said the digital business would be profitable by 1997. If he hits that target, it will go a long way toward quieting critics who say Kodak has never been able to compete in any arena except film. This is a real test of whether Kodak can grow from within to solve its problems, rather than just buying and selling businesses.

Too many companies have fallen into the trap of slicing off problem businesses after pouring millions into trying to make them work. The 1990s have been marked by corporate America's attempts to undo some of the problems created by too many deals in the 1980s. AT&T, for example, announced it would split itself into three pieces, in the aftermath of some botched mergers, such as the one with the NCR Corporation. Too little attention was paid to the front end of the deals, to asking simple questions, like Why are we doing this? The CEOs, like AT&T's Robert Allen, are rewarded for buying and selling companies; then, when they decide to bail, they are often deemed heroic for being gutsy enough to exit a business. Trouble is, they are usually the ones who foolishly bought the business in the first place. During 1996, AT&T's Allen finally started to take some heat from investors about the company's lackluster performance; some said he should step aside. As the company began looking for Allen's successor in the fall of 1996, Kodak's George Fisher, who got his start at AT&T's Bell Labs, was on the list of candidates.

Fisher was also mentioned as a possible contender for the post of commerce secretary following the death of Ron Brown. His response to the overtures? Publicly, he has said he'll stick around. But his spokesman notes that "employees ought to get used to" seeing Fisher's name mentioned in every search. Good chiefs are hard to find, even when boards offer multimillion-dollar packages to jump ship. Fisher extended by two years his five-year contract and says he won't leave Kodak until he feels good about its performance and sees a strong leadership team ready to carry on. His likely successor is Dan Carp, who was named president and chief operating officer in December 1996. No one really knows when Fisher will leave, but the next generation of leaders inside Kodak had better be ready. Fisher clearly has a lot of people courting him.

While insiders lamented Fisher's possible departure, they continued to grouse about his compensation. For 1995, Fisher earned $2 million in salary, $2.28 million in bonus, and a hefty $5 million in long-term compensation—among other payments, including another $2 million in loan forgiveness, part of his original employment pact. That's more than $11 million in a year, when others inside the company were being told they could no longer count on annual raises.

Others in the senior ranks of Kodak have profited nicely during Kodak's restructuring. Bill Prezzano, one of Fisher's lieutenants, was paid a $1.35 million bonus as a "special recognition award" for his work in selling off Kodak's drug businesses.

Kodak overpaid when it bought Sterling Drug, a move that many deemed one of its biggest blunders. The company never succeeded when it strayed from its core business into the unknown territory of drugs and household products, such as Bayer aspirin and Lysol cleaning products. All of the resulting

debt and unfocused management forced Kodak to cut thousands
of jobs to stem its losses. The senior people who orchestrated the
moves didn't pay the price for their mistakes. Instead, the rank
and file paid, through lost jobs. Whitmore was forced out, but he
got a million dollars on the way out the door. And after leaving
Kodak, Whitmore took the job he always really wanted: he runs a
missionary program for the Mormon church in England.

The people he left behind weren't so lucky. Insiders joked that
the reward for doing a good job now was that you got to keep
it. Bill Davis, whose family has logged 160 years as Kodak
employees, stood up at an annual meeting to say that he was considering selling his Kodak shares to protest recent changes in the
company's policies. Senior management get hefty bonuses, while
the rank and file get very little. He cited the Advantix launch:
"People involved in the program were called together for hot dogs
and hamburgers to tell them what a great job they had done."
Then the company announced an end to cost-of-living adjust-
ments for workers. "The leaders got scandalous raises. The
workers got hot dogs and an admonition to tighten their belts as
living costs increased," Davis said. "This is not fair."

He was right: it wasn't fair. But little about big business today
is fair, when you consider how corporate senior managers are
sheltered and pampered even when they screw up. Often, the
worst thing that happens to them is that they get fired and exit
with a generous buyout.

So how can a company like Kodak balance the need of shareholders to see a return on their investment, against the paternalistic culture in which employees think they're entitled to a job?
For starters, people must realize that no one CEO can be blamed
for all the problems, or all the successes, of any company. No
single chief can do it alone, especially against the backdrop of a
rapidly changing global marketplace. Nor can CEOs expect to fix
a company by slicing off its limbs. It seems there should be some
middle ground between the likes of "Chainsaw Al" Dunlap, who
fires thousands of workers when he restructures companies, and
Aaron Feuerstein, the mill operator who kept his 3,000 employees
on the payroll even after a fire destroyed the plant. Dunlap is

deemed evil because he slashes companies and takes home millions in compensation. Feuerstein is lauded as a hero because he didn't close up shop and throw thousands of people out of work. "I have a responsibility to the worker, both blue-collar and white-collar," he said. "I have an equal responsibility to the community. It would have been unconscionable to put three thousand people on the streets and deliver a death blow to the cities. . . . Maybe on paper our company is worth less to Wall Street, but I can tell you it's worth more. We're doing fine."

Unfortunately, not every company can afford to be that generous, but there should be some alternative between treating employees like cattle sent to slaughter and an excessive, unprofitable paternalism. The smartest CEOs realize when a business or plant needs to be shuttered to improve the entire company's performance. But this should be a decision made over the course of time and backed up with worker retraining so employees can move from one job to the next, rather than to the unemployment lines.

By the same token, American workers need to realize that the days of the Yellow Father, Big Blue, and Ma Bell are over. Companies cannot promise jobs for life, continual raises, and promotions, just because workers show up most days. What they do need to offer is incentives so their workforce is invested in a company's future. Rewards for solving problems shouldn't be limited to those at the top. If Kodak and other companies want employees to share in the pain, they must share in the gains, too. If American workers are ever going to move beyond their old entitlement mentality, they must share the riches, not just get the pink slips.

Kodak must make more of its employees real owners, who have more than just a few shares of stock; Fisher has expanded the use of stock options. Kodak has also eliminated automatic 2 percent to 4 percent annual raises; raises are now based primarily on merit. At the same time, the annual wage dividend has climbed to 8.22 percent in 1996, up from 6.82 percent in 1990, giving a $40,000-a-year employee a bonus of about $3,300. To take the dividend a step further, by March 1998, everyone down through mid-level managers will receive their wage dividend in stock options. That's a good move, because shareholders who are also employees can see how difficult it is to balance one set of demands against the other. Then maybe more attention will be paid to solving problems for the long haul rather than managing companies from quarter to quarter or from sale to sale. The board of directors should practice some of the accountability measures that are now imposed throughout the rest of Kodak. They could learn a few things from their sister company in Tennessee, where directors ask the question "Are *we* doing our jobs?" And they invest in the company, too.

No one, whether director or factory worker, should be entitled to keep a job unless he or she is producing results. If they don't deliver, companies can always find others who will. Jobs and production of goods can now be moved virtually anywhere, thanks to technology and transportation that make the world a smaller place. And consider: a U.S. software engineer earns in one month what a similar engineer in India makes for the entire year.

Likewise, Rochester must learn to carry on without handouts from its Yellow Father. Communities must generate more private and public partnerships to address core issues, like improving public schools, reducing crime, and creating jobs. Rochester mayor William Johnson warned residents in his 1996 State of the City address that the city's problems should worry everyone: "All around, we see warning signs: property values on the decline, families struggling to make ends meet, young people troubled by violence. These are not just city problems."

In the end the story of Kodak is the story of American business in the 1990s. Those who figure out how to change can succeed, regardless of the global competition. American workers can also adapt to the changes, which are bound to continue as more companies figure out how to rebuild rather than just downsize. The moment for the old corporate ways has passed, as we see in the passing of the old Kodak. The company's next hurdle will be to achieve the goals set by George Fisher, and take the company into the digital age of photography, in the next century. Fisher believes they can pull it off. "I have long believed that in great companies, people not only accept change, they embrace and lead it. The people at Kodak, through resilience, creativity, and skill, are making it happen." In the years to come, the world will learn whether or not George Fisher is right.

NOTES

Most of the information in *Changing Focus* came from interviews with more than 300 current and former employees of Eastman Kodak, residents of Rochester, consultants, and industry analysts. Information was also gathered from George Eastman's letters and documents on file at the Eastman House. News coverage of Kodak in the Rochester *Democrat & Chronicle* and *Times Union* provided historical details on past management and products. Other information was gathered from *The Wall Street Journal, Business Week, Fortune,* and other publications, as noted below.

Introduction

4   "You may think of this as a corporation": *Democrat & Chronicle,* March 7, 1994.
5   Layoff figures from Challenger Gray, a firm that tracks corporate cutbacks across the country.

1.   Country Club

11   Information about George Eastman comes from interviews and from his letters and other documents at the George Eastman House, Rochester, NY. Some information was found in *George Eastman* by Carl Ackerman (New York: Houghton Mifflin, 1930).
11   Quote about poverty found in October 1920 interview published in *System: The Magazine of Business.*
14   Disney information from *Democrat & Chronicle,* April 23, 1995.

16   Quote about Eastman and women found in *Smugtown U.S.A.*, by Curt Gerling (Rochester, N.Y.: Plaza Publishers, 1957; reprinted 1993), p. 8.

17   a line of people at Lenin's tomb: *Democrat & Chronicle*, July 10, 1995.

19   "a few clean shirts": Gerling, op. cit., p. 1.

21   "we sleep well" This quotation and other information about Fallon comes from interviews and news coverage of his tenure published in the Rochester newspapers.

23   "It never is the dawn": *Democrat & Chronicle*, Aug. 24, 1986.

2.   Slippery Slope

27   Surveillance information found in *Democrat & Chronicle*, Oct. 4, 1979.

32   "high level of nervousness": *The Wall Street Journal*, May 22, 1985.

33   GAF takeover rumors reported in *USA Today*, Feb. 27, 1986.

33   Boesky, Belzbergs, and Steinberg buying shares: *The Wall Street Journal*, Feb. 28, 1986.

33   A security guard watched: *The Wall Street Journal*, Feb. 13, 1986.

33   "I'm just too old": *Rochester Times Union*, April 30, 1986.

34   some board members left the meeting early: *The Wall Street Journal*, May 15, 1986.

40   "The gang that can't shoot straight": *The Wall Street Journal*, Sept. 19, 1989.

3.   Hitting the Wall

42   The company suffered: *Nihon Keizai Shimbun*, Feb. 15, 1993.

51   Steffen's impact on stock price: *The Wall Street Journal*, Jan. 22, 1993.

51   "the other half": *The Wall Street Journal*, April 28, 1993.

52   "The market thinks": *The Wall Street Journal*, April 29, 1993.

52   "saw his own mortality": *The Wall Street Journal*, April 30, 1993.

54   Whitmore went alone: investor meeting reported in *The Wall Street Journal*, Aug. 6, 1993.

58   "Only 9,999": *Democrat & Chronicle*, Aug. 19, 1993.

59   "I am really appalled": *Democrat & Chronicle*, March 28, 1994.

60   "Good luck": *Business Week*, Nov. 8, 1993.

4.   Downscaling the American Dream

72   The national savings rate: *Atlantic Monthly* report on middle class, May 1994.

73 "working poor": *Democrat & Chronicle,* April 2, 1994.

75 From July 1984: Associated Press report, Dec. 19, 1993.

81 "Nothing in the boomers' upbringing": Katherine S. Newman, *Declining Fortunes: The Withering of the American Dream* (New York: Basic Books, 1993), p. 13.

5. White Knight

99 "graceful leapfrogging": Robert W. Galvin, *The Idea of Ideas* (Schaumburg, Ill.: Motorola University Press, 1991), p. 49.

100 Management training information found in *Harvard Business Review,* July–August, 1990.

101 more than 4 million pagers: figures from *Fortune,* April 18, 1994.

103 House information from *Democrat & Chronicle,* May 20, 1994.

105 Rich Bob: *The Wall Street Journal,* Feb. 25, 1994.

105 "What really matters": *Newsweek,* Feb. 26, 1996.

6. Wake-up Call

127 One White House official: *The Wall Street Journal,* May 24, 1996.

7. Pawning Rolexes in Smugtown

139 "biased and restricted measure": from "The State of Greater Rochester" (Rochester, N.Y.: Center for Governmental Research, 1993).

139 Census figures vs. unemployment numbers: *Democrat & Chronicle,* Feb. 19, 1996.

140 For the impact on inner cities, see William Julius Wilson, *When Work Disappears: The World of the New Urban Poor* (New York: Knopf, 1996), p. 19.

141 Chiles personally courted Al Dunlap: Associated Press, March 14, 1995.

142 "important" probated wills: Curt Gerling, *Smugtown U.S.A.* (Rochester, N.Y.: Plaza Publishers, 1957; reprinted 1993), p. 96.

142 "More fun": from a September 1923 story in Hearst's *International Magazine.* Quoted in Carl Ackerman, *George Eastman* (New York: Houghton Mifflin, 1930), p. 382.

143 The American Red Cross has had trouble: *Democrat & Chronicle,* July 6, 1994.

146 "more than a sports program": *Democrat & Chronicle,* April 2, 1993.

149 "a dinosaur": *Democrat & Chronicle,* July 10, 1994.

152   Kodak tax assessment found in *Democrat & Chronicle*, January 30, 1996.

153   Real estate rankings found in *Money*, September 1994.

153   New housing figures found in *Democrat & Chronicle*, January 21, 1995.

156   Kodak's chemical emissions: For Kodak's environmental problems and fines, see coverage in the *Democrat & Chronicle*. 1988–1996.

156   Cancer study cited in *Democrat & Chronicle*, March 22, 1991.

8.   Changing the Picture

196   "going back on Kodak's promises": *Democrat & Chronicle*, July 22, 1995, and Aug. 13, 1995.

10.   Beyond the Yellow Box

243   He pledged the company would: *The Wall Street Journal*, Jan. 16, 1997.

Epilogue

244   For the Funsaver cameras at the Olympics, see *Democrat & Chronicle*, Aug. 6, 1996.

245   For Fuji winning the Wal-Mart business, see *Democrat & Chronicle*, July 9, 1996.

245   For the World Trade Organization taking the Kodak case, see *The Wall Street Journal*, Sept. 20, 1996.

246   For production problems and other snafus, see *The Wall Street Journal*, Aug. 7, 1996.

247   For the Fisher and Prezzano bonuses see the Kodak proxy, March 14, 1996.

249   "I have a responsibility": *Parade*, Sept. 8, 1996.

249   the annual wage dividend has climbed: *Democrat & Chronicle*, March 8, 1996.

250   The comparison of software engineers' wages appeared in *The New York Times*, Sept. 3, 1995.

250   "All around, we see": *Democrat & Chronicle*, Jan. 18, 1996.

ACKNOWLEDGMENTS

And now for the easy part—saying thanks to everyone who made this book possible.

So many people helped me shape the story of life after layoffs. I am particularly grateful to the "Class of '93," especially those who gave me access to their lives during more than three years of research. Bob and Meredith Couture and their lovable Newfoundland, Rosie, along with Al and Mary Waugh, welcomed me back for countless visits. Likewise, Paul and Ruth Langlois, John and Janet Wise, Tom and Gerry Walker, Patty and Skip Minisce, and Michael Donnelly spent a lot of time with me and never hesitated to answer my endless questions. I couldn't have told the story without them. I focused on a handful of people, but I'm also grateful to the other 300-plus people who shared their thoughts for the project.

At the Rochester *Democrat & Chronicle*, Bill Patalon offered his friendship and encouragement. He is a talented reporter whose daily coverage of Kodak gave me a local perspective on the ever-changing company. And in the final rounds of editing, he made me laugh and reminded me that yes, the book would someday be finished. The newspaper's editors granted me access to the paper's morgue, so I could look up stories from earlier times in Kodak's history.

At Eastman Kodak and Eastman Chemical, many people helped me throughout the long process of reporting the book: Paul McAfee, Paul Allen, Charlie Smith, and Mike Benard were patient, despite my endless lists of questions. Chris Veronda, Ed Hurley, and Tim Elliott guided me through Rochester plants, while Rod Irvin and Nancy Ledford helped me in Kingsport, Tennessee.

The book benefited from the remarkable access I had to senior and middle management, along with employees throughout Kodak's plants and offices. Former CEO Kay Whitmore declined to be interviewed for the book. However, the new CEO, George Fisher, understood the importance of telling Kodak's side of the story, so I'm grateful for his time and the access he provided to the rest of the company. And, he didn't hesitate even when we asked him to climb up a ladder for a rooftop photo. Ann Fisher gave a candid perspective that is often lacking in business stories, largely because most CEOs are reluctant to see their spouses talk to the press.

Throughout Kodak, those who have endured years of restructuring were receptive to numerous interviews. I can't name them all, but I thank them for being so generous with their time.

No project like this survives without a support system of family and friends who never question your sanity . . . at least not publicly. My ten-year-old nephew, Benjamin Hill, offered his computer when mine was in the repair shop. More important, he offered constant smiles and hugs, a tonic for anyone. Likewise, Maribel Allison Swasy and Alexis Hill were ready to do whatever I needed to keep the project on schedule. Amy Kase should win some sort of prize for transcribing a boxful of taped interviews. I am also grateful for her family's hospitality during my trips to Rochester. The Friday Night Supper Club, also known as Dave and Deb Dunlap, toasted each chapter and listened to me babble on and on about the book. Phone calls and visits with Tim Schellhardt, Lynne Anderson, Terry Mutchler, Tracy and Kevin Riley, Charlotte Sutton, and Mary Jane Park kept me forging ahead. Dean Mills served once again as unpaid editor, a thankless job, while his sidekick Sue offered her usual encouragement. Phil Barach provided the perspective of a former CEO. And Blair Gardner got to try his hand at book editing, proving that he has a second skill should he ever give up the lawyer's trade.

Paul Steiger, managing editor of *The Wall Street Journal,* along with many others at the newspaper, wished me well when I ventured off to write a second book. Joan Rigdon offered her perspective as a former Kodak watcher. And I found a lot of useful insights in stories written by Clare Ansberry, Jim Hirsch, and Wendy Bounds.

A book on Kodak needed some great photographs. Charles Bertram, a prize-winning photographer from Lexington, Kentucky, lent the project his talents and sense of humor. He has the ability to put anyone at ease in front of a camera. And his photos helped bring the story to life.

Kris Dahl and Dorothea Herrey at ICM offered their usual support during the long journey. At Random House and Times Books, Ann Godoff, Enrica Gadler, Karl Weber, and many others helped take the book from proposal to publication. I am grateful for so many fine editors and everyone who worked behind the scenes to produce the book.

At the *St. Petersburg Times,* Paul Tash and Neil Brown were incredibly patient when I needed time to do "just one more rewrite." Thanks for cheering me on during that long home stretch. Kyle Parks and the entire business staff endured, even when I whined. You guys are great!

Finally, extra thanks go to three people who deserve much more than one dedication page. Alexis Hill and Amy Kase, two of my wonderful sisters, are a source of joy and inspiration. They share the dedication of the book with a dear friend, Pat Stricharchuk, who died of breast cancer. We miss you.

In remembering Pat, we should all remember to live each moment.

—ALECIA SWASY
St. Petersburg, Florida

INDEX

ABOUT THE AUTHOR

ALECIA SWASY is business editor of the *St. Petersburg Times*. Previously, she worked as a staff reporter for *The Wall Street Journal*. She is the author of *Soap Opera: The Inside Story of Procter & Gamble*. She lives in St. Petersburg, Florida.